The Iran Wars

THE
Iran Wars

SPY GAMES, BANK BATTLES,

AND THE SECRET DEALS THAT

RESHAPED THE MIDDLE EAST

Jay Solomon

RANDOM HOUSE | NEW YORK

Published in the United States by Random House, an imprint
and division of Penguin Random House LLC, New York.

RANDOM HOUSE and the HOUSE colophon are registered trademarks of
Penguin Random House LLC.

LIBRARY OF CONGRESS CATALOGING-IN-PUBLICATION DATA
NAMES: Solomon, Jay (Reporter)
TITLE: The Iran wars : spy games, bank battles, and the secret deals that
reshaped the Middle East / Jay Solomon.
DESCRIPTION: New York : Random House, 2016. | Includes index.
IDENTIFIERS: LCCN 2016016783| ISBN 9780812993646 | ISBN
9780812993653 (ebook) Subjects: LCSH: United States—Foreign
relations—Iran. | Iran—Foreign relations—United States. |
Economic sanctions, American—Iran. | Nuclear weapons—Iran.
| Nuclear arms control—Iran.
CLASSIFICATION: LCC DS63.2.I68 S65 2016 | DDC 327.1273055—dc23
LC record available at https://lccn.loc.gov/2016016783

Printed in the United States of America on acid-free paper

randomhousebooks.com

246897531

First Edition

Frontispiece photograph by AP Photo/Mehr News Agency, Raouf Mohseni

Book design by Barbara M. Bachman

To my son, Hudson,
my father, Richard Solomon,
and to Michael Adler.
The future, present, and the past

Contents

Cast of Characters

Mark Dubowitz, executive director of Foundation for
Defense of Democracies

THE NUCLEAR PLAYERS

Mohsen Fakhrizadeh, former head of Iran's Physics
Research Center

Fereydoun Abbasi-Davani, director of Atomic Energy
Organization of Iran, 2011–2013

Ali Akbar Salehi, foreign minister of Iran, 2010–2013;
head of Atomic Energy Organization of Iran, 2013–

Mohamed ElBaradei, director general of International
Atomic Energy Organization, 1997–2009

Yukiya Amano, director general of International Atomic
Energy Organization, 2009–

Olli Heinonen, deputy director general of International
Atomic Energy Agency, 2005–2010

Benjamin Netanyahu, prime minister of Israel, 2009–

Mahmoud Ahmadinejad, president of Iran, 2005–2013

Alireza Jafarzadeh, Washington spokesman for the
Mujahedin-e Khalq

David Albright, president of the Institute for Science and
International Security

THE AXIS OF RESISTANCE

Ayatollah Ali Khamenei, supreme leader of the Islamic
Republic of Iran

Bashar al-Assad, president of Syrian Arab Republic

Hassan Nasrallah, secretary general of Hezbollah

Khaled Meshaal, chairman of Hamas Political Bureau

Imad Mugniyah, late Hezbollah military commander

Mustafa Badreddine, late Hezbollah military commander

SPY MASTERS

Major General Qasem Soleimani, commander of
Revolutionary Guard's Qods Force

General Abdul Reza Shahlai, a deputy commander of
Qods Force

Henry Crumpton, deputy chief of CIA's Counterterrorism
Center, 1999–2001

Gary Berntsen, leader of CIA's Jawbreaker operation in
Afghanistan, 2001–2002

David Petraeus, commander of Multi-National Force in
Iraq, 2007–2008; CIA director, 2011–2012

Zalmay Khalilzad, senior director at National Security
Council, 2001–2003; ambassador to Afghanistan,
2003–2005, and to Iraq, 2005–2007

James Dobbins, State Department special envoy on
Afghanistan, 2001–2002, 2013–2014

The Iran Wars

Prologue

A Diplomatic Ruse

SINCE THE 1980S, THE ISLAMIC REPUBLIC OF IRAN STEADILY, THOUGH erratically, developed the technologies needed to build nuclear weapons. Though the West constructed expansive defenses to stop these advances, it achieved only limited success. This would all change during the second term of President Barack Obama.

On September 26, 2013, Secretary of State John Kerry, just six months on the job, attended his first international meeting on the Iran nuclear crisis in a dilapidated conference room at the United Nations headquarters in New York. The top diplomats of the five permanent members of the UN Security Council—the United States, Russia, China, France, and the United Kingdom—plus representatives from Germany and the European Union gathered around the table to reach a major advance toward making a nuclear deal with Iran, or so they thought. On Kerry's left sat the Iranian delegation, headed by its U.S.-educated foreign minister, Javad Zarif, known for his impeccable English and disarming smile. The wooden conference table was bathed in an eclectic mix of purple, red, and gray reflecting off the room's decades-old wallpaper. Journalists from across the globe jammed into stakeout positions outside the hall anticipating the results of the highest-level meeting ever between diplomats from Washington and the Islamic Republic. Circumstances seemed ripe for a thaw in their relations.

The meeting between Iran and the so-called P5+1 diplomatic bloc was also the first opportunity for the two sides to discuss their positions on the nuclear talks since Kerry's appointment and the election of the moderate Iranian president Hassan Rouhani three months earlier in Tehran. Years of failed talks had stoked real fears in the Obama White House and Europe that Israel might attack Iran's nuclear facilities. This meeting, the diplomats hoped, could ward that off. The Iranian politician and cleric had won the vote on a pledge to improve his country's ties with the West and end Iran's economic isolation. U.S.-led sanctions, aimed at curbing Tehran's nuclear program by targeting oil profits held in banks around the world, were crippling Iran's economy. The penalties cut Iran's oil revenues in half and diminished the value of its currency, the rial, by two-thirds. Aides to Rouhani privately warned the president that their country could run short of hard currency and face a crisis if Tehran wasn't able to quickly get its hands on tens of billions of dollars of oil revenue frozen in Asian, European, and Middle Eastern bank accounts. Iran's Islamic revolution, which Rouhani had championed since his twenties, was in jeopardy.

Zarif didn't let on to the dire state of Iran's finances and made a self-assured presentation to the room, according to diplomats who took part in the meeting. He described the standoff over Iran's nuclear program, which had dragged on for nearly a decade, as a "manufactured crisis." He said his government had no intention of developing nuclear weapons and that it was willing to allow international inspectors from the UN significantly more access to Iran's nuclear sites. Tehran was also willing to diminish its stockpiles of nuclear fuel, which included enough medium-enriched uranium for at least two nuclear weapons. He said a deal should be easy to put in place.

"We hope to be able to make progress toward resolving this issue in a timely fashion based on respecting the rights of the Iranian people to nuclear technology for peaceful purposes," Zarif told reporters after the meeting. "At the same time, [we need to make] sure that there is no concern at the international level that Iran's nuclear program is anything but peaceful."

Kerry and Zarif, however, weren't exactly being straight with the foreign ministers assembled at the meeting or with the media outside, many of whom thought this meeting marked only a first step. The two statesmen, whose countries had been enemies for nearly four decades, were collaborating in an elaborate diplomatic ruse for the benefit of their presidents and, they believed, peace.

The meeting at the UN was a coming-out party. For more than two years already, Kerry had been secretly reaching out to Iranian leaders to attempt a compromise on a nuclear agreement. The former Democratic presidential candidate had started this secret diplomatic work in late 2011, while still serving as chairman of the Senate Foreign Relations Committee. He'd used the position for a range of other diplomatic missions, such as attempting to broker a peace deal between Syria and Israel and mending U.S. ties with the mercurial Afghan leader Hamid Karzai. But his efforts on Iran were particularly high stakes and included secret trips to the Persian Gulf country of Oman, where he discussed building bridges to Iran with Oman's sultan, Qaboos bin Said al Said. Oman's monarch was one of the only Arab rulers who had strong ties to Tehran's paramount political figure, Supreme Leader Ayatollah Ali Khamenei. Kerry sent messages to the ayatollah through the sultan's offices, indicating that the United States was willing to make significant concessions on the nuclear dispute, which had remained deadlocked since Tehran's vast infrastructure was revealed in 2002.

The standoff focused more than anything else on Iran's demands that it had the right to produce nuclear fuel on its soil through the enrichment of uranium. The technology was threatening international stability because it could be used both for powering a nuclear reactor and for producing the core of an atomic weapon. Kerry indicated to Khamenei for the first time that the United States could accept Iran enriching uranium, provided significant monitoring be put in place. Through the Omanis, the politician also discussed confidence-building measures with Iran, such as prisoner swaps and joint efforts to fight terrorism.

Kerry wasn't acting alone, nor was he the only American going through Oman. His efforts bolstered President Barack Obama's own secret initiative to have direct talks with the Iranian regime, which began at the start of his presidency in 2009—like Kerry's meetings, initially behind the backs of the Security Council and the United States' closest Middle East allies, including Israel and Saudi Arabia. In 2012, more than a year before Kerry, Zarif, and the rest of the P5+1 met in the conference room in New York, White House and State Department officials sat down with an Iranian delegation in the Omani capital, Muscat, in the first direct meeting between the United States and Iran on the nuclear issue since the revolution in 1979. Kerry was not present. That encounter was kept secret because of the White House's fears that Israel and the Arab states, and their allies in Washington, might try to upend the diplomacy if they got word. The United States knew that any moves toward rapprochement between Washington and Tehran would be viewed as a threat to these countries, which feared a stronger Iran.

This first meeting made little progress. But the escalating U.S. sanctions on Iran and Rouhani's election in June 2013 accelerated the diplomacy to the point where many of the terms of a framework for an accord were already agreed to by the time of the meeting at the United Nations in New York. Zarif hinted at some of the broad outlines of a deal to the P5+1. But neither he nor Kerry let their diplomatic partners know just how far the bilateral track had advanced, or how close they were to an initial nuclear agreement. "I think all of us were pleased that Foreign Minister Zarif came and made a presentation to us," Kerry told reporters, giving no sign of a larger deal already in the works.

Exiting the meeting, Kerry and Zarif met privately in an adjacent room at the United Nations not much larger than a phone booth. A scheduled fifteen-minute meet-and-greet turned into a substantive forty-five-minute discussion. The two men exchanged personal email addresses and cellphone numbers to lay the groundwork for what they anticipated would be stepped-up negotiations in the ensuing months. Their staffs were instructed to do the same. Both men privately said they remained deeply skeptical of the other, due to their governments' historical hostility. But at the same time, they expressed hope their efforts could forge a diplomatic thaw between the United States and Iran, ending more than forty years of estrangement.

THE SEPTEMBER 2013 MEETINGS in New York marked an important advance in a frantic period of direct diplomacy between Washington and Tehran that ultimately resulted in Iran and the P5+1 signing a landmark nuclear accord in July 2015. The deal was President Barack Obama's signature foreign policy achievement. Some of his supporters equated it with Richard Nixon's secret outreach to China in the 1970s that led to a normalization of relations between Washington and Beijing. It cooled a growing feud between Washington and Tehran that the White House believed risked escalating into a military confrontation. "The president and I both had a sense that we were on an automatic pilot towards a potential conflict, because no one wanted to talk to anybody or find out what was possible," Kerry told me in an interview in early 2016. "I have no doubt we avoided a war. None."

Iran, under the deal, agreed to cap or reduce large parts of its nuclear infrastructure, including the number of centrifuges enriching uranium as well as its stockpile of fissile material, for at least a decade. It also agreed to enhance the ability of the UN's nuclear watchdog, the International Atomic Energy Agency (IAEA), to access and monitor Iran's nuclear sites to guard against Tehran secretly developing atomic weapons. In return, the United States and Western countries rolled back the crippling economic sanctions they had imposed on Iran over the past decade.

President Obama, from his first days in office, pursued an opening to Iran and Supreme Leader Ali Khamenei with an obsessive commitment. The White House thought a link to Khamenei would be a critical step toward stabilizing the Middle East and avoiding another regional conflict. Tehran and its military proxies had tentacles spread into most Middle East countries, and they posed direct threats to U.S. allies in Israel, Saudi Arabia, and the United Arab Emirates. Obama sent at least four letters to Khamenei, called for better relations in speeches and national addresses to the Iranian people, and communicated to Tehran via third-party countries that the United States wasn't seeking regime change in Iran. This marked a sharp reversal of the George W. Bush administration's policy, which largely shunned Tehran and sought to keep it outside the diplomatic tent. Iran, for its part, undermined Bush's major Middle East projects, including the wars in Iraq and Afghanistan and the peace process between Israel and the Palestinians, by backing anti-U.S. militias. Obama viewed détente with Shiite-dominant Iran as crucial to stopping the spread of nuclear weapons, calming the region, and underpinning efforts to counter radical Sunni groups such as the Islamic State and al Qaeda. He saw Iran as part of a solution. Rapprochement with Iran, the White House calculated, would aid the U.S. effort to pivot away from a foreign policy consumed by the Mideast to one focused more on the booming economies of Asia.

Obama's hope for an opening was a first step on the way to the historic Iran nuclear deal, which ranks among the riskiest diplomatic bets made by an American president in modern U.S. history. Indeed, while the United States hopes the nuclear deal will curb the spread of nuclear weapons in the Mideast, there's the threat it could fuel an arms race. Many of the terms of the agreement lapse after a decade, and Iran will then be allowed under international law to rapidly expand its nuclear program and produce weapons-grade fuel. Iran is also developing an expansive ballistic missile program. In preparation for these threats, Saudi Arabia and other Arab countries have vowed to match Iran's nuclear and military capabilities over the next decade.

The agreement, what it took to get there, and the tens of billions of dollars now flowing to the Iranian regime could also undermine hopes for a democratic transition in Tehran. Millions of pro-democracy supporters took to the streets in 2009 to protest the allegedly fraudulent reelection of President Mahmoud Ahmadinejad. The political revolt was widely seen as the greatest opening for political reform since the country's 1979 revolution. But President Obama and his advisors offered almost no support for the demonstrators out of fear that backing the protestors would diminish Khamenei's willingness to hold direct negotiations on the nuclear dispute. Communications between the two leaders had already begun by then, and the moment for political change in Tehran passed. There are no guarantees, U.S. officials concede, that the nuclear agreement will breed more moderate Iranian behavior, and it could entrench the hard-line regime.

The story of the nuclear agreement, and the decade of U.S.-Iranian conflict that preceded it, marked a new era in the annals of U.S. national security and diplomacy. The Obama and George W. Bush administrations deployed weapons never used before against an enemy state. These included sanctions on Iran's entire banking, transportation, and energy sectors and the deployment of cyber weapons, including the Stuxnet virus, which briefly crippled the Iranian centrifuges used to produce nuclear fuel. All of this was aimed at forcing Iran into negotiations on the nuclear issue. In many ways, the United States' conflict with Iran created and fine-tuned new forms of American warfare that encompassed virtually every corner of the world.

Iran, for its part, unleashed its militias and its elite military unit, the Islamic Revolutionary Guard Corps, against American troops fighting in Iraq and Afghanistan, killing hundreds of U.S. soldiers through the deployment of sophisticated munitions on those battle-fields. Tehran intensified support for its military proxies in Iraq, Syria, Lebanon, and Yemen in a broader bid to challenge the influence of the United States and its allies. Iran also honed its own cyber skills, targeting the computer systems of American banks, oil companies, and government offices, including those controlling critical infrastructure such as dams.

Who won the decade-long feud is up for debate, but certain facts are not. Iran was severely crippled by years of extreme sanctions when it first seriously approached the negotiating table. Iran's leaders, emboldened by the nuclear agreement, have not softened their stance toward the United States—the "Great Satan"—even if the deal amounts to a momentary truce.

The cost to the United States was substantial. The Obama White House needed to cut diplomatic deals with Russia and China to gain their support for increasing sanctions on Tehran. The White House's decision to secretly engage in direct talks with Iran in 2012 significantly hurt its relations with the United States' allies in the Mideast—Israel, Saudi Arabia, and the other Persian Gulf states—who view Tehran as a direct threat to their national security. These countries would increasingly follow foreign policies more independent of Washington's and generate even more instability in the Middle East. Saudi Arabia, Turkey, and Qatar armed and funded Islamist militias in Syria precisely as a means to challenge Tehran and its Shiite allies, giving rise to the Islamic State terrorist organization.

The Obama administration also touted the Iran deal as a tool to loosen Iran's notoriously oppressive regime. U.S. officials hope the lifting of sanctions and Tehran's increased economic engagement with the West will help to open up Iranian society. Supreme Leader Khamenei and other revolutionaries are aging and are expected to exit the scene over time, opening the door, the United States hopes, for leadership more in sync with Iran's youthful and significantly pro-American population.

In attempting to fix one problem, hoping it would solve many others, the administration appeared blind to new threats mounting in the Middle East. Some U.S. officials believed that the White House's obsession with the Iran deal handcuffed the administration, preventing it from acting decisively in Syria. President Obama warned he would use military force to end the civil war in Syria but then repeatedly backed down. This hesitancy came with a cost: hundreds of thousands of civilians died in Syria, and the conflict fueled the rise of Sunni extremist groups such as the Islamic State. Because Syrian president Bashar al-Assad was Iran's closest Arab ally, "there was definitely a fear that strikes in Syria could alienate the Iranians and make them walk away from diplomacy," said Fred Hof, who oversaw Syria policy in the State Department during Obama's first term.

Contrary to American hopes, Khamenei dug in, reaffirming his country's anti-West position, regardless of the White House's actions. "Whether the deal is approved or disapproved, we will never stop supporting our friends in the region and the people of Palestine, Yemen, Syria, Iraq, Bahrain, and Lebanon," Khamenei said in a speech marking the end of the Islamic holy month of Ramadan, just days after the negotiations in Vienna concluded. "Even after this deal, our policy toward the arrogant U.S. will not change. We don't have any negotiations or deal with the U.S. on different issues in the world or the region."

Obama has wagered that Khamenei and his revolutionary allies won't outlast the terms of the nuclear agreement. If they do, the United States risks unleashing an even larger nuclear cascade on the Middle East. "The White House bet the farm on reaching an accommodation with the Iranians," said a senior Israeli official who regularly discussed Iran with U.S. officials. "But they never truly seemed to understand who they were dealing with."

The Persian Domino

I N THE NORTHERN HILLS OF TEHRAN LIES A TRIBUTE TO THE ISLAMIC Republic's war dead. The Holy Defense Museum is a multimillion-dollar facility founded in 2004 that chronicles the violent campaign Iran's Islamist leaders have waged in their region, beginning with the 1979 Islamic revolution. While memorializing the fallen, the monument also looks to Iran's future goals, documenting Tehran's obsession with establishing a new world order based on Islamic principles and its opposition to the United States, Zionism, and Western values as a whole.

At the front of the facility, trash cans wrapped in Israeli flags and human skulls line a walkway. Tanks captured during Iran's eight-year war with Iraq are on display. Exhibits herald the republic's growing military might, with replicas of Iran's long-range Shahab missiles pointed to the sky and fighter aircraft that appear poised for takeoff.

Starting with the museum's main hall, a guide takes visitors through the chaotic final days of the revolution and the overthrow of Iran's last monarch, Shah Mohammad Reza Pahlavi. One exhibit tracks the day-by-day story of the Iranian students who held fifty-two American diplomats hostage for 444 days at the U.S. embassy. Galleries vividly recount the lives of the hundreds of thousands of Iranians who died fighting Saddam Hussein's forces during the 1980–88 Iran-Iraq War. Three-dimensional holographs of Iran's martyrs eerily stare down visitors as they pass by. It's an illustration, says the guide, that the fallen continue to watch and protect the living.

The Holy Defense Museum is a monument to Iranian nationalism, the Islamic revolution, and the country's historic role as the self-declared greatest historical power in the Middle East. Maps of the original Persian Empire show neighboring countries, such as Bahrain and Azerbaijan, as they are meant to be in the eyes of Tehran—under Iran's writ. The Islamic Republic's founder, Ayatollah Ruhollah Khomeini, is honored as one of the world's greatest theologians. His successor, Supreme Leader Ayatollah Ali Khamenei, seen in photographs and videos, preaches the ideals of the revolution to supplicants and world leaders.

Beneath this patriotism, however, the visitor confronts the repeated mantra that Iran has been wronged and persecuted throughout its history, particularly by its Arab neighbors in collusion with the West. A section dedicated to Saddam Hussein characterizes the Iraqi leader as the tyrannical face of the Arabs who were committed to destroying Iran's revolution from its earliest days. A photo of Saddam in his olive-green fatigues shaking hands with former U.S. defense secretary Donald Rumsfeld in 1983 is a reminder of their collaboration, the guide says. (During the height of the Iran-Iraq War the Reagan administration supplied intelligence to Baghdad that Saddam then used to launch chemical weapons attacks against Iranian targets.)

"How could you have worked with Saddam?" a guide named Mehdi asks me, an American, as we stare up at a photograph of the Iraqi dictator. The picture has been altered so that half his face is bathed in a satanic red. "You then had to fight him yourselves!"

Outside, on a concrete strip overlooking Tehran, sits the most chilling exhibit, the ghostly remains of four sedans once owned by Iranian nuclear scientists who were blown up or shot by hooded assassins. The cars are wrapped in white shrouds with red dye seeping through the fabric. Red tulips, an Iranian symbol of martyrs, stick out through the windows. Photos of the scientists peer out at visitors.

Massoud Alimohammadi was murdered when a remote-controlled bomb detonated near his car on January 12, 2010, in Tehran. The fifty-one-year-old, according to the gold-plated plaque displayed near his photo and car, was working as a university professor when agents from Israel's intelligence service, the Mossad, killed him. The scientist was devout and never took actions in life "without deep understanding and complete study," reads the inscription.

Darioush Rezaienejad was shot six times in his car in 2011 by two alleged Mossad assassins, says the plaque. The thirty-four-year-old was a research director in nuclear physics at a Tehran university who was clever and kind and who respected his parents. He died "in the presence of his wife and little daughter."

Here, Iran's defiance against its enemies through its commitment to its nuclear program is on full display. The head of the Atomic Energy Organization of Iran, a U.S.-educated scientist named Ali Akbar Salehi, inaugurated the grisly exhibit when it opened in 2012. A former foreign minister, Salehi was seen as a relative moderate in Iran's theocratic system by American and European diplomats. But the scientist's words underscored his commitment to Iran's revolution and global struggle. "The memorial to the innocent nuclear martyrs is an image of honorable victors and chivalric offspring of science and technology . . . against the cruelty of global arrogance headed by the U.S. and Zionism," he said.

THE DIPLOMACY BARACK OBAMA and John Kerry were pursuing in 2013 was challenged not just by Iran and words such as Salehi's, and not just by opposition from U.S. allies including Israel, Saudi Arabia, and the United Arab Emirates, but by history itself. Thirty-five years of frozen relations since the 1979 Islamic revolution have created a generation of Americans and Iranians who have known only conflict. In that time, the bureaucracies in both countries have become entrenched and invested in containing the other side.

The Iranian revolution in 1979 altered U.S. foreign policy in a way that few other events in our time have. Gone almost overnight was the shah, Washington's closest Mideast ally outside Israel, who helped safeguard the nearly 40 percent of the world's oil supply that moved through the Persian Gulf. In his place emerged a theocratic government that was fundamentally opposed to Western capitalism, democracy, and foreign policy and was committed by its ideology to fomenting revolutions in Muslim countries across the Middle East as well as Central and South Asia. There were parallels in the Iranian threat to that posed by Soviet communism. Both relied on heavy promotion and investment in a radical ideology and support for militant proxies internationally.

U.S. animosity toward Iran was seared into the American collective conscious from the early days of the revolution because of the attacks on American military advisors and the capture of the U.S. hostages. The embassy seizure in Tehran is widely viewed as having put an end to President Jimmy Carter's reelection hopes in 1980. And it fed into a sense of despondency and hopelessness in the United States following the Vietnam War—a time also marked by economic malaise, sky-high oil prices, and the Soviet Union's territorial advances.

The Iranian regime is driven by an Islamist ideology that sees the United States as its principal rival for dominance in the Middle East. Furthermore, while a president is elected every four years in Tehran, the country's power rests almost solely in the hands of its supreme leader. This cleric directly controls the country's most powerful military force, the Revolutionary Guard, and oversees clerical bodies that manage the judiciary, the legislature, and the executive. The president may be the public face of the regime, but that's about it.

During the shah's rule, the United States built Iran into its staunchest ally in the Persian Gulf and a policeman of the region's oil traffic. Washington sent billions of dollars in arms to the Iranian monarchy and showered the country with U.S. loans and development experts from American universities, the State Department, and the World Bank. President Obama's closest political advisor, Valerie Jarrett, lived in Iran in the 1950s when her father ran a children's hospital in the city of Shiraz. The United States, ironically, lent support to a nuclear program the shah pursued in partnership with the German conglomerate Siemens AG. The ruler touted the economic benefits of nuclear power, though he also hinted at its military application. Tehran's Islamist government inherited the nuclear sites, but it appeared initially uncertain about using them.

The shah's demise immediately placed the world's oil supply in jeopardy and resulted in a clerical regime overtly hostile to the United States and its allies. The capture of the American hostages traumatized the American public, and Tehran moved quickly to attempt to spread its revolution into Saudi Arabia, the Gulf emirates, and the wider Mideast region, though with only limited success. It also sent military advisors to support Palestinian and Lebanese militias fighting Israel.

Out of the public eye, the covert war brewing between the United States and Iran was even more pronounced and extensive than most Americans understood or realized in the 1980s and 1990s. From the ashes of the shah's despotic state, Ayatollah Khomeini created an ideologically driven military command, called the Islamic Revolutionary Guard Corps (IRGC), that was wholly focused on maintaining the religious purity of the new Islamic state. The IRGC, in turn, formed an overseas military and intelligence unit, called the Qods Force, which was tasked with exporting the Islamic revolution and aiding Tehran's allies in the Middle East. Qods is the Arabic name for Jerusalem, symbolizing the Iranian leadership's commitment to taking back the holy city from Israel for Muslims worldwide. The shah, by contrast, had been one of the Jewish state's only military allies in the region.

Just three years after the shah's fall, the IRGC also oversaw the creation of the Lebanese Shiite militia Hezbollah, or the "Party of God," which in the 1980s conducted a string of kidnappings and suicide bombings targeting American diplomats, military officers, and academics based in Lebanon. Hezbollah's largest attacks were the 1983 bombing of the U.S. embassy in Beirut and the attack on the Marine Corps barracks there the same year. The strikes killed more than three hundred Americans—the largest terrorist attacks against U.S. interests before 9/11.

For American security strategists, the Revolutionary Guard and their allies presented an unprecedented security challenge because of their ability to mix radical ideology, military training, and guerilla warfare tactics to threaten U.S. interests. Hezbollah's use of suicide bombers in Beirut in the early 1980s was among the first times the United States faced a contemporary foe willing to sacrifice its own people to inflict such wide-scale damage. Hezbollah commanders would go on to train al Qaeda in bombing tactics, according to U.S. intelligence reports.

Iran, Hezbollah, and their allies fined-tuned their intelligence capabilities and focused on U.S. and allied targets across the Middle East. The 1983 bombing of the U.S. embassy in Beirut occurred on a day when, as the Revolutionary Guard's and Hezbollah's informants had learned beforehand, more than a half dozen of the CIA's Mideast officers were assembled in the American diplomatic compound there for a liaison meeting. Eight CIA personnel died, including the Agency's top Middle East analyst and Near East director, Robert Ames, and station chief Kenneth Haas.

This successful attack marked the beginning of a blood feud between the CIA and the IRGC, which continues today. Indeed, some of the staunchest critics of the nuclear negotiations have been American military and intelligence officers. Former American and

Mideast officials argue the United States has not done nearly enough to punish Iran for the attacks in Lebanon. Some in the Reagan administration called for the bombing of Tehran after the attack on the Marine Corps barracks, though no such retaliation occurred. Iran was emboldened, they argue, by the lack of reprisal.

"You both respect them, but also realize that the Iranians will go to almost any end to inflict damage," said Bill Murray, a former CIA operative who was based in both Tehran and Beirut. "You waver on whether they're rational players or not."

This profound lack of clarity about Iran's intentions, Tehran's decision-making process, and its willingness to take big military risks vexed the United States' attempts to calculate the regime's future actions. Did Iran really want to strike Israel, as its leaders claimed? Would they be willing to form some sort of accommodation with the West? Would business and economic engagement temper the Iranian leaders' revolutionary zeal? The United States just didn't know.

Operations by the Qods Force and Hezbollah in Lebanon were followed in the 1990s by equally spectacular global strikes on U.S. and Israeli targets. In 1994, Iran's government employed Hezbollah suicide bombers to blow up the Jewish community center in Buenos Aires, killing more than 150 Jewish Argentines. Two years later, Iranian-controlled terrorists in Saudi Arabia blew up the United States' Khobar Towers military compound in Dhahran, killing 19 Americans and injuring 271.

Iran's belligerence has inspired a schizophrenic U.S. strategy toward Tehran over the past thirty-five years. It has alternated between seeking to woo the regime and trying to overthrow it. Following the onset of the 1980–88 war between Iran and Saddam Hussein's Iraq, the Reagan administration vacillated about which side to support. The United States supplied intelligence and advanced weaponry to Saddam's military in an effort to weaken Tehran in the years immediately after the revolution and the hostage crisis. But by the mid-1980s, the White House, with the aid of Israel, concocted a plan to ship missiles to Iran in exchange for the release of American hostages held in Lebanon. Some officials in Israel and Washington also hoped the deal could support what were believed to be moderate leaders in Iran's revolutionary government by showing the West's goodwill. The scheme became known as the Iran-Contra scandal and nearly led to the impeachment of President Reagan. Some involved in the scandal said the United States never identified any moderate Iranian leaders to begin with.

In the months before President George W. Bush's 2000 election, a little-known Middle East strategist named David Wurmser wrote a treatise for the American Enterprise Institute (AEI), a conservative Washington think tank. It presaged the U.S. obsession over the coming decade with isolating, weakening, and overthrowing the Islamic Republic of Iran. Wurmser's work, *Tyranny's Ally*, championed the cause of toppling the Iraqi dictator, Saddam Hussein. But the scholar didn't make his case based solely on Baghdad's alleged efforts to develop nuclear weapons or its ties to international terrorism. Rather, Wurmser argued, Saddam's fall would drastically remake the Mideast's political and religious map and eventually lead to the removal of a much greater threat to the United States, Israel, and the West—Iran's theocratic government. Iraq had the world's largest Arab Shiite population and was home to ayatollahs and other religious leaders who directly challenged Tehran's theocratic system and Supreme Leader Khamenei's claim to speak for the world's Shiites. They were suppressed, however, by Saddam Hussein's Sunni Baathist regime. His fall, Wurmser argued, would free Iraqis to challenge the Iranian state.

"An effective policy on Iraq offers the United States an opportunity to endanger and ultimately triumph over Iran's Islamic Revolution as well," Wurmser wrote in the 1999 book, which drew almost no notice at the time. "Launching a policy and resolutely carrying it through until it razes Saddam's Baathism to the ground will send terrifying shock waves through Tehran." He argued that Iraq's Shiite population would emerge as a rival to Tehran's government.

In a broader sense, this challenge to Iran, Wurmser wrote, could lead to the undermining of Tehran's political and religious legitimacy and break apart its regional system of alliances, known as the "resistance axis," which comprised Syria's Assad regime and the militant groups fighting Israel: Hezbollah in Lebanon and Hamas in the Palestinian territories. Wurmser argued that this alliance was among the largest sources of anti-American and anti-Western terrorism and militancy in the world, and Iran was its powerful core. Any weakening of Tehran, he argued, would fray this alliance and serve as the key to a new and stable Middle East, with restored American power.

"Lebanon-based terror is a major tool used by Iran and Syria to erode American prestige and regional influence," Wurmser wrote. "For the United States, any strategy that would compromise the eclipsing influence of Iran's revolutionary clerics . . . would usefully promote American interests."

Wurmser's short book, written in near obscurity, encapsulated the strategic rationale some in the George W. Bush administration had for invading Iraq, with a weaker Iran as the ultimate goal. Indeed, Wurmser was one of the few neoconservative strategists to last through nearly all eight years of the Bush administration, alternating between posts at the Pentagon and State Department before becoming Vice President Richard Cheney's top Middle East advisor. During this time, the conflict he had written about in 1999 played out along the very fault lines he envisaged, though not necessarily with the outcome he predicted. A struggle between the United States and Iran for control of the Middle East was taking place with hot wars and proxy battles in Iraq, Afghanistan, the Persian Gulf, Lebanon, and the Palestinian territories. These regional conflicts quickly eclipsed Washington's focus on al Qaeda and Sunni extremism and exposed the limits of American strategic planning.

IN THE YEARS FOLLOWING September 11, 2001, the U.S. conflict with Iran emerged as the largest national security challenge for both the

George W. Bush and Barack Obama administrations, as hundreds of thousands of American troops occupied Iran's neighbors Iraq and Afghanistan. American diplomats and military strategists struggled to define a coherent policy somewhere between subverting Iran and trying to negotiate with it. In 2003, Iran's ambassador to France, a relative of Khamenei's, sent a memo to the U.S. State Department in Washington though the Swiss ambassador, who represented American interests in Tehran. The correspondence was delivered in the months following the U.S. invasion of Iraq and overthrow of Saddam Hussein, which raised fears in the Iranian government that they could be the next Mideast country targeted by the Pentagon. The letter explained that Iran sought to conduct an extensive dialogue with the United States in a bid to normalize relations. Among the concessions Iran was considering making, according to a copy of the letter, was a suspension of its nuclear program, an end to arming and financing of Hezbollah and Hamas, and Iranian assistance in helping to stabilize Iraq. In return, Iran wanted normalized relations with Washington, an end to international sanctions, and guarantees the United States wouldn't seek to promote regime change in Iran. U.S. officials didn't believe the offer was sincere, or that it came from the top.

To this day, American and Iranian officials differ over whether Tehran's 2003 offer was legitimate and had been approved by Supreme Leader Khamenei. Two high-ranking Iranian officials told me in interviews the memo was written by one of Khamenei's relatives through marriage: Sadegh Kharrazi, Iran's ambassador to France at the time. His uncle was Foreign Minister Kamal Kharrazi. Both had significant political cover to pursue their diplomatic initiatives because of their relationship with Iran's most powerful man. "You think we wouldn't have checked every paragraph with the Leader?" said an Iranian official involved in the memo's drafting. "We would never have risked that."

Senior members of the Bush administration, however, including Deputy Secretary of State Richard Armitage, never believed that the

Iranian overture was serious. If it had been, they argued, Iran would have made the offer directly through the U.S. ambassador at the United Nations or via Washington's European allies. Hawks in the Bush administration thought the letter was floated by some Iranian diplomats as a defensive ploy to ward off a possible American attack. The letter was dismissed at the time either as a fake or as a desperate attempt to temporarily relieve U.S. pressure.

"We thought we were being set up. Dealings with Iran had severely damaged both President Reagan and Carter," said Zalmay Khalilzad, a top White House and State Department official in the Bush administration. "We were willing to deal with Iran authoritatively. But this was not taken seriously."

THE RESPONSE TO THE LETTER revealed how wary the United States had grown over any communications with Tehran. This uncertainty was no help in developing a unified and coherent policy toward Iran. Rather, it exposed deep divisions within Washington's national security establishment and fueled turf wars and ideological fights involving the State Department, Pentagon, White House, CIA, and FBI. At times these clashes produced internal charges of spying and treason, with catastrophic ramifications for the security of the United States and its allies.

Nowhere were these divisions more apparent and pronounced than in the buildup to the Iraq War. Hard-line and neoconservative strategists in the National Security Council and Pentagon believed conquering Baghdad would weaken Tehran, as outlined in Wurmser's book. But many in the State Department and Pentagon, as well as officials in Israel, Saudi Arabia, and Jordan, feared Saddam's overthrow would only empower Tehran regionally, by removing one of its foremost enemies and opening Iraq to Iranian influence. They took the position exactly opposite to Wurmser's, arguing that Iraq's Shiite majority would closely align itself with Iran after Saddam's fall—which is, in fact, what happened. "I never understood the rationale for the war when it came to the challenge of Iran," said Michael Oren, who served as Israel's ambassador to the United States during Obama's first term. "I can remember telling members of Congress that Iran would move much closer to Israel's borders once Baghdad fell."

The battle over Iran policy also played out inside Washington's intelligence services. Since 2002, evidence had been mounting that the Iranians were moving quickly toward a nuclear weapon, which could have placed the United States on a path toward war with Iran. But in late 2007, the collective offices of the United States' sixteen American spy agencies released a report on the state of Iran's nuclear program. The report, a National Intelligence Estimate (NIE), was requested by Congress and represented the most expansive study to date by the U.S. government on Tehran's nuclear work. Its conclusions stunned the White House and Israel by arguing that Tehran had ceased a coordinated effort to develop nuclear weapons, akin to the United States' Manhattan Project, in 2003. The NIE, according to U.S. officials, was based in part on intercepted emails and telephone calls made by the suspected head of Iran's nuclear weapons program, a Revolutionary Guard officer named Mohsen Fakhrizadeh. He complained in his communications that the Iranian government had cut off funding for his operations.

The NIE sent shock waves across the international diplomatic community. Iranian president Ahmadinejad cited the study as a "gift from God" and proof that Tehran wasn't secretly developing nuclear weapons. Many White House officials and allies in Israel, France, and Britain, meanwhile, believed the intelligence report ended the possibility that the Bush administration would use military force against Iran during its final years in office.

Republicans and some officials inside the White House publicly charged the authors of the intelligence report with launching a policy coup against President Bush. They noted that the authors of the report, former State Department counterproliferation and terrorism experts, had been among the most vocal in challenging the intelligence assessments on Saddam Hussein's alleged nuclear program in the months heading into the 2003 Iraq War. Vindicated after revelations about Iraq that showed no nuclear weapons, these officials were now seeking further payback against the hawks and the so-called neoconservatives in the Bush administration, and trying to prevent another war.

"You couldn't read the key judgments [of the report] and not assume that this was intended to change policy," said John Bolton, who served as President Bush's ambassador to the UN and the State Department's top counterproliferation official. "It shredded the Bush administration policy."

BARACK OBAMA FACED NO FOREIGN POLICY issue more pressing than this when he took office in 2009. Despite the NIE's conclusion, Iran continued to expand and refine its ability to enrich uranium, and UN inspectors could see in the course of their regular visits to Iran that it was close to being capable of producing weapons-grade fuel. The debate focused on when—not if—this might happen, and whether Tehran would take the risk of developing actual weapons. Obama and his aides worried Israel might make good on its threats to attack Iran's nuclear infrastructure, setting off a regional war. "We just thought this would be a catastrophe. We thought it would collapse the painstaking international house of cards we built," Benjamin Rhodes, President Obama's deputy national security advisor, told me in a 2016 interview about the potential for an Israeli attack. "It would invite the Iranian response, so we'd be in the worst of all worlds." Tehran's support for militias fighting American forces in Iraq and Afghanistan, meanwhile, placed Iran in the position of being able to either support or sabotage Obama's plans to end the wars in those countries.

Obama administration officials say that in their first term U.S. policy toward Russia, China, and Europe was largely viewed through the lens of American efforts to gain these countries' support for sanctioning Tehran. President Obama shelved missile-defense plans in Europe to win the Kremlin's buy-in. American diplomats exhaustively sought to find new energy suppliers for China so that Beijing could wean itself off Iranian oil.

Obama's White House planned to escalate sanctions by quietly building on the work begun by the Treasury Department during the Bush administration. The Treasury had already cut off Iran's major banks and financial institutions from the global banking system, but now Washington sought to dry up Iran's global oil exports, which, for most of the past two decades, were the second- or third-largest within the Organization of the Petroleum Exporting Countries (OPEC). The Obama administration expanded this financial war by recruiting every country in Europe, the Middle East, and Asia to block trade with Iran and by targeting every sector of Iran's economy.

The growth of Iran's nuclear program, meanwhile, galvanized Washington's and Israel's intelligence services to use cyber attacks to thwart Tehran's acquisition of an atomic bomb. Beginning in 2009, U.S. intelligence agencies covertly inserted a computer virus, called Stuxnet, into the computer systems controlling Iran's uranium enrichment facility in Natanz. The virus caused the destruction of thousands of Iran's delicate centrifuges, programming them to spin erratically at supersonic speeds and eventually explode. The computer attacks are the first known use of cyber warfare against a sovereign state.

Tehran and the IRGC responded by establishing the Cyber Army in 2010 to conduct computer attacks on its domestic and international enemies. Major U.S. banks such as Bank of America, JPMorgan Chase, and Morgan Stanley sustained tens of millions of dollars in damages as a result of cyber attacks in late 2012 that U.S. officials said they traced to Iran. The Department of Justice indicted seven Revolutionary Guard hackers, one for allegedly trying to break into the control system of a New York dam.

An ugly game of spy-versus-spy intensified between the United

States and its allies on one side and Iran on the other as Tehran's nuclear program progressed. Israeli officials were convinced Iran was close to the bomb, regardless of American intelligence. Beginning in 2008, masked assailants targeted more than a half dozen Iranian nuclear scientists for assassination as they traveled through downtown Tehran commuter traffic or delivered their children to school. Many of them are memorialized at the Holy Defense Museum. Among them was Fereydoun Abbasi-Davani, who later became Iran's vice president and the head of the Atomic Energy Organization of Iran. The assailants, who Iran claimed were Israeli agents, placed a magnetized bomb on the bottom of his car; Abbasi-Davani jumped out just before it detonated. He was the only scientist to survive the wave of attacks.

Iran responded by launching a string of its own terrorist attacks on U.S. and Israeli diplomats and tourists. Most of the targets were in Third World countries, such as Thailand, India, Georgia, and Azerbaijan. But in late 2011, U.S. authorities announced that they had uncovered a plot led by the IRGC to kill the Saudi ambassador to Washington, Adel al-Jubeir, while he dined at a posh Georgetown restaurant, Café Milano, which was frequented by Washington politicians and diplomats.

As President Obama eyed his second term, there were growing fears in both Tehran and Washington that all-out war could break out because of the escalating nature of the tit-for-tat conflict. In response to the sanctions and assassinations, U.S. officials said, Iran was using Hezbollah to take aggressive positions across the Middle East in 2011 and 2012 in a bid to hedge against Western aggression. But it was a battle that neither the Americans nor the Iranians believed they could sustain. On the American side, President Obama was loath to open a third major war in the Middle East in a little over a decade and thought even more sanctions might provoke Iran rather than bring the regime to its knees. For Iran's rulers, even Supreme Leader Ayatollah Ali Khamenei, there was a growing belief that Iran's economy could be bankrupted by the U.S. financial war, which was already in full swing. In a little over three years, Iran's international financial transactions had collapsed by around 80 percent, while the value of its currency, the rial, had fallen by nearly 70 percent against the U.S. dollar. Nonetheless, Tehran remained defiant and dangerous.

THE AMERICAN INVASIONS OF IRAQ and Afghanistan dominated global headlines and cost the United States thousands of lives and hundreds of billions of dollars. The emergence of China, India, and Russia as economic and military powers captivated the Pentagon's long-term strategic planners. And the specter of al Qaeda terrorism continued to weigh on the American public. But over the past fifteen years, no single country has influenced the U.S. foreign policy agenda so aggressively or has so directly threatened American allies across the Middle East as Iran and its theocratic leadership.

Although the nature of the U.S. conflict with Iran has been highly visible in many ways, played out in the exhaustive diplomatic efforts Washington has pursued to curb Tehran's nuclear program and choke off its finances, much of the conflict has played out covertly, in the shadows, and in ways most Americans never saw or comprehended. The wars in Iraq and Afghanistan devolved into proxy battles between the United States and Iran, with the two sides overtly and secretly supporting opposing political parties and militias. The wave of revolutions that swept the Middle East and North Africa beginning in late 2010—the so-called Arab Spring—fractured the region and led to a new fight between the United States and Iran for influence in a rapidly shifting political landscape. This competition has played out in Lebanon, Yemen, the Palestinian territories, Egypt, and Bahrain.

Nowhere has the fallout from this U.S.-Iranian standoff been more tragic, though, than in Syria, where Iran and the IRGC have propped up and armed President Bashar al-Assad against a nationwide political revolt that's descended into civil war and left as many as half a million Syrians dead. The chaos has allowed Sunni extremists, in particular the Islamic State, to fill the power vacuum. Iran's ability to save the Assad government has until now provided Tehran with a major strategic victory over the United States and its allies. The United States, conversely, appeared powerless to stop the carnage in Syria (if not uninterested in doing so), providing only limited supplies to a rebel movement it never entirely trusted.

The conflict between the United States and Iran has grown ever more intense and sophisticated over the past decade. This book, based on interviews and reporting trips across the Middle East, Europe, and the United States over the past five years, sheds light on just how far Tehran and Washington have gone to combat each other's roles in the Middle East since 9/11. It also shows the enormous costs both sides have borne in a competition that continues to this day.

Many in America and Iran are intent on turning the page. But the fifteen years of the Iran wars have been an exercise in engaging an enemy we don't fully understand or trust. Negotiating the future of the relationship from a point of such uncertainty, Washington and Tehran face dubious prospects for moving forward peacefully.

"There are two futures. One future will be greater conflict, greater tension, greater mistrust—basically, more of the same as we had in the past. But more of the same may not be easily manageable," Iran's foreign minister, Mohammad Javad Zarif, told *The New Yorker* as the diplomacy with the United States gained momentum in 2014. "And it may even get worse, and more dangerous. So that's one option, which I hope will not be before us."

CHAPTER 2

The Missed Chance

I N THE WEEKS AFTER THE SEPTEMBER 11, 2001, TERRORIST ATTACKS ON New York and Washington, D.C., the people of Iran expressed more sympathy for the United States and American victims than did the citizens of any other Middle East or Muslim county. Iranians held candlelight vigils at universities and public squares to honor the dead. President Mohammad Khatami, a reformist cleric, restated his call for a "dialogue among civilizations." Ayatollahs from the holy city of Qom decried the attacks on the United States as a corruption of Islam.

Even Supreme Leader Khamenei voiced alarm about the global terrorist threat, though in a speech that managed to counter empathy with blame. "In the final analysis, we doubt the sincerity of the American government's intention to combat terrorism," the ayatollah said in a speech on September 27, which directly focused on the attacks on New York and Washington. "It is insincere, and does not tell the truth. It has other aims."

The cleric's tone was revealing, betraying both his deep-seated anti-American feelings and his long-standing enmity to radical

Sunni groups such as al Qaeda and the Taliban government in Afghanistan, which sheltered al Qaeda there. He accused Washington of helping to create them by arming and funding the Afghan militants who fought and expelled the Soviet Union in the 1980s, essentially inviting an attack on the United States itself. Osama bin Laden was among those in the Pakistan-based insurgency that the United States indirectly supported. Though he despised the Sunni extremists, Khamenei discounted the possibility that Iran would formally ally with Washington in a battle against al Qaeda. "Everybody should know that Iran, the Islamic Republic, will not participate in any movement that is led by America," he told a national audience.

Tehran had been a strident enemy of the Taliban government that had taken power in Kabul following the 1996 end of the Afghan civil war. Osama bin Laden and his al Qaeda movement, meanwhile, viewed Iran's predominantly Shiite faith as a sacrilege that corrupted the world's Muslim faithful. It's a belief held by a surprising number of Sunnis and spread by clerics in Persian Gulf countries such as Qatar and Saudi Arabia. Some al Qaeda leaders categorized Shiite Muslims as even lower than Jews, for skewing the teachings of the Prophet Muhammad. The Taliban, upon coming to power, treated Afghanistan's Shiite minority, known as the Hazara, as second-class citizens.

The schism between Sunni and Shiite is a profound feature of the Middle East's conflicts and traces back more than a thousand years to the death of Islam's Prophet Muhammad in AD 632. The two sects believed power should have been passed along different familial lines: the Sunnis arguing that Muhammad's father-in-law, Abu Bakr, was the new caliph, or leader of the Islamic world, while the Shiites backed Muhammad's son-in-law, Imam Ali. This battle between the two branches of Islam continues to this day, as Shiite-dominant Iran competes with the leading Sunni states, particularly Saudi Arabia, Egypt, and the Persian Gulf's oil-rich monarchies, for the hearts and minds of the world's 1.6 billion Muslims.

In Afghanistan, enmity between Iran and the Taliban grew so

pronounced that the two nations nearly went to war in 1998. During a military offensive on the northern Afghan city of Mazar-i-Sharif that year, the Taliban laid siege to Iran's consulate and killed nearly a dozen Iranian "diplomats" who were stationed there. Many of these men were members of Iran's elite military unit, the Revolutionary Guard. The Taliban was reported to have rounded up and summarily executed hundreds of Hazaras living in the ancient city during the siege. This was an affront to Iran's theocratic rulers, who view it as their mission to protect the world's Shiites. Iran's supreme leader, Khamenei, responded by ordering his military to mass seventy thousand troops on Iran's nearly six-hundred-mile border with Afghanistan. Many countries in the region believed this was the buildup to an invasion. Although tensions eventually subsided after the United Nations intervened to mediate the dispute, the conflict would lead Tehran to become one of the most active supporters of the Northern Alliance, the rebel movement that sprang up in Afghanistan to fight the Taliban. Some of its commanders said they might not have survived during that time without Tehran's largesse.

The months after 9/11 were a period of growing optimism that America's feud with Iran could be extinguished, or at least placed on hold. "A huge opportunity appeared after 9/11 for the U.S. and Iran to cooperate against al Qaeda and the Taliban," said Hossein Mousavian, an Iranian diplomat and academic who served as a member of Tehran's most important strategic body, the Supreme National Security Council, in the months after the al Qaeda attack. "It [the threat] made clear that Tehran and Washington, despite all of the acrimony, actually shared many vital interests," such as combating Sunni extremism.

ALMOST IMMEDIATELY AFTER THE al Qaeda attacks, President Bush ordered the CIA to insert a small team of operatives, code-named "Jawbreaker," into Afghanistan. Jawbreaker's mission was to link up with the insurgent Northern Alliance, headquartered in the Panjshir Valley, and to plan a joint military operation against the Taliban. The six-man team was specifically tasked with mapping out the battlefield in Afghanistan and guiding U.S. allies in the fight there.

Located just forty-five miles northeast of Kabul at the foot of the Hindu Kush mountain range, the Panjshir Valley links the capital to northern Afghanistan and Central Asia. Foreign forces have used the Panjshir to insert their armies into Afghanistan dating back to the time of Alexander the Great. It had been a rebel stronghold for the mujahedeen fighters who had successfully driven the Soviet Red Army out of Afghanistan in the 1980s. Its minerals, including diamonds and emeralds, have lured outsiders for centuries. And it was where the Jawbreaker team came face-to-face with the Qods Force, Iran's most feared military organization.

Tehran's theocratic rulers established the Qods Force in 1990 as the overseas arm of the Revolutionary Guard, and charged it with exporting Iran's Islamic revolution to bordering countries and other Muslim lands. Qods commanders instigated instability in a range of Muslim countries across the Middle East by arming and training proxy groups, either to undermine strategic rivals such as Saudi Arabia and Israel or to promote the cause of fellow Shiites.

Revolutionary Guard operatives in the early 1980s created the Lebanese militia and political party Hezbollah as a powerful military threat to Israel on its northern border. The Qods Force also serves as a major supplier of arms to the Syrian army and the Palestinian militant groups Hamas and Islamic Jihad. Closer to Iran's borders, the Qods Force supported the Shiite ethnic group in Yemen, called the Houthis, in their fight against the government in San'a, and has for decades backed Iraqi Shiite militias. U.S. officials believe the Qods Force is one of Iran's most powerful organizations, combining an intelligence and paramilitary arm with diplomatic and economic responsibilities. It's a CIA, Pentagon, and State Department all rolled into one.

A tough-talking southerner named Henry "Hank" Crumpton headed the Jawbreaker team from the CIA's offices in Langley, where he oversaw the covert operations of the Agency's recently created Counterterrorism Center. Two of the CIA's most experienced overseas operatives, Gary Schroen and Gary Berntsen, were stationed on the ground, with Crumpton monitoring from Virginia. Each man had experience dealing with both the Afghans and the Qods Force and Iranian intelligence. Schroen had tracked the Iranian movement of arms and cash into the Balkans in the 1990s in their bid to bolster Muslim communities in Bosnia and Kosovo. Berntsen helped U.S. allies in Arab countries fend off efforts by the Qods Force to destabilize their political systems and incite their Shiite populations. Crumpton had been based in Africa, where Hezbollah was active among the expatriate Lebanese Shiite populations there.

Jawbreaker's mission was complicated by the fact that the ally they sought, the Northern Alliance, was partially a creation of the Qods Force itself. Throughout the late 1990s, as the Taliban gathered strength in the Pashtun areas of southern Afghanistan, Tehran had transferred weapons, funds, and trainers to the Northern Alliance. Although militias from Afghanistan's minority Tajik, Uzbek, and Hazara populations dominated the rebels' ranks, it was India and Russia, two countries that also feared the rise of a radical Sunni movement in their region, that joined Iran in backing the Northern Alliance. The Iranians, as well as the Russians and the Indians, hoped their Afghan ally could serve as a bulwark against the Taliban spreading their radical ideology outside Afghanistan's borders.

Among the United States' principal interlocutors in the Northern Alliance prior to 9/11 was its commander, Ahmad Shah Massoud, an ethnic Tajik. The French-educated soldier had been an on-and-off ally of the CIA during the 1980s and served as defense minister in Kabul after Afghanistan's civil war briefly ended in the early 1990s. Massoud returned to his life as a rebel after the Taliban took power in 1996. He was a fierce opponent of the movement's radical interpretation of Islam and its repressive stance toward Afghanistan's minorities, though he himself was a conservative Muslim. The Iranians and the Americans both saw Massoud as the one Afghan who could unite the country's feuding warlords and clans against al Qaeda and the Taliban. Tehran particularly felt an affinity for the commander, as Iran shares strong linguistic and cultural ties to Tajikistan and its ethnic community. The CIA even inserted its officers into Afghanistan to support Massoud's men in their fight against Taliban and al Qaeda militias prior to the 9/11 attacks. The Agency's Counterterrorism Center established limited ties with the Northern Alliance in an unsuccessful effort to prevent such a major terrorist strike from happening.

Tehran, Moscow, and New Delhi, as well as the Americans, all sought to push back the tide of Sunni fundamentalism that was spreading across Central and South Asia. Their rivals were the Taliban's financiers and arms suppliers: Pakistan, Saudi Arabia, and the Persian Gulf states, such as the United Arab Emirates. Washington was uncomfortably stuck in the middle: allied with the Saudis, but increasingly concerned about the Afghanistan-based activities of one of the Saudi kingdom's most famous sons, bin Laden, who had found safe haven there. The Qods Force, meanwhile, with its experience in funding and training proxy armies, helped strengthen the Northern Alliance with arms and monies. By building a compliant ally from within Afghanistan, as Iran had done in Lebanon, Syria, and the Palestinian territories with Hezbollah and Hamas, Iran's ayatollahs and generals sought above all to entrench their influence in the wider Mideast and reconstitute, in some ways, the vanished power of the Persian Empire.

As CRUMPTON'S TEAM MADE contacts in the Panjshir Valley in late September, the CIA was immediately caught in a shadowy game for influence with Iran's spy agencies. The Americans on the ground didn't trust the Iranians. Many inside the CIA held a deep disdain for the Revolutionary Guard and their proxies, particularly Hezbollah, dating back to Lebanon's civil war in the 1980s. Gary Berntsen began his career at the Agency the same week, U.S. officials believe, Tehran ordered Hezbollah to blow up the American embassy in Beirut in 1983. The attack killed nine of the Agency's top Middle East hands, including the legendary spy Robert Ames. "My first day at the CIA was the day the bomb went off in Beirut," Berntsen said. "We really, really hated these people."

Crumpton, Berntsen, and other Agency staff were fully aware of the presence of Qods Force agents intermixed among the Tajik, Uzbek, and Hazara fighters who constituted the Northern Alliance. But Jawbreaker was instructed to steer clear of any dealings with the Iranians. This placed the Afghans in the middle of two rival camps as they geared up to confront the Taliban.

"I told the Afghans: 'You need to deliver a message to the IRGC. If they approach, or appear anywhere near the battlefield, we will view them as hostile,'" Crumpton said in an interview after he retired from the Agency in 2005. "We knew the Iranians were scared shitless of us." Crumpton claimed the Revolutionary Guard dreaded any direct confrontation with the United States.

Berntsen said he was even more blunt. He penned a letter to the Iranians operating in Afghanistan and asked a Northern Alliance intermediary to deliver it. The New York–born Berntsen, now fifty-eight, declared in his missive that he would kill any Revolutionary Guard he confronted on the battlefield. "[This] horrified the Afghans," he said. They didn't want to get caught in the middle of a geopolitical feud.

The Northern Alliance's leaders made no secret of the fact that the IRGC kept a liaison office in the Panjshir to help coordinate training and battlefield tactics. While wary of the IRGC's actions, the CIA came to see this as an asset and a means to monitor the activities of the secretive Iranians. U.S. intelligence officials had struggled mightily to gain useful or accurate information on Iran, whether on its nuclear program or on its military activities across the Middle East. "This was a good thing for us," Crumpton said. "We had information on Iran through our Afghan friends."

In the early weeks of the Jawbreaker operation in late 2001, the Afghans took to trying to separate the operations of their two bene-factors: the CIA and the IRGC. The Northern Alliance was inti-mately aware of the tensions between the two spy agencies, but Afghanistan's long history was riddled with short-lived military alli-ances and examples of Western powers quickly tiring of the savage fighting in the country. It was beneficial for the Northern Alliance to keep both Washington and Tehran close for as long as possible.

Gary Schroen traveled to the battlefront just a few days after landing in late 2001 to map out the Taliban positions so Pentagon warplanes could target them. The Northern Alliance's military com-mander, General Mohammed Fahim, accompanied the American to the war zone. The Tajik officer instructed Schroen and the CIA to keep a very low profile as they neared the front. "It turned out that the Iranian Revolutionary Guard Corps had a two-man observer team assigned with the [Northern Alliance] forces on the Kabul front," Schroen wrote in his account of the Jawbreaker mission. "Fahim was anxious that the Iranians not discover the presence of U.S. personnel, at least not this early in the deployment."

At the time, Tehran conveyed messages to Washington signaling Iran's willingness to cooperate in the war effort—though they were greeted with skepticism by the Bush administration. The Iranians said they would help any American fighter pilots shot down near or in Iranian territory. Tehran indicated supply routes that could be opened up through Iran's borders to bring arms and food to the front. And some American officials said the Iranians had even sug-gested intelligence sharing, though Crumpton said this never oc-curred.

The CIA worked to set up a coherent leadership structure within the Northern Alliance from their base in Afghanistan's north as the war against the Taliban gathered pace. The Taliban and the Pashtun tribes dominated the south. The Agency would have banked on its relationship with Ahmad Shah Massoud to serve as the glue to pull together the rebel factions in the fight. But just two days before the

9/11 strikes on Washington and New York, a pair of al Qaeda assassins killed Massoud at his headquarters in the Panjshir. The operatives posed as journalists and carried a letter forged by Osama bin Laden's deputy vouching for their credentials. The two men detonated an explosives-laden camera and battery pack recorder when Massoud sat down for the interview; Massoud died just hours later. Al Qaeda viewed it as a critical blow to its Afghan rival. "Massoud was a gentleman," Berntsen said. "He was a smart political operator, and knew how to work the media. Al Qaeda used that against him."

Massoud's deputy, General Fahim, took power after 9/11, and the Northern Alliance was able to pull together many of the same warlords and militia leaders the United States had armed and funded during the 1980s. Among them were Abdul Rashid Dostum, the head of Afghanistan's Uzbek community, and Ismail Khan, a Shiite warlord who controlled the western Afghan city of Herat, the principal trade bridge between Iran and Afghanistan. After the Taliban's fall, Herat would be electrified through a grid on the Iranian side of the border, a cogent symbol of Tehran's influence in the region.

The U.S. and British militaries stepped up their air strikes on Taliban positions through October and November 2001. And on November 13, the Northern Alliance pushed into Kabul, finding the city largely deserted. The Taliban's leadership fled to the southern city of Kandahar, its traditional base. And al Qaeda's leadership crossed the mountainous Afghan border into a sanctuary in Pakistan.

After the capture of Kabul, officials at the White House, CIA, State Department, and Pentagon remained divided over whether Iran and its Revolutionary Guard were a help or a hindrance to the allied war effort. Crumpton and Berntsen said the Qods Force's men largely disappeared after receiving the Americans' threats and neither helped nor hindered their operations against the Taliban. "The only reason they even pretended to help was that they were scared out of their minds," Crumpton said.

Others in the Agency, however, believed the Bush administration piggybacked on the groundwork the IRGC did in creating the Northern Alliance after the United States abandoned Afghanistan in the 1990s at the end of the Cold War. These American officials believed the United States never properly acknowledged the work Tehran did against the Taliban. "The Iranians had given much more lethal assistance to the Northern Alliance than we ever did," said a former CIA officer who worked in Afghanistan after 9/11 and viewed Pakistan as a bigger threat to the United States than Iran because of the Pakistanis' support for the Taliban. "We were just giving [the Northern Alliance] a hug and maybe some cash."

In fact, Khamenei and the IRGC initially supported the U.S. mission to topple the Taliban, according to Iranian officials. The Supreme National Security Council allegedly gave the green light. Even the commander of the Qods Force, the powerful Major General Qasem Soleimani, joined in. The officer controlled all of the Iranians' paramilitary and intelligence operations in Afghanistan. He vocally supported the idea of cooperating with the United States in the months after 9/11, according to the Iranians. "Qasem is a very pragmatic commander. He's willing to cooperate with the West if it serves Iran's interest," said Hossein Mousavian, the former member of Iran's Supreme National Security Council, who said he attended the meeting.

By November 2001, Jawbreaker, in cooperation with the Pentagon, succeeded in driving the Taliban and al Qaeda out of Kabul to sanctuaries along the Afghanistan-Pakistan border. It was a win for Iran as well.

As the Taliban's government fell in November 2001, the Bush administration accelerated its efforts to put a new Afghan government in place. The White House and the Pentagon initially argued in late 2001 that they didn't foresee a long-term American military presence in the impoverished country, or a substantial exercise in nation-building. Instead, American diplomats were instructed to quickly cobble together an interim government made up of the Northern Alliance and other rebel factions, and set up a clear and steady process that would lead Afghanistan toward holding national elections. Meanwhile, U.S. Special Forces and the CIA were to continue to focus on the hunt for senior Taliban and al Qaeda members, including, of course, Osama bin Laden, who had fled to the mountainous border region between Afghanistan and Pakistan.

The American official given the job of delivering a new Afghan government was James Dobbins, a career State Department diplomat with a history of rehabilitating strife-torn countries. Dobbins, now seventy-three, had worked extensively in the Balkans in the 1990s to end ethnic conflict and establish stable regimes in Kosovo and Bosnia. He had served in Somalia as well as Haiti, following U.S. military operations that uprooted local despots and militia commanders there.

Dobbins didn't bring any ideological baggage to his new job as the special U.S. envoy to the Afghan opposition, colleagues say. He had a reputation as a straight shooter, independent and capable of working with unsavory diplomats and bureaucrats in Third World countries often hostile to the United States. Dobbins was a contemporary of high-flying American diplomatic stars such as Richard Holbrooke, Christopher Hill, and Strobe Talbott, who had also made their names during the Clinton administration by ending the Balkan war and navigating post–Cold War Russia, though Dobbins kept a lower profile.

When Dobbins assumed his job, just two weeks after 9/11, he had a sense of urgency. The Taliban and its al Qaeda allies were weakening militarily at a pace much faster than many in the Pentagon or CIA had anticipated. Afghanistan, as a perpetual battleground for competing regional powers, would soon need the support of its neighbors, principally Russia, Pakistan, India, Saudi Arabia, and Iran, in order to create a new government in Kabul. The State Department envoy needed to bring them all on board, or risk outsiders undermining the political transition.

Dobbins's job turned to shuttle diplomacy—some meetings secretive, some not. He traveled from New York to Rome and from Pakistan to Germany in the final two months of 2001. He met often with the Afghan tribal leaders and royals who would eventually play key roles in bringing Hamid Karzai to power. Karzai was a Pashtun leader, with strong ties to the West, who sought the Taliban's overthrow from sanctuary outside Afghanistan. In Islamabad and New Delhi, Dobbins worked to assuage Pakistani and Indian diplomats, whose decades-old enmity at times risked sparking a nuclear conflict in South Asia and who threatened to derail Dobbins's mission of forming a new Kabul regime. The Indians didn't want to see the Taliban or any political group tied to Pakistan in power in Kabul. The Pakistanis armed and funded the Taliban in a bid to guarantee as much Pashtun representation in Afghanistan as possible.

To the surprise of Dobbins and his team, a trump card for their diplomatic mission emerged in the relationship they formed with Iran's Foreign Ministry, and in particular the U.S.-educated envoy Mohammad Javad Zarif. Zarif was Iran's deputy foreign minister under the government of the moderate President Mohammad Khatami, and the most effective Iranian diplomat at engaging with the West.

Zarif was living in the United States at the time of the Iranian revolution. He had earned his undergraduate degree in San Francisco and then moved to the University of Denver to earn his Ph.D. in political science. After the shah's fall, however, he quickly moved to New York to help run Iran's UN mission and sustain the revolution while Tehran's new Islamist government found its feet. Zarif spent so much time in the United States that his children were born in New York, making them U.S. citizens.

American academics and journalists grew to know the Iranian diplomat from the European conference circuit he frequented during the 1990s. He preached Khatami's line about the need to build bridges with the West and wooed interlocutors with his American English. "Zarif was the face the regime liked to put forward to show the warmer side of Iran," said Karim Sadjadpour, an Iranian American scholar who regularly met with Zarif while Khatami was in power. "It was never clear, though, if he truly spoke for the regime. It was like that with many officials in that government." Indeed, the status of Zarif's relationship with Khamenei and the Revolutionary Guard proved to be a mystery to U.S. officials.

Dobbins quickly came to believe that Zarif and the Iranian government, more than any other regional power, was the key to making or breaking Afghanistan's first post-Taliban government. Tehran had tremendous leverage over the Northern Alliance, and Zarif seemed committed to a deal. It was through Zarif's mediation, Dobbins thought, that Iran could build cooperation within the international community for all regional actors to help combat the terrorism and narcotics smuggling that emanated from Afghanistan. Iranian officials regularly reminded Western governments that its population bore the brunt of Afghanistan's instability, as evidenced by the high number of heroin addicts inside Iran who got their drugs from Afghan smugglers. "They were pretty specific that they were willing to work with us on a range of issues," Dobbins told me in multiple interviews after leaving government. "We had a crucial opportunity."

The Bush administration was initially noncommittal on whether Dobbins was authorized to directly engage Tehran on the Afghan issue. Some of the more hawkish officials in the White House and Pentagon viewed any contacts with the Iranians as a sign of weakness, which would only encourage Tehran to spread its influence into the region's hot spots. Successive U.S. administrations had formally barred any direct contacts with Iranian officials that weren't first cleared by the State Department (colloquially known as Foggy Bottom, after its neighborhood in Washington).

But eventually Secretary of State Colin Powell gave Dobbins the green light. The retired general had himself sought to forge common ground with Tehran in the weeks after 9/11. Attending the annual meeting of the UN General Assembly in New York in November 2001, Powell had gone out of his way to shake hands with his Iranian counterpart, Kamal Kharrazi, who had told the assembly that Iran stood with the United States in the fight against terrorism. "Powell thought that our interests in Afghanistan were parallel with Iran's," Dobbins said. "And we saw this as an avenue for rapprochement with Iran."

Weeks of globetrotting by Dobbins and the American diplomatic team culminated in the UN negotiations on Afghanistan transferring from the UN General Assembly in New York to a December conference in the former West German capital, Bonn. A large state guesthouse, called the Petersberg, housed the mishmash of UN bureaucrats, high-powered diplomats, and Afghan warlords who showed up for the meetings. Between talks about the shape of a new Afghan constitution and government, the envoys peered down on the Rhine River and the vineyards that dotted the German landscape.

Dobbins met with Zarif and his staff every morning at ten o'clock in a large banquet area at the Petersberg. Italian and German representatives also attended the get-togethers, as did the Afghan-born U.S. diplomat Zalmay Khalilzad, who would become President Bush's ambassador to both Kabul and Baghdad in the years to come. Zal, as he was called, spoke Dari, closely related to the Persian language Farsi, which made him a useful tool in eavesdropping on the Iranian team's thinking. "The Iranians would sometimes beat down my door with their ideas," Khalilzad told me about his time in Bonn.

As the conference gathered steam, Dobbins and Zarif saw Washington's and Tehran's views on the Afghan constitution converge. Surprising both Dobbins and Khalilzad, Zarif was even more progressive than the Bush administration on certain political issues in Afghanistan, both men recounted. In particular, Zarif advocated enshrining a specific time frame for democratic elections in the Afghan constitution and wanted Kabul to overtly pledge itself to combating terrorism.

"Should we not insist that the new Afghan regime be committed to cooperate with the international community to combat terrorism?" Zarif said with a smile during one morning meeting, as Dobbins recounted in a book he wrote. The Americans saw this in part as a jab at the United States, which regularly accused Tehran of being the world's largest state sponsor of terrorism because of its support of Hezbollah and Hamas. The Iranians claimed these organizations were legitimate liberation movements seeking to end the Israeli occupation of Arab lands. But at the same time, the United States believed Zarif was serious about getting the world behind the fight against the Taliban.

By the tenth day of the conference, the diplomats had agreed on the terms of the new Afghan constitution and that Hamid Karzai should be leader of an interim government. But the Northern Alliance and the other Afghan factions were still battling over how to apportion seats in a new cabinet. The Alliance's envoy to the talks, Yunus Qanooni, was demanding that his faction get three-fourths of the seats. His position threatened to collapse the Bonn meeting.

The conference was close to a stalemate when Javad Zarif pulled Qanooni into a corner of the breakfast room for a quick talk, according to Dobbins and Khalilzad. Minutes later, the Afghan diplomat conceded to lessening the Northern Alliance's chokehold on the cabinet, which allowed a comprehensive agreement to be formalized at Bonn. U.S. officials said Zarif reminded the Afghan warlord how reliant economically the new government in Kabul would be on Tehran—another indication, Dobbins and others believed, of Iran's ability to aid or undermine U.S. plans for Afghanistan.

Dobbins said he believed the Iranian government probably had a more coordinated approach to Afghanistan than the Bush administration, which was fractured by rivalries between individuals and offices. The American said he didn't see any split in approach between Iran's diplomats and its military apparatus, including the IRGC. They were a united front, Dobbins told me.

———

EVEN AS THE UNITED STATES and Iran appeared to reach common ground while creating a new Kabul government, powerful figures inside the Bush administration were already positioning themselves for what they believed was an inevitable clash with Tehran in the post-9/11 world. Among them were a couple of Iran experts at the Pentagon, Harold Rhode and Larry Franklin, both vocal internal critics of engaging Tehran. These officials believed the Islamic Republic was ideologically incapable of making any accommodation with the United States and that the Revolutionary Guard was setting traps to ensnare the United States in Afghanistan, just as they had done in Lebanon during the 1980s. Only regime change in Tehran could bring real stability to the broader Middle East, they argued.

Rhode, a native New Yorker, studied Farsi in the Iranian city of Mashhad a year before the Islamic Revolution and received his Ph.D. in Islamic history from Columbia University. He worked at the Office of Net Assessment, an in-house Pentagon think tank, where he focused on Middle East issues and specifically Iran. Even though Rhode dealt in military matters, his analysis of Tehran was deeply informed by his study of both Persian culture and the ideology that infused the Islamic Republic. "Iranians do not consider their own weaknesses as a reason to engage an adversary in a compromise, but rather an opportunity to destroy them," Rhode said. "It is for this reason that goodwill and confidence-building measures should be avoided at all costs."

Franklin, a reserve Air Force colonel, acquired his knowledge of Iran through work and self-study, rather than higher education. He taught himself Farsi at night while working as a Middle East analyst at the Pentagon's Defense Intelligence Agency, all while supporting five children and a wife who was wheelchair-bound due to spinal disease. His service as the U.S. defense attaché in Tel Aviv during the 1990s, meanwhile, exposed him to Iran's ability to project power internationally through its use of proxies, such as Hezbollah, Hamas, and Palestinian Islamic Jihad. As soon as the Bush administration began preparing to topple the Taliban, Franklin was immediately concerned about the IRGC's abilities to target American and coalition forces inside Afghanistan.

The incoherence of the U.S. strategy toward Iran became dangerously apparent and threatened the Afghanistan diplomacy. In late December, just as Dobbins was forging the Bonn agreement, Rhode and Franklin secretly traveled to Rome with White House approval to meet with a group of Iranian opponents of the regime, at least one purportedly a high-ranking Iranian intelligence official. The gathering was held in a nondescript residential building near the city's tourist-heavy Piazza di Spagna, famous for the Spanish Steps and high-end boutiques. The office apartment belonged to Italy's main overseas intelligence agency, the Servizio per le Informazioni e la Sicurezza Militare, or SISMI. No State Department or CIA officials were invited, which raised alarm bells at State — though participants in the meeting told me that the U.S. ambassador to Rome at the time, Mel Sembler, was informed.

The meeting had been arranged by Michael Ledeen, a former National Security Council official and historian who studied totalitarian movements at a number of prominent conservative Washington think tanks. Ledeen had been a central player in the early machinations of the Iran-Contra scandal, which rocked the Reagan administration in the mid-1980s. He had written a detailed account of the Iranian revolution, called *Debacle*. The California native shared Rhode and Franklin's deep concerns about Iran and agreed with them about the need to overthrow the Islamic Republic. He believed Iran's Islamist ideology posed a growing threat to the West and its values, not unlike fascism in Europe during the 1930s and 1940s. Ledeen also believed that the Iranian people were ready to topple the mullahs running the government if they received an assist from the West.

The former academic and journalist had coordinated with the Israeli government of Shimon Peres in efforts during the 1980s to establish a channel to the Islamic Republic, an initiative that led to the White House shipping arms covertly to Tehran to aid that country's war effort against Iraq. The White House hoped the missile shipments would help secure the release of American hostages kidnapped by Hezbollah in Lebanon.

One of Ledeen's sidekicks in the deal was a Persian businessman and onetime intelligence agent for the shah, Manucher Ghorbanifar. Ghorbanifar resettled in France after the revolution and did a side business swapping information with the CIA and European intelligence services on developments inside the Islamic Republic. The balding, cigar-smoking exile claimed to have maintained high-level contacts in Iran.

But by 1984 much of the information he had provided proved inaccurate, according to former Agency officials, earning Ghorbanifar a "burn notice" from the CIA. When senior Reagan administration envoys, including Robert "Bud" McFarland and Oliver North, secretly traveled to Tehran in 1986 to attempt to secure the release of American hostages, none of the meetings Ghorbanifar had supposedly arranged for them actually came to pass. "Ghorbanifar, in the end, was only good at taking care of Ghorbanifar," said George Cave, the CIA's representative on the trip to Tehran, who noted that the Iranian exile still profited from the arms sales to Iran. The CIA veteran called him "a con artist of the first kind."

Ledeen, however, maintained his ties to Ghorbanifar throughout the 1990s, believing that his information had often been accurate and that his contacts inside Iran remained strong. The American despised the CIA, viewing the Agency as incompetent and incapable of appreciating the quality of the intelligence the Iranian exile had passed on. Ledeen also believed the CIA had scapegoated Ghorbanifar for the failure of the Iran-Contra operation. In the weeks after 9/11, Ledeen said, he began receiving communications from Iranian sources, via Ghorbanifar, concerning the Qods Force's deployment of assassination teams inside Afghanistan that were targeting American forces. In an interview, Ledeen said the information was incredibly specific as to which American units could be targeted and where. He said Ghorbanifar's informants told him the Qods Force and the IRGC were "laying a trap."

"This was good information, and if we had the opportunity to save American lives, why shouldn't we try?" Ledeen said to me. "The information passed to U.S. Special Forces was proven accurate, and the assassins were eliminated," he stressed.

Whether Ghorbanifar's information was good or not, however, James Dobbins and Colin Powell believed the Rome meetings were an attempt to sabotage cooperation with Tehran at a time when the United States needed Iranian assistance. It was yet another example of how competing factions inside the U.S. government undercut the formation of an Iran policy.

THE MEETINGS AT THE SISMI office in Rome went on for three days, beginning on December 21. Present were Ledeen, Ghorbanifar, Pentagon representatives, Italian intelligence officials, and the Iranian defectors. The talks, according to Ledeen, focused on the IRGC's purported activities in Afghanistan and discontent among the Iranian military. But the Iranians and Ghorbanifar also pushed the Americans on a plan to topple the regime, according to former CIA officials and leaked State Department documents.

Directly after the meeting, Harold Rhode sent a classified cable back to the Pentagon via the telex room at the American embassy in Rome. The defense official reported that his team had "made contact with [active] Iranian intelligence officers who anticipate possible regime change in Iran and want to establish contact with the United States government," according to parts of the cable obtained by the Knight Ridder news agency (now the McClatchy Tribune news service). "A sizable financial interest is required."

Details of the meetings outlined in the cables unnerved the State Department and CIA. The fact that two Pentagon officials seemed to be discussing a regime change operation with disaffected Iranian officers and a man formally burned by Langley raised fears of another scandal of Iran-Contra proportions. Also, given Ghorbanifar's past, Agency officials worried he could be concocting a financial scam. The Iranians, if aware of the Rome encounter, would view it as a hostile act on the part of the United States.

The CIA's station chief in Rome quickly wrote a memo back to Langley raising the prospect that an "unauthorized covert action" had taken place at the SISMI office. Colin Powell, Jim Dobbins, and other State Department officials, meanwhile, raised concerns with the White House that any such activities could undercut Washington's efforts to stand up the Karzai government in Kabul and stabilize Afghanistan.

Ledeen, in interviews, denied that the Rome meeting was unauthorized and stressed that it had been cleared beforehand by Deputy National Security Advisor Stephen Hadley, an old friend from the Reagan administration. (Hadley has never refuted this claim.) Still, the White House made sure that Ledeen's Rome channel didn't move forward. A Senate committee began probing the possibility that elements inside the Pentagon and the neoconservative movement had been secretly hatching a regime change plan.

Manucher Ghorbanifar, meanwhile, continued to offer Washington his intelligence information—for a price, some believed. Beginning in 2003, his longtime assistant in Paris, a former Iranian minister named Fereidoun Mahdavi, began sharing information on alleged Iranian terrorist activities with Congressman Curt Weldon of Pennsylvania, then the vice chairman of the House Armed Services Committee. This correspondence ended up forming a major portion of a book Weldon wrote in 2005, called *Countdown to Terror*. Among the explosive accusations was a claim that the Iranians had tried to blow up the Seabrook nuclear power plant in New Hampshire. Langley tasked Bill Murray, then the CIA's station chief in Paris, to check out the veracity of Mahdavi's claims. "None of the information bore any ties to reality," Murray said.

——

THE ROME EPISODE UNDERSCORED the divisions between the White House, parts of the Pentagon, the State Department, and intelligence agencies over Iran policy as the Afghanistan war gathered strength and the buildup to the Iraq invasion began. Some saw Tehran as a potential ally, others as a clear adversary. Strategists inside the Bush administration understood that Tehran could sabotage American efforts to stabilize and democratize both Afghanistan and Iraq. Still, given the history of Washington's secret wars with the Islamic Republic, many in the White House and Pentagon didn't trust Tehran's intelligence services and believed 9/11 offered a unique opportunity to punish the country they viewed as the Middle East's worst actor.

Contacts between American and Iranian officials continued nonetheless. In March 2002, just weeks before he left the State Department, James Dobbins met in Geneva with an Iranian delegation that he said included a senior Qods Force general. The conference was focused on developing Afghanistan's security forces. The Iranian military officer, according to Dobbins, offered to build barracks for and train twenty thousand Afghan troops, as part of a larger U.S.-led program to help stabilize Afghanistan—this despite the fact that President Bush had just named Iran as a member of an "axis of evil," with North Korea and Iraq.

Dobbins said his response to the Iranian general was that the United States and Iran might have difficulty conducting joint training exercises because of competing military doctrines. But the American diplomat said he still believed the outreach was a potential watershed moment in U.S.-Iranian relations. Dobbins raised the Iranian overture during a meeting at the White House a few weeks later, which included Secretary Powell, National Security Advisor Condoleezza Rice, and Defense Secretary Donald Rumsfeld. But he received no formal response, and said that Rumsfeld was particularly suspicious of Tehran's intentions.

"This was a remarkable moment that we failed to seize," Dobbins said. "We should have at least accepted their offer in principle, and seen what we could make of it." No cooperation with Iran in Afghanistan ensued.

WHITE HOUSE ENVOY ZALMAY Khalilzad also continued to meet with Javad Zarif and other Iranian diplomats through 2002 and 2003, on both Afghanistan and Iraq. The irony wasn't lost on Khalilzad that many of the Iraqi politicians and leaders whom the United States was cultivating for a post-Saddam regime were also close allies of Iran's—some even living in Tehran.

In December 2002 Khalilzad led the American delegation to a conference in London that was aimed at unifying the Iraqi opposition behind the war in Iraq and the overthrow of Saddam Hussein. The event was formally convened by the State Department. But many of the Iraqi delegates had close ties to Iranian intelligence and the Revolutionary Guard. Among them were leaders of the Badr Corps, an Iraqi Shiite militia that had served as a veritable intelligence arm of the IRGC in its operations against Saddam Hussein during the 1980s.

Javad Zarif headed the Iranian delegation at the London meeting. In ways reminiscent of the diplomacy on Afghanistan, he supported the U.S. plan to quickly assemble a government to replace Saddam, Khalilzad said. Iraq's population was more than 60 percent Shiite and hostile to the Sunni elites who had run their country for decades. The Iranians believed any free election in Iraq would naturally bring to power a Shiite government committed to strong ties with Tehran. "The Iranians were very supportive in London," Khalilzad said. "They wanted to move as quickly as possible toward a government formation in Baghdad."

Khalilzad had three more meetings with Zarif and other top Iranian officials in Geneva as the countdown to the Iraq invasion ticked down. Zarif was fixated on purging any new Iraqi government of members of Saddam's Baath Party. It was a position Khalilzad said he knew could be destabilizing for Iraq and deepen splits between Sunnis and Shiites. But that was the policy the Americans eventually pursued over the objections of many U.S. administration officials. "Zarif was pushing for things we eventually did," Khalilzad said. "It was ironic."

Washington's engagement with Tehran on Iraq, however, like its efforts on Afghanistan and most previous diplomatic encounters, eventually ground to a halt because of mutual suspicions. In the months surrounding Kabul's fall, American intelligence officials tracked senior al Qaeda leaders fleeing Afghanistan and crossing into Iran. These Arab operatives didn't seem to be living openly in Iran, but were being closely monitored by Tehran and kept under some form of house arrest. U.S. officials believed Iran's leaders were holding the men both as insurance against al Qaeda launching attacks on Iran and as future chips in Tehran's conflict with the United States. The al Qaeda fighters could simply be released to plot new attacks against the West if U.S.-Iranian relations deteriorated.

Among the al Qaeda leaders in Iran were Osama bin Laden's son Saad and the senior al Qaeda military commander, Saif al-Adel, according to U.S. officials. Abu Musab al-Zarqawi, who would become the commander of al Qaeda's military operations in Iraq, used Iran as a transit zone through which to enter Iraqi Kurdistan, where he set up training camps for Islamist fighters preparing to fight coalition forces inside Iraq.

The United States pressed Iran to hand over the al Qaeda leaders. Such a move would be seen as concrete evidence of Iran's interest in working with the United States. And Washington didn't see that Iran would pay any political price; after all, it had openly announced its support for the campaign against al Qaeda.

The Iranians, however, were hard bargainers, and wanted something concrete in return: access to the Iraq-based camps of the Mujahedin-e Khalq, or MeK, an Iranian opposition group from the 1970s that the United States had designated as a terrorist organization. The MeK had aligned with Saddam against Tehran, and the Pentagon planned to control its facilities after deposing Saddam. Iran's leadership was committed to apprehending and trying (or executing) the movement's leadership, in particular its Iraq-based chief, Massoud Rajavi, for a string of attacks they had launched against the Iranian government going back to the 1980s. Zarif and others said Tehran viewed the transfer of the MeK members as its own yardstick through which to judge the Bush administration. The United States feared that handing them over would violate international statutes due to the likelihood that some would be executed. Some in the Pentagon also saw the MeK as potentially useful intelligence assets.

As Khalilzad was set to meet Zarif and an Iranian delegation again in Geneva in May 2003, a series of bombs ripped through three compounds in Riyadh, Saudi Arabia, that were housing American and British military contractors training the Saudi National Guard. The blasts killed more than 30 people, including 9 Americans, and injured 160. American intelligence officials said they traced the attack's planning back to al Qaeda leaders based in Iran, including the military commander, Saif al-Adel. Though there were disagreements inside the Bush administration over how much advance knowledge the Iranian government had of the attack, it was another example of how little the United States understood of Iran's relationship with the Sunni terrorist group.

Iran's government at the time formally denied any knowledge of the attack and reiterated its commitment to fighting al Qaeda. But the diplomatic track between Tehran and Washington, and the possibility for close cooperation in Afghanistan and Iraq, largely ended at this stage. The hopes held by some in Washington and Tehran that 9/11 and shared interests could lead to a rapprochement between the rivals were evaporating, and the two countries were again marching directly into renewed conflict. "We felt like we couldn't keep this going if they were hosting senior al Qaeda members," Khalilzad told me, though he said he did keep open some communication lines with Iranian officials while serving in Kabul, Baghdad, and New York. "The trust between the two sides had broken down."

Many in Washington believed Tehran was willing to cooperate with the United States on security issues, at least on its eastern border. Afghanistan had long been a source for the opium that flooded Iran's markets and produced the world's largest population of heroin addicts. Afghanistan was also not technically the Middle East, where Iran sought to lead the Islamic world in its campaign against Israel and its American backers. Still, there remained doubts that Khamenei or the IRGC could ever really form a common front with Washington. These doubts would linger as the United States entered Iraq and risked a confrontation with Iran.

CHAPTER 3

The Shiite Crescent

As the U.S. military began steadily massing its forces in the Persian Gulf in early 2003, Saddam Hussein's military-intelligence services were warily watching developments on Iraq's eastern border. With war nearing, Baghdad was in many ways more concerned about the intentions of Iran than the United States.

Going back to the Iran-Iraq War in the 1980s, Iran's Islamist government and the Revolutionary Guard had invested heavily in recruiting and training Shiite allies from Iraq, employing them for sabotage operations, intelligence gathering, and propaganda purposes against their sworn enemy in Baghdad. Many of Iraq's top Shiite politicians and clerics relocated to Tehran in the years after the 1979 revolution to avoid imprisonment or execution. Among them were future Iraqi prime ministers Ibrahim al-Jaafari and Nouri al-Maliki and Shiite religious leaders such as Mohammad Baqir al-Hakim. Hundreds of thousands of Iraqi Shiite refugees fled with them into Iran.

These Iraqi exiles became military assets for Tehran during its eight-year war with Saddam, sharing intelligence and launching cross-border attacks. Iran's government nurtured pro-Iranian political movements such as Dawa and the Islamic Supreme Council of Iraq (SCIRI) to give voice to their country's Shiites, who made up at least 60 percent of Iraq's Muslim population. (The Sunnis make up around 20 percent.) Dawa and SCIRI supported Iran's battle against Saddam, both inside Iraq and in the wider Persian Gulf region. The Revolutionary Guard trained these Iraqi proxies at camps along the Iran-Iraq border. They plotted terrorist attacks against the United States and Arab states in retaliation for their support of Saddam in the war. The most active of these Iran-based militias was the Badr Corps, formed by Mohammad Baqir al-Hakim's family, one of Iraq's most powerful Shiite dynasties.

The stronghold of the Badr Corps inside Iraq was in Najaf. The city is considered the holiest in Shiite Islam because it is home to the Imam Ali Mosque. Millions of pilgrims from Iran, Lebanon, and the Persian Gulf states visit Najaf annually to worship at the grave of the Prophet Muhammad's son-in-law. The Badr Corps maintained large networks of informers, charities, and political supporters inside Iraq's southern Shiite-dominant regions and on Iraq's eastern border.

Following the 1991 U.S. invasion of Iraq during the first Gulf War, the militia had played a key role in rallying Iraq's Shiite majority to try to overthrow Saddam and his Baath Party, with the encouragement of the George H. W. Bush administration. The Iraqi Republican Guard responded with a vicious military crackdown that killed tens of thousands of Iraqi Shiites and Kurds in the early 1990s.

In 2002, as the calls for war grew louder in the United States, Saddam's spies detected stepped-up military preparations by the Revolutionary Guard and their Iraqi allies as well. According to Iraqi intelligence files captured by the Pentagon after the invasion, the Iraqis believed that Tehran was preparing for its own invasion of Iraq, or at the very least would seize on the chaos and instability brought by the American attack to send their agents and military allies into the Shiite-dominated regions of Iraq, outmaneuvering the Iraqis and the Americans simultaneously.

"[Military maneuvers in Tehran] are aimed at improving the combat preparation of the Iranian units and preparing the Guard Forces and Basij Forces for the forthcoming American attack that would affect Iran and the Iranian people," the director of Iraq's military-intelligence unit wrote Saddam's office on December 30, 2002, referring to the Revolutionary Guard and its paramilitary force, called the Basij.

The Badr Corps and other groups linked to Iran were indeed increasingly mobilizing their operations inside Iraq. Saddam's intelligence services caught Iran's military distributing communications equipment to its Iraqi allies in January 2003. Iraqi border guards captured Badr Corps members moving supplies into its safe houses in eastern Iraq. And Iraqi spies reported that Iranian "agents" looted Iraqi government buses and trucks operating in Maysan province, near the Iranian border.

As the date for the American invasion drew closer, Iraqi intelligence was on high alert. Of particular concern to Baghdad was intelligence showing that leaders of the Badr Corps and SCIRI had been liaising with senior Bush administration officials in Washington, Europe, and the Middle East ahead of the invasion of Iraq. Though U.S. officials knew of SCIRI's close ties to Tehran, Washington still sought to cultivate its leaders, including its chairman, Mohammad Baqir al-Hakim, and his brother, in an effort to forge a unified Iraqi government in Baghdad after Saddam's fall. According to Baghdad's spies, Iran's supreme leader, Ayatollah Ali Khamenei, personally signed off on Badr's Washington contacts, suggesting to Baghdad an unprecedented—and secretive—alliance between Washington and Tehran. Bush administration officials, however, publicly spoke of wooing these Iraqis away from Iran in the months before the invasion. These conflicting messages and intelligence only underscored to the United States' Arab allies the incoherence of U.S. policy. And it heightened their fears that Saddam's overthrow would strengthen Khamenei.

"During his visit to Kuwait, Mohammad Baqir al-Hakim agreed to send elements of the Badr Corps there in order to guide the American forces when the aggression against Iraq begins (God forbid)," read another January 2003 dispatch from Iraq's military-intelligence unit to Saddam Hussein's office. The U.S. invasion commenced weeks later, and Saddam and his forces were powerless to stop the American onslaught. He quickly ceded Baghdad to the U.S. coalition and retreated to the Sunni-controlled areas in central and western Iraq, where his forces began planning a lethal insurgency. The Iranians began to activate their networks inside Iraq as well.

THE BUSH ADMINISTRATION SOLD war in Iraq as a campaign of necessity—urgently required to stop Saddam Hussein from developing nuclear weapons and to sever his regime's links to international terrorism, including al Qaeda. President Bush and some of his strategists at the Pentagon, including Paul Wolfowitz and Douglas Feith, talked of the nobility of helping to establish a democratic foothold in the heart of the Middle East, which would then provide the impetus for the spread of progressive values and free markets beyond Iraq's borders. Some Bush administration veterans would later claim they did in fact achieve this end (admittedly a few years after the invasion) when political rebellions surged across the Arab world from Tunisia to Syria in early 2011. There was evidence to support the idea that Saddam's demise altered the mindset of the Arab street by uprooting one of the main obstacles for political change in the region. "We certainly sought to shake things up by removing Saddam," Feith said in an interview in 2012. "History will still judge the greater fallout from the Iraq war." But the cost of fueling this change would be immense, and Iran was the best positioned to profit from it.

A less publicly stated—or debated—aim of Saddam's overthrow, according to Bush administration strategists, was to increase the military and political pressure on Iran's clerical rulers, and to a lesser extent on Syrian president Bashar al-Assad's government. It was the dynamic laid out in David Wurmser's writings heading into the Iraq War, embraced by some in the Bush administration, that a U.S. takeover of Iraq would isolate Iran. A popular refrain repeated by U.S. government officials in the days after the invasion was "Today Baghdad, tomorrow Damascus, and then on to Tehran." But the level of Iranian influence in Iraq was not well understood in Washington. And, as evidenced in Saddam's intelligence files, Iran was actually lying in wait for the invasion to begin.

The presence of hundreds of thousands of American troops on Iran's eastern and western borders in Afghanistan and Iraq would hem in Tehran's ability to threaten its neighbors and destabilize the Persian Gulf, many Americans officials believed. And they thought that the sight of Iraq's majority Shiite population voting in open elections and choosing a government not ruled by clerics would galvanize the Iranian citizenry, which was seen as perhaps the most pro-American population in the Middle East outside of Israel. To some extent, they would be proven right. In 2009, massive protests broke out in Iran following the reelection of President Mahmoud Ahmadinejad, which was believed to be fraudulent. But Khamenei and his forces would brutally put down the revolt.

The key in the long term, U.S. officials believed, was freeing the Iraqi city of Najaf, traditionally the most powerful and important center of Shiite learning, from Saddam's repressive rule. The seminaries there, overseen by Ayatollah Ali Sistani, rejected the Iranian government's philosophy that one supreme leader, known as the *velayat al-faqih* in Persian, served as a pope-like leader for all Shiite Muslims worldwide. Indeed, most Muslim scholars held that this belief system, established in Tehran after the 1979 revolution and backed by the Iranian clerics in the holy city of Qom, was antithetical to the true teachings of Shiism, which respected the division between church and state while accepting some blending of politics and religion. Sistani preached a "quietist" brand of Islam that kept the clerics and the seminaries strictly out of politics. Changes in Iraq, beginning with freeing quietist Shiite scholarship, would gradually force changes in Iran, some U.S. strategists believed.

"If you can release Najaf, you can cure one of the great rifts in Islam," said Ladan Archin, an Iranian American who worked for Wolfowitz and Feith as an Iran analyst in the Office of the Secretary of Defense from 2001 to 2005. "That was one of the underlying themes of the U.S. strategy."

Inherent contradictions within the Bush administration's policy toward Iraq and Iran, however, soon became clear to Arab governments throughout the Middle East, and in Israel as well. For decades the United States and the Sunni states had seen Saddam Hussein as the bulwark against any expansion of Iranian influence into Iraq and westward into the Levant, particularly in Shiite-dominant areas. Saudi Arabia, the United Arab Emirates, and other Sunni states had sent billions in financial aid to Baghdad during its eight-year war with Iran in the 1980s, specifically to blunt Tehran's advances. By removing Saddam Hussein, the United States would empower the very Iraqi Shiite politicians whom Tehran had nurtured and financed for years, including SCIRI, the Badr Corps (SCIRI's military wing), and Dawa.

Israeli officials grumbled that Iran's borders would effectively move hundreds of miles closer to the Jewish state's once the Baathists were gone and the Shiites took power in Baghdad. As co-religionists with Iran, Iraq's new government would naturally sympathize and cooperate with Tehran. Sunni leaders in Arab countries such as Jordan, Egypt, and Saudi Arabia agreed. Some thought that the United States and Iran had forged a secret compact to overthrow Saddam. They spoke of a "Shiite Crescent" running from Iran through Iraq and into Syria. In their view, only Tehran would benefit from this war. But the Bush administration continued to argue the opposite — that Iran would be weakened.

The conferences for Iraqi opposition leaders, staged by Zalmay

Khalilzad in London in late 2002, brought the point home. Many of the politicians who attended—particularly the Iraqi Shiite politician Ahmad Chalabi—had been cultivating both Washington and Tehran for years, if not decades. Chalabi was the scion of a prominent Baghdad family that had grown rich during the time of the Ottoman Empire as privileged members of the Baghdad royal court. Chalabi and his relatives were forced to flee the Iraqi capital in 1958 when the Iraqi military staged a coup d'état against King Faisal II and massacred the royal family. Ahmad Chalabi went into exile, first living in Lebanon and then moving between Jordan, London, and the United States. A brilliant mathematician, Chalabi received his Ph.D. at the University of Chicago (which had also produced some of Bush's top advisors, including Paul Wolfowitz and Khalilzad). He eventually grew close to many conservative politicians and strategists in Washington and shared intelligence with the CIA.

Many in the White House and Pentagon in 2003 had hoped Chalabi could emerge as Iraq's first democratically elected president after Saddam's fall. But while living in Beirut and London in the 1990s, Chalabi had also maintained an office in Tehran for his political organization, the Iraqi National Congress (INC), which was solely focused on galvanizing international support to unseat Saddam. The U.S. Congress was providing the INC with $25 million per year, even though lawmakers knew some of these funds were going to pay for the offices in Iran. The organization secured a special waiver from the U.S. Treasury to allow the aid to legally go into Tehran, despite American sanctions that prevented the U.S. government from conducting any business with Iran. This was not an insignificant achievement, given the hostility toward Iran on Capitol Hill.

Weeks before the invasion, Chalabi traveled to Tehran to meet with Iranian leaders and give them insights into Washington's plans, according to his aides. Among those he met with was Major General Qasem Soleimani, commander of the IRGC's Qods Force. Soleimani was a veteran of the Iran-Iraq War who had quickly risen through the ranks of the IRGC thanks to his experience in conducting both conventional and guerilla warfare (he was in charge of targeting Afghan drug smugglers who operated in Iran's eastern tribal regions). His position as Qods Force commander made him Iran's top international spymaster. But his power went beyond that, according to Iranians who worked with him. His responsibilities included serving as one of Tehran's top diplomatic envoys to foreign governments, a conduit for arms shipments to Iranian proxies, and a manager of the IRGC's foreign business operations.

Chalabi and his aides viewed establishing ties with Soleimani and the Iranians as a positive development for the United States—which was kept in the dark about these developments. Francis Brooke, a close aide of Chalabi's who helped run the offices of the Iraqi National Congress in Washington, traveled to Tehran with the INC team shortly before the war. Brooke said the Iranians fully supported the toppling of Saddam but wanted assurances the Americans weren't planning a prolonged military occupation that eventually could be used as a base to threaten Tehran. What Soleimani and others sought was the quick demise of Saddam followed by a rapid transition to a new, Shiite-led government, made up of the very politicians both the United States and Iran had cultivated. Many senior officials in the White House and Pentagon had initially envisaged the same thing.

But Chalabi's meetings with Soleimani were never shared with Washington. And it would eventually feed a belief in Washington that the Iraqi politician was working for the other side, particularly as his post-Saddam activities became clearer. By 2004, many officials in the Bush administration came to believe that Chalabi was an Iranian spy. The Pentagon formally accused the Iraqi of supplying Iranian agents with American computer codes that allowed Tehran to listen in on U.S. communications traffic inside Iraq. American troops raided the Baghdad offices of the INC that year, carting away computers and files, though they never arrested Chalabi. The politician repeatedly denied any wrongdoing, though he never renounced his good relations with Iran.

Once the invasion began, Iran's government pursued a two-pronged strategy inside Iraq. On one hand, Tehran and Soleimani were happy to allow politicians from Dawa and SCIRI—the parties once exiled in Iran—to gain power in Baghdad, knowing they'd pursue a generally pro-Iranian line and break from the policies of Saddam's Baath Party. This is what quickly happened with the election of Dawa's Ibrahim al-Jaafari as president in 2005, followed by Nouri al-Maliki the following year.

But on the other hand, Soleimani and his Qods Force were also arming and funding a wide network of militias and terrorist organizations that could quickly fan the flames of violence in Iraq if Tehran chose to do so. One aim of this strategy, according to Americans and Arabs who studied it, was to keep the U.S. military under constant harassment and prevent the Bush administration from developing the type of pro-Western society it wanted. The other was to make Iran the ultimate arbiter of any political evolutions and alignments on the ground. The Iranian regime wanted to displace the Sunnis from central Iraq and push them out of power in the new Iraqi order.

The Bush administration was being drawn into an Iranian trap. While Wurmser and other U.S. strategists believed toppling Saddam Hussein was a chance to weaken Tehran, General Soleimani saw the opposite: an opening to project Iranian power as the United States removed Tehran's enemies. It was the outcome many Arab and Israeli officials had predicted.

Indeed, in the months after the war began, the United States seemed unable to stop a constant flow of businessmen, clerics, aid workers, and spies flowing into Iraq from Iran. Because of their shared Shiite faith, these agents of influence could establish aid programs and small businesses much more easily than their American counterparts and competitors. And to U.S. soldiers, who didn't speak

Farsi or Arabic, the Qods Force and its operatives were virtually invisible.

MICHAEL RUBIN WAS AMONG the first U.S. officials to recognize the speed at which Iran moved to capitalize on the overthrow of Saddam. Rubin, just thirty-one years old in 2003, was one of the directors of the Pentagon's Office of Iran and Iraq, which reported to Secretary of Defense Donald Rumsfeld. But following the invasion, the Pentagon sent him to help build Iraq's first post-Saddam government. Rubin had also been a member of the Office of Special Plans, the military unit that played a key role in planning the invasion. Democrats would later charge that the office had failed to assess the sheer enormousness of the task of rebuilding the country.

Rubin's position in Iraq was attached to the Coalition Provisional Authority (CPA), the post-invasion U.S. body tasked with preparing Iraq for elections. President Bush's special representative to Baghdad, Ambassador L. Paul Bremer, headed the CPA. But Rubin kept a special line open to many of his colleagues back at the Pentagon, men and women who believed that Washington needed, without delay, to prepare to confront Iran inside Iraq.

During his first few weeks in Baghdad, Rubin grew increasingly concerned by what he viewed as a blasé attitude within the CPA and allied governments about the presence of Iranian agents inside Iraq. Tehran was quickly moving to consolidate power for its allies, Rubin believed, while Bremer and the civilian U.S. leadership were too overwhelmed with the day-to-day realities of running a new Iraq to try to check Iranian actions. Meanwhile, Rubin thought that the Pentagon's generals didn't want to run the risk of sparking a wider war by directly targeting the Revolutionary Guard. As a result, Tehran and its clients were largely allowed to operate without harassment.

"We should be very, very careful of what the Iranians are up to, but our friends in [the State Department] and the British Foreign

Service seem to be pooh-poohing the Iranian presence and intentions," Rubin wrote to higher-ups in the Pentagon just weeks after arriving in Baghdad in July 2003. "We are in very serious trouble here." He was describing a clandestine Iranian invasion.

Rubin decided to travel into Baghdad's markets and universities and visit Shiite villages in the south. He relied heavily on Iraqi sources he'd cultivated in Kurdistan and Europe during Saddam's reign. Moving without American military personnel, he rose at three or four in the morning and drove while it was still dark to mitigate the effects of traveling in 120-degree heat and to avoid detection by insurgents.

He soon saw that Iranian consumer products had flooded into Iraqi households. Tehran's merchants had beaten America's to the market, another indication of the growing Iranian influence. Iraqi students in Shiite cities such as Najaf and Karbala had raised portraits of Iran's two supreme leaders, Ayatollahs Ruhollah Khomeini and Ali Khamenei, on their universities' gates. And Iranian-backed radio stations, newspapers, and television networks had begun distributing Tehran's message, often speeches by Khamenei, almost immediately after Saddam was deposed.

Najaf was a key barometer for gauging Iranian influence. Rubin visited Najaf in August 2003 and had the uneasy feeling that the Iranians were lying in wait. He met the director of an Islamist job creation center who was seeking American aid to help develop computer and sewing classes for Shiite women. It was the sort of project Rubin believed the Americans should be funding. But as Rubin and the man continued to talk, Rubin learned that the Iraqi was moonlighting as a correspondent for Al-Alam, Iran's Arab-language satellite television channel. The man said he'd been contacted by the Iranians shortly before the U.S. invasion and given a car, a salary, and a videophone so that he could roam and report.

"It seems like the Iranians knew exactly who to hire, went out and did it," Rubin reported back to his Pentagon counterparts. "My informal sense from visiting numerous houses is that 90 percent of the people who watch regular broadcast television choose al-Alam over the U.S.-sponsored Iraqi Media Network." Iran was beating the Americans to the punch in the propaganda war and selling their vision of post-Saddam Iraq.

Rubin began to look at the activities of SCIRI and its militia, the Badr Corps. The White House and some Pentagon officials had initially focused on placing Ahmad Chalabi into power. Others believed that former Baathists who had allied and then broken with Saddam, such as the Shiite politician Iyad Allawi, could emerge as major political players in a new Iraq. But Rubin's reporting showed that SCIRI, with both financial and military support from Tehran, was quickly taking control of large swaths of Iraqi territory right under the noses of the Americans and British. Their political power would give Iran tremendous influence in running Iraq.

In the southern Iraqi city of Al-Amarah, Rubin saw that SCIRI had already virtually taken over the place. The Badr Corps set up its operations in the city hall, which had once served as the Baath Party headquarters. Covering the building's walls were slogans such as "Death to America" and "Death to Sharon" (referring to Israel's prime minister at the time, Ariel Sharon).

The Shiite sheikh Muhammad al-Abadi was a member of SCIRI and with the help of the party and its militia was Al-Amarah's de facto ruler. Rubin sought an audience with the cleric at his house on the banks of the Tigris River. Members of the Badr Corps ushered him into the living room, where a picture of Ayatollah Khomeini hung on the wall. The American reported back to the Pentagon that the sheikh had said "the U.S. would not have peace in Iraq, even if we stayed here 18 years."

Toward the end of his first year in Iraq, Rubin's impression was that Iraq's oil-rich south was becoming an Iranian protectorate. Iranian intelligence officials often worked covertly, but Rubin sensed that they were controlling the local population through fear. A more effective U.S. administration in Iraq's south should limit Tehran's influence, he thought.

In September 2003, Rubin was invited to address a town hall meeting in the southern city of Nasiriyya. At the meeting, a number of the local politicians complained that a "hidden hand" was dictating events in their town, though they refused to speak publicly about Tehran's activities due to fear of retribution. Rubin was alarmed by the Iraqis' paranoia. "People simply are afraid to come out and criticize Iran," Rubin emailed his colleagues back in Washington. "They realize that the Iranians do not hesitate to use violence, and the U.S. has proven itself unwilling or unable to defend the border and the local Iraqi population."

In January 2004, Rubin traveled to Qadisiyah province in east-central Iraq to interview its governor, Khalil Jalil Hamza. Hamza had lived in London during Saddam's rule and spoke fluent English. He was the type of Iraqi Rubin saw as a natural ally as the United States prepared the country for its first legislative elections post-Saddam.

Hamza, however, repeated the concerns Rubin had heard from other Iraqis: that Iran was using cash, drugs, and intimidation to ensure that the elections scheduled there would be dominated by Iran's allies, particularly SCIRI and Dawa. Beginning the previous May, the governor said, Iraqi refugees from Saddam's rule had started streaming back across the border from Iran, finding absolutely no security guarding the border. Iranian intelligence agents joined in this convoy.

In the ensuing months, Iran's political allies appeared to receive a stamp of approval from the U.S. government and Bremer, Hamza said. The CPA and Bremer chose Mohammad Baqir al-Hakim of SCIRI and Ibrahim al-Jaafari of Dawa for seats on the interim Governing Council in Baghdad. The governor told Rubin that "the legitimacy [the United States] bestowed . . . encouraged both [of the politicians' organizations] to begin greater activities throughout the south."

Over the summer, Iranian emissaries, purportedly on the direct order of Supreme Leader Khamenei, had brought ten trucks of high-cost Persian carpets into Diwaniya as gifts for tribal leaders, the governor was told. SCIRI set up a command center in the local offices of Baghdad's Governing Council to channel funds coming in from Iran (including counterfeit U.S. dollars) to Iraqi provinces. Hamza, however, said he wasn't provided any funds by the U.S. government for development projects or to build the government's credibility among moderate constituents in his province.

"He said that [SCIRI] would win throughout the south . . . because [of] Iranian money, intimidation, and because the process which Bremer proposed and the Governing Council accepted would disproportionately favor the Islamists," Rubin wrote in a memo to his CPA higher-ups. "The Iranians are thinking three or four steps ahead of the game; I am not sure we are thinking more than one or two. If we are embarking on a process we believe will have even a 20 percent chance of resulting in [Iraq becoming another] Islamic Republic, we need to reconsider right now."

Frustrated with the Iraqi operation, Rubin returned to Washington in 2004 to take up residence at the American Enterprise Institute, the conservative Washington think tank. He and others from AEI were proponents of the invasion but would emerge as critics of both the Bush and Obama administrations' handling of the occupation. They particularly warned that Iran was using the conflict to gain de facto control of Iraq. Rubin's warnings were often challenged by Democrats and other critics of the Iraq War who feared the Bush White House might directly target the Iranians.

AFTER THIS INITIAL IRANIAN SURGE into Iraq following the U.S. invasion, Tehran appeared content with allowing Baghdad's political process to play itself out. The first two democratically elected governments in Baghdad in 2005 and 2006, headed by Ibrahim al-Jaafari and Nouri al-Maliki, promoted good relations with the Islamic Republic and a sharp break from the confrontational foreign policy of the Baathist governments. Diplomats in Baghdad at the time said neither man was just an Iranian stooge. Iraqi Arabs, even Shiite ones, were wary of Persian domination, they said. For example, Maliki pursued military operations against the Iranian-funded Mahdi Army, headed by the radical cleric Muqtada al-Sadr, when his militias sought to control parts of Baghdad, Najaf, and the southern city of Basra. Still, Maliki aligned Iraq closely with Iran on key regional strategic issues, such as oil pricing by OPEC and diplomatic support for Shiite populations in Lebanon, Bahrain, and Yemen. Post-Saddam Iraq also began providing huge business opportunities for Iranian companies in everything from consumer products to banking and construction. Many of these companies were tied to the IRGC. Trade between Iran and Iraq would go from virtually zero during Saddam's rule to billions of dollars annually.

Iran and the Revolutionary Guard began to intensify their military involvement inside Iraq, both through their intelligence activities and via support for Iraqi militias, following the election of Iranian president Mahmoud Ahmadinejad in 2005. A onetime mayor of Tehran, he was elected to replace the reformist cleric Mohammad Khatami as president and had been backed by the IRGC in the vote. Tehran subsequently took an increasingly confrontational stance toward the United States and the West on issues ranging from Iran's nuclear program to the Arab-Israeli conflict. Ahmadinejad was a former officer in the IRGC's paramilitary wing, the Basij, and didn't share any of his predecessor's desires for reconciliation with the West. Rather, he wanted to challenge it.

Ahmadinejad quickly reversed some key foreign policy initiatives promoted by the Khatami government. Among them was Tehran's diplomacy with three European powers focused on Iran's nuclear program. Khatami's ministers had agreed to freeze Iran's enrichment of uranium beginning in 2003 in pursuit of a lasting deal with the West and the removal of what at the time were very limited Western sanctions. The talks stalled after Iran argued that it had failed to quickly receive any economic boosts from the deal. Ahmadinejad subsequently ended the freeze and rapidly expanded Iran's nuclear work starting in 2005. The Bush administration responded by pushing the first of four rounds of economic sanctions on Iran through the UN Security Council in 2006. The U.S. Treasury Department, meanwhile, initiated a global campaign to freeze Iran's major banks out of the international financial system.

Ahmadinejad voiced an even greater willingness to support the militant groups fighting Israel from Lebanon and the Palestinian territories. He appalled Western leaders when he called for the Jewish state to be "wiped off the face of time" and questioned the historical reality of the Holocaust. Tehran was hardening its line. In just Ahmadinejad's first year in office, the flow of Iranian arms to Shiite militias inside Iraq began to dramatically increase. "In 2006, Iran seemed to make a tactical decision to significantly turn up the heat in Iraq," said Stephen Hadley, then President Bush's national security advisor. "We believe it was in response to our economic pressure on the nuclear program."

Iranian leaders and clerics also spoke of Iran's religious duty to protect the Shiites of Iraq. The conflict in the country was quickly morphing into a sectarian war between Iraq's two major sects. This was fueled by al Qaeda's assassinations of Shiite leaders with whom the United States had sought to cooperate, such as SCIRI chief Mohammad Baqir al-Hakim in Najaf, and the slaughter of tens of thousands of Shiites in mass bombings throughout the country. In early 2006, the commander of al Qaeda's Iraq franchise (called al Qaeda in Iraq), the Jordanian terrorist Abu Musab al-Zarqawi, orchestrated the destruction of the al-Askari mosque in the city of Samarra, one of the most renowned mosques in the Shiite world. Many Shiites took this as a call to war. Zarqawi spoke of wiping out the Shiites on the way to maintaining Sunni dominance in Iraq. His position was so extreme that al Qaeda's leaders, such as Ayman al-Zawahiri, warned him that too much violence could alienate Muslims, including Sunnis.

———

AS THE VIOLENCE IN Iraq intensified, Major General Qasem Soleimani inserted himself more aggressively into the conflict. And he greatly changed the direction of the war, earning a nearly mythic status among American, Israeli, and Arab intelligence officers. A veteran of the Iran-Iraq War, the Qods Force's commander rose to fame inside his country with operations he led for the Islamic Revolutionary Guard Corps deep inside Iraqi territory during the eight-year conflict. Iranian media described him as a deeply devout Muslim who courted his own martyrdom against Saddam's forces. He often appears in public sans his military uniform, dressed in the simple clothes of a Hezbollah adherent—a plain, collarless shirt and threadbare jacket. He also sports a graying, closely cropped beard, a standard fashion among Iran's revolutionary leadership.

Soleimani, who was in his early twenties at the start of the Iran-Iraq War, moved up the ranks of the IRGC in the mid-1990s by overseeing military operations against Central Asian narcotics smugglers and by cultivating the Qods Force's military proxies in Afghanistan, Lebanon, and the Palestinian territories. Born in Iran's southeast Kerman province, he was raised in a tribal society where the Iranian government had only a limited presence and very little control. Growing up in such an atmosphere made Soleimani adept at rallying Islamist militias, tribal warlords, and Arab businessmen far from Iran.

"Soleimani can be brutal or cunning, depending upon what's required," said Mouwaffak al-Rubaie, who served as the Iraqi government's national security advisor for six years under Prime Minister Maliki. "His ultimate goal is to further the revolution." This means opposing U.S. foreign policy across the region and Washington's Arab allies.

U.S. intelligence officials describe Soleimani as a Persian version of Karla, the Soviet spymaster depicted in John le Carré's Cold War novels, who is habitually playing geopolitical chess against his British nemesis, MI6, and its intelligence chief, George Smiley. Like Karla, Soleimani's endgame has always been to blunt the West's advances and to cement ties with Washington's adversaries, using any means possible.

The general's work eventually made him one of Supreme Leader Khamenei's closest strategists and confidants, one who may yet have a future political career in Tehran. Iranian state-controlled newspapers regularly carry photos of General Soleimani standing next to Khamenei at the front during the Iran-Iraq War in the 1980s. This may mean that Soleimani could emerge as a future president.

As tensions in Iraq between the United States and Iran began to boil over in 2005 and 2006, Soleimani and his Qods Force executed an increasingly aggressive plan to empower Tehran's political and military allies in Iraq and bleed American forces there. Members of Iraq's Shiite political bloc were intimidated and bribed. Soleimani also established a vast network of arms smuggling, military training, and religious indoctrination that ran through paramilitary camps established by the IRGC and Qods Force inside Iran. Tehran's close Lebanese ally, Hezbollah, helped oversee this network and sent its own men into Iran and Iraq to run training missions and operations.

The Qods Force, in many ways, acted like an old-world mafia in Iraq during the U.S. military occupation, keeping a close watch on local politicians who threatened Tehran's interests and objectives. Persian officers were generally polite and diplomatic, but the threat of violence lurked just below the surface. They made it clear to the Iraqis that Tehran was the dominant power in the region. Even Iraqi Shiite leaders and parties would be targeted.

Iraq's autonomous Kurdish region became a central area of conflict between the United States and Iran. Kurdistan has long been a fault line between the Middle East's Arab, Kurdish, and Persian peoples. The United States became the region's protector after the first Gulf War, policing its borders with American aircraft.

The Kurds in northern Iraq were in a political bind because of their close ties to both Washington and Tehran. Both countries wanted the autonomous Kurdish region as their ally. The Kurdish politician Noshirwan Mustafa reported angrily to Americans that two senior officers in Soleimani's Qods Force had come to his home in the Kurdish capital and warned him and his party against running in local parliamentary elections scheduled to be held that May. "What you are doing is very dangerous, and the situation might become very dangerous [for you]," Mustafa told the Americans.

Soleimani also gained leverage over Iraq's affairs by investing in competing political factions. Tehran's ties to Prime Minister Maliki and his Dawa Party traced back decades to the party's formation in Iraq. But later in the U.S. occupation, Iran also began funding and training fighters from Muqtada al-Sadr's Mahdi Army, which was a competitor to Dawa. Sadr hailed from one of Iraq's most beloved and powerful Shiite families, which never left Iraq during Saddam's rule and therefore was hailed for its bravery, martyrdom, and nationalist ethos. Indeed, despite being Shiite, the Sadrist movement was historically suspicious of Iran, if not actually hostile to it.

The Mahdi Army, however, quickly became a central force in the Shiite insurgency against the United States. Despite its anti-Iranian position, its fighters increasingly received training and funding from Tehran. Sadr's forces became so powerful that they directly challenged the Iraqi government for control of Najaf and parts of Baghdad, leading to a virtual state of war between the Iraqi government and the Mahdi Army. U.S. officials watched incredulously as General Soleimani sought to be the only international official capable of brokering a truce between the two sides, largely because the Qods Force had been arming both the government and the militias, while the Americans had less leverage with either.

Indeed, General Soleimani would travel into Baghdad's so-called Green Zone, the U.S.-controlled seat of the Iraqi government, to meet with government officials, sometimes behind the Americans' back. But in April 2006 the U.S. embassy and military intercepted communications showing that the Qods Force commander planned to meet Iraqi prime minister Ibrahim al-Jaafari ahead of key Iraqi elections. According to the U.S. ambassador at the time, Zalmay Khalilzad, the Bush administration decided to let Soleimani travel into Baghdad unhindered because intelligence showed he was going to ask the Iraqi leader to stand down. The United States sought the same goal because it believed that Jaafari, a Shiite politician, was incapable of healing the political rift between Sunni and Shiite that was fueling the internal conflict in Iraq. "He came to get rid of Jaafari in the spring of 2006," Khalilzad said of General Soleimani. "He thought we didn't know."

Around that time the Pentagon, with coalition and Iraqi forces, began piecing together the magnitude of the training and arms smuggling network established by Soleimani and the Qods Force to empower their Iraqi allies. Up until that year, the United States had detected only a relatively small influx of arms and roadside bomb technology coming in from Iran, though the Pentagon and CIA were aware of the Qods Force's links to the Badr Corps and Mahdi Army. The Americans' primary focus in Iraq at that point had been the Sunni insurgents and al Qaeda. But now the death toll of American troops attributable to Iranian-supplied bombs was skyrocketing. In the last quarter of 2006, the Pentagon concluded, these munitions were responsible for nearly 20 percent of the deaths of coalition forces in Iraq.

Soleimani and the Qods Force, the U.S. and Iraqi militaries learned, had created a virtual underground railroad for Iraq's Shiite fighters to get training inside Iran, Syria, and Lebanon. The Iranians had established at least a half dozen military training camps, some centered around Tehran and others close to the Iran-Iraq border. Recruits were taught the religious philosophy of the Islamic Republic's founder, Ayatollah Ruhollah Khomeini.

U.S. military intelligence also learned that Hezbollah operatives from Lebanon were playing a central role in the Qods Force's operations. Many of the Iranian military trainers couldn't speak fluent Arabic and relied on these Lebanese Arabs to communicate with the Iraqis. Hezbollah had extensive experience in conducting guerilla warfare from its twenty-year conflict with Israel and had become expert in the use of roadside bombs, suicide attacks, and snipers.

The U.S. military and Iraqi security captured and interrogated dozens of Shiite fighters beginning in 2006. They described remarkably similar paths that took them to training camps both inside and outside Iran. American officials began calling these pro-Iranian militias "special groups," due to their focus on military attacks rather than political maneuvering.

The experience of one Iraqi captured by coalition forces in 2007 outlined the extensive networks Iran and its allies in Syria and Lebanon had established to fight the war against the Americans in Iraq. The militant, whose name was redacted from the Pentagon's interrogation record, traveled, like many in Tehran's underground pipeline, to the southern city of al-Amarah, where he and a dozen other men hid in a safe house that was described as a "garage." There they were given fake passports and waited for Iranian couriers to contact them for the trip across the border. They secretly traveled in a boat that plied the southern marshlands dividing Iran and Iraq.

Once inside Iran, the trainee and his companions took buses and planes to reach an IRGC military compound near Tehran. The men were given uniforms and bunked in small sleeping areas, four to a room. Every morning they received training in small arms, counterinterrogation techniques, and physical surveillance. They would also be schooled in the tenets of the Iranian revolution. "The schedule was demanding, and several of the students felt that the course was too demanding," the militant told his interrogators.

But the men's odyssey had only just begun. After nearly three weeks at the camp, the trainee and other fighters were flown to Damascus. In the Syrian capital, they were quickly shuttled over the Lebanese border into the Bekaa Valley, the stronghold of Hezbollah. There they were given a second round of military training, conducted by Hezbollah members, that focused on the somewhat staid tasks of project planning and weapons warehousing, as well as on coded communications and small weapons use.

"The instructors were members of Lebanese Hezbollah," said the Iraqi militant. "They had complete control of the area, the students and the familiarity with all of the management process needed to run a paramilitary organization." It was only after he returned to Iraq that the man's Iranian handlers paid him—in U.S. dollars. The amount wasn't cited in the documents. But Americans believe it was in the hundreds of dollars, indicating how well funded the operation was.

A second Iraqi insurgent captured by coalition forces in 2007 also described traveling with about a dozen recruits to Iran via al-Amarah and the southern marshlands. The trip involved multiple stops in smaller Iranian cities, such as Kermanshah and Mashhad. Along the way the trainees were allowed to do some sightseeing: they visited the holy shrine of Imam Reza in Mashhad and the local zoo.

In Tehran, the men were taken to a military base, Sayid Shuhada, run by the IRGC on the outskirts of the capital. There they were given instruction in using Russian Dragunov sniper rifles. They were also taught how to use night-vision goggles to identify coalition forces in the dark.

After thirty days, the Shiite militants returned to Iraq and were deposited in one of three locations: Baghdad or the southern cities of Diyala and Kut. One who went to Kut told his interrogators that he was put in charge of training other local insurgents fighting the U.S. forces. The man was associated with the Mahdi Army, which often went by the Arabic acronym JAM. He told his interrogators that he wanted "to take the opportunity in detention to learn if what everyone else said about the [coalition forces] is true," he said. "Everyone in JAM tells everyone that the CF will use people and throw them away in prison."

Still, many of Iran's Iraqi recruits voiced little love for their Iranian trainers or Soleimani's Qods Force. They viewed them as arrogant, with an air of cultural superiority toward Arabs. Their alliance, they noted, wouldn't last forever. And this played into the hope of American strategists that Iraq could eventually be broken from Iran. "Iraqi [Special Group] trainees do not like their Iranian trainers," said one of the captured militants. "The Shia in Iraq would be led by an Iraqi. Even a bad Iraqi leader is better than a good Iranian leader."

U.S. officials hoped this Arab-Persian divide would eventually allow Washington to peel the Iraqis away from Tehran. But the sectarian war between the Sunnis and the Shiites wouldn't allow the United States to truly test this proposition. Some Americans believed Tehran was intentionally fueling this conflict as a way to ensure their control over any reconciliation efforts.

SOLEIMANI'S OFFENSIVE FINALLY CAPTURED the attention of the Pentagon's top brass as the numbers of roadside bombs and militants coming in from Iran increased in 2006 and 2007. During the early stages of the war, the Bush administration was almost singularly focused on containing the Sunni insurgency and the waves of suicide bombers launched by al Qaeda and Zarqawi. Now they began taking countermeasures.

In the fall of 2006, the Pentagon's Iraq command set up a special unit, called Task Force 17, to work against Iran and its allies. American intelligence officials in Baghdad believed that Soleimani's men were all over the country, posing as diplomats, businessmen, journalists, and Shiite pilgrims. Iran's ambassador to Baghdad, Hassan Kazemi Qomi, was a known Qods Force officer. And IRGC and Qods Force officers—including possibly General Soleimani himself—continued to pay visits to the heavily fortified Green Zone.

The U.S. Special Operations Command intensified its efforts to directly target the Qods Force. General Stanley McChrystal headed the Special Operations unit from its headquarters in Fort Bragg, North Carolina, but increasingly worked out of forward U.S. bases in Iraq as he prepared his operations. He closely studied the nexus between Soleimani's men and the Iraqi "special groups," according to his advisors.

On December 21, 2006, General McChrystal's men made their first major capture of a senior Qods Force officer inside Iraq. U.S. intelligence showed that a commander named Mohsen Chizari, a key lieutenant of Soleimani's, was staying at the compound of an Iraqi politician associated with SCIRI, just across the Tigris River from the Green Zone. General Chizari commanded an operations staff inside the Qods Force, called Department 600, which the United States believed was playing a central role in smuggling arms to the Shiite groups. Other senior Qods Force officers were believed to be at the SCIRI compound with him, including men focused on Iranian operations inside the Persian Gulf and Yemen.

In a lightning operation, the Special Operations unit raided the SCIRI office, using drones and U.S. military helicopters. The United States held and interrogated Chizari and his cohorts for ten days before their eventual release. The U.S. action drew heavy protests from both the Iraqi prime minister's office and the Iranian government. "They were totally shocked," General McChrystal said. "But it was a necessary first step" to push back the Iranians. Khalilzad said he pressed the Iraqis to obtain the travel documents of those Iranians who had been detained, which they didn't. "We had good information on the IRGC's role," he said.

Three weeks later, on January 11, the U.S. military raided the Iranian government's liaison office in Erbil, capital of the autonomous Kurdish region, to look for Qods Force officers. Both Iranian and Kurdish officials said Tehran's mission there was a regular diplomatic compound, legally hosting trade, energy, and cultural delegations, and was in the process of being upgraded to a formal consulate. The Iranian government had maintained the office since 1992, they said. But McChrystal's team believed a senior delegation of IRGC and Qods Force officers were transiting through Erbil that day.

At daybreak American military helicopters landed on the roof of the Iranian compound, and U.S. soldiers quickly sprinted into its offices at gunpoint. The Americans took away five of the Iranians who were sleeping there and confiscated a trove of computers and Iranian-government documents. The men were moved to Camp Cropper, the prison for high-value targets where Saddam Hussein had been detained.

Iraqi and Kurdish officials vehemently criticized the U.S. operation, saying it violated international law and that the men were accredited diplomats. Massoud Barzani, president of the Kurdistan Regional Government, said the Americans had actually captured the wrong men. "The Americans came to detain this delegation, not the people in the office," Barzani said. "They came to the wrong place at the wrong time."

The Americans, however, learned that the men they had detained were traveling with fake civilian identification papers. General McChrystal and other Americans insist that at least three of the men detained were senior Qods Force officials and that they provided the United States with substantial intelligence following their capture.

The Iranians retaliated. On the evening of January 20, 2007, a dozen armed insurgents raided a joint U.S.-Iraqi military command in the city of Karbala. The militants were dressed in American combat uniforms and carried U.S.-made weapons. Iraqi guards later said they waved the men through in their Suburban vehicles because some spoke English.

The squads used concussion bombs to enter the barracks housing the Americans. One U.S. soldier was killed in a firefight at the base. But the commando team kidnapped four other Americans and fled the scene under pursuit by U.S. military attack helicopters, apparently trying to get back to the Iranian border. Two of the U.S. soldiers were found dead in the back of a Suburban abandoned by the assailants, shot in the chest and head execution-style. The body of one of the other soldiers was found in a ditch, while the fourth

American survived his capture but died en route to a hospital after he was rescued by American soldiers.

U.S. Special Forces eventually tracked the assailants back to Najaf. Two days later they raided a compound there and arrested four men for overseeing the Karbala attack. Two of them, Qais and Laith al-Khazali, were brothers and former members of the Mahdi Army. In 2006 they had established a much more radical splinter group, called Asaib Ahl al-Haq, or "League of the Righteous," which U.S. officials said was central to Iran's arms smuggling network. Another man, Ali Musa Daqduq, was identified as a senior Lebanese Hezbollah member whose activities inside Iraq had been approved by the Shiite movement's senior leadership.

During lengthy interrogations, both Qais al-Khazali and Daqduq provided detailed information on the Qods Force's role in the attack. (Daqduq initially refused to talk to his captors, pretending to be mute. But after weeks of detainment and interrogation he eventually talked.) The Qods Force had developed detailed intelligence on the Karbala military structure and the movement and shifts of the U.S. troops based there, which they passed on to the attack team. The Iranians had also assisted by acquiring the American uniforms and arms used in the deception. "Daqduq contends that the Iraqi special groups could not have conducted this complex operation without the support and direction of the Qods Force," Brigadier General Kevin Bergner, a spokesman for the multinational force in Iraq, said at the time. General McChrystal added during that interview that the Karbala attack might well have been the most dangerous incident inside Iraq in terms of possibly sparking a direct conflict between the United States and Iran, saying, "They did a very good job of doing a lot of damage."

IN JANUARY 2007 GENERAL David Petraeus became the top U.S. military commander in Iraq and quickly moved to refocus the Pentagon on Iran's role in fueling the insurgency. Petraeus's star was rising in the Pentagon and Washington thanks to the performance of forces under his command in Sunni-dominated areas in northern Iraq during the early stages of the war. He had been able to pacify the area by forming alliances with Sunni tribesmen, often using cash, to fight against al Qaeda and insurgents. His operations were viewed as a model for the later efforts to fight al Qaeda in Iraq with an influx of troops, known as the "surge."

Petraeus fixated on the Qods Force and General Soleimani, for whom he developed a personal hatred because the Iranian targeted American personnel and seemed to want to destabilize Iraq. Petraeus was furious that the Iranians publicly assured the world that they were promoting stability in Iraq while covertly funneling arms and trained militants across the border and buying off Iraqi politicians.

Petraeus and Soleimani communicated with each other via the Iraqi politicians who courted both Washington and Tehran. In early 2008, according to U.S. military officials, Soleimani sent an electronic message to Petraeus in Baghdad via Jalal Talabani, the Kurdish politician and Iraqi president. The message arrived as U.S. forces were supporting an Iraqi government crackdown on the Mahdi Army in Baghdad's largest Shiite slum, called Sadr City. Soleimani stressed to Petraeus that stability in the Iraqi capital could only be achieved with his involvement. "General Petraeus, you should know that I, Qasem Soleimani, control the policy of Iran with respect to Iraq, Lebanon, Gaza and Afghanistan," the electronic message read, according to the officials who saw it.

Petraeus answered that the Iranian commander should know that the United States and the Western world were aware of what the Qods Force was doing inside Iraq and that this was only going to further isolate Tehran economically and diplomatically. "General Petraeus mentioned that we continue to see on average one rocket and one [armor-piercing bomb] attack daily," a State Department diplomat in Baghdad wrote to Foggy Bottom in a cable, recounting a recent meeting between the American general and Talabani. "The next time Talabani spoke to Qasem Soleimani, he might pass along that we are concerned about Iranian actions," Petraeus told Talabani, according to a recounting of the conversation to Washington.

Petraeus sent another message to Soleimani in 2008, this time using an Iraqi Shiite militia leader close to Tehran. At the time, American forces were being targeted by a particularly lethal munition called an IRAM. The Pentagon's intelligence networks showed the Revolutionary Guard was providing theses bombs to its Iraqi allies and training them on their use.

"If we sustain casualties from one of these IRAMs, there's going to be a very significant response," Petraeus told Soleimani via Hadi al-Amiri, a leader of the Badr Corps and future lawmaker. The Americans didn't see another IRAM attack for twelve to eighteen months. "The Iranians would have had a death wish if they wanted to go head-to-head with the United States," Petraeus believed. "They always stopped short of this."

But now, five years after the invasion, it was clear that Washington's strategy had backfired in Iraq in regard to curbing Iran's influence. Rather than weakening Khamenei and the state, the war had empowered Tehran to spread its power and influence farther into Arab lands. Iran could target American troops in Iraq at will, and U.S. allies were even more vulnerable. And Iran would be able to use this leverage against the United States and Europe, particularly on the nuclear issue.

CHAPTER 4

The Axis of Resistance

T HE TRAINING AND ARMING OF SHIITE INSURGENT FIGHTERS BY IRAN
hamstrung the U.S. military in Iraq as the war intensified. But
Tehran's closest regional ally, Syrian president Bashar al-Assad, was
facilitating the movement of an equally deadly enemy across Iraq's
western border: al Qaeda's jihadist fighters and suicide bombers.
Iran and Syria, to the horror of the United States and Baghdad's
leaders, were backing competing sides in Iraq's civil war—Shiite
militias and Sunni insurgents—in an effort to sabotage the Bush
administration's ambitious Middle East project. The result was the
slaughter of hundreds of thousands of Iraqis in a gruesome Sunni-
Shiite sectarian war. "It was a very cynical alliance in every respect,"
said Mouwaffak al-Rubaie, a long-serving national security advisor
to Iraqi prime minister Nouri al-Maliki, describing the Syrian-
Iranian strategy.

Assad publicly signaled Syria's preparations to undermine U.S.
military operations in Iraq from the early days of the American
buildup to war in 2003. The Syrian dictator and his government
were convinced that any American campaign to topple Saddam

Hussein would invariably also seek to destabilize, if not overthrow, the Baathist regime in Damascus at a later stage. Assad and Saddam were hardly allies: in 1991 the Syrians joined a U.S.-led coalition in 1991 that drove Iraqi troops out of Kuwait. But the two Baathist states shared an ideology based on terrorism and state-sanctioned violence, particularly political assassinations, connecting them in the West's eyes in the years after 9/11.

Assad felt particularly vulnerable at the time of the Iraq invasion, according to his presidential aides, because he was still in the process of consolidating power after succeeding his father in 2000. Bashar didn't trust the old guard of his party and military, and he feared they would link up with the United States and other Western powers to unseat him. Subverting the U.S. project in Iraq, Assad believed, was a preemptive move. "The United States and Britain will not be able to control Iraq. There will be much tougher resistance," Assad told Lebanon's *as-Safir* newspaper after the invasion started in March 2003. "But if the American-British designs succeed — and we hope they do not succeed and we doubt that they will succeed — there will be Arab popular resistance anyway and this has begun."

Syria's grand mufti, Sheikh Ahmad Kuftaro, the highest-ranking Sunni Muslim in the country, publicly called for martyrdom operations against coalition forces in Iraq in a six-point statement he put out at the time. He also called on Muslims worldwide to disrupt the U.S. war effort in Iraq. "Muslims must use all possible means to repel the aggressors, including martyr operations," he announced. "Muslims all over the world must boycott American and British products and those from coalition forces."

Damascus International Airport emerged as the primary pipeline for al Qaeda fighters and other Sunni militants traveling to Iraq from all over the Middle East. Syrian government officials repeatedly denied to the Bush administration that they had the ability to control the movement of these jihadists or to seal Syria's border with Iraq. Assad also stressed that his government was among the most committed in the region to fighting Sunni extremists, including al Qaeda, citing his father's war in the 1980s against the Muslim Brotherhood, a global Islamist movement, which killed tens of thousands of Syrians in the western city of Hama. The Assad family was a member of Syria's minority Alawite sect, an offshoot of Shiite Islam, which many Sunni clerics considered heretical. These religious ties bonded the Assad regime even more closely with Iran and alienated them from the region's Sunni Arab powers, particularly Saudi Arabia.

But the Pentagon and U.S. intelligence agencies didn't buy the Syrian line that it was committed to the fight. The Assad family regime, often in collaboration with Iran, had for decades manipulated extremist groups, terrorists, and militias to control Lebanon and to fight Israel. Assad's brother-in-law, Assef Shawkat, headed Syria's military-intelligence unit and was a master of using proxies to fight Damascus's battles. Shawkat and Iran's Revolutionary Guard were central players in building up Hezbollah and Hamas, even though the latter didn't share the Shiite faith. Damascus's and Tehran's intelligence services became intertwined in the 2000s. U.S. officials grew convinced that Shawkat either turned a blind eye to the sophisticated smuggling networks being established by al Qaeda in his country or directly ran them. His intelligence apparatus inside Syria was so pervasive that Shawkat couldn't be unaware of the movement of Sunni fighters across his borders, American officials believed.

Damascus made little effort to hide its support for the Iraqi insurgency as the war in Iraq gathered steam in 2003 and 2004. Directly across the street from the U.S. embassy in the Syrian capital, in the upscale suburb of Abu Roumaneh, Iraqi Sunnis opened a recruitment office to lure young Arab men, both Syrians and foreigners, to the fight. The facility was guarded by Syrian intelligence and military officers twenty-four hours a day, according to eyewitness accounts. The recruits quickly boarded buses that took them directly to Baghdad and other Iraqi cities where the insurgency was intensifying.

The recruitment became so overt that Washington's ambassador to Syria in 2003, Ted Kattouf, repeatedly filed protests with the Syrian government, demanding they break up the human-smuggling operation. Syrian authorities first responded by denying these activities were taking place and then simply moved the recruitment center to Damascus's fairgrounds, at the center of the capital, where the transfer of foreign fighters to Iraq continued unabated. "The Damascus fairgrounds are owned and operated by the government of Syria," said David Schenker, a former Pentagon official who oversaw U.S. defense policy toward Syria during the first George W. Bush administration. "There's no way the regime couldn't have been involved in overseeing these types of activities."

Iran's and Syria's joint efforts to undermine the American war effort in Iraq strengthened their "Axis of Resistance," as Iranian and Syrian officials called it. This alliance included other movements and militias across the Middle East committed both to fighting Israel and to challenging U.S. foreign policy. These included Hezbollah, Hamas, Palestinian Islamic Jihad, and Shiite militias in Iraq, Yemen, and Afghanistan. The Resistance Axis would only strengthen as American involvement in their region grew, with disastrous consequences for U.S. interests.

DAMASCUS, UNDER PRESIDENT BASHAR AL-ASSAD's leadership, became the forward operating base for Iran's Axis of Resistance during the 2000s. The Arab capital, considered the world's oldest continuously inhabited city, had maintained its sophisticated Levantine culture, architecture, and cuisine. The streetscape of Damascus is a sweep of Ottoman-era mosques, Byzantine churches, and French-colonial cafés and restaurants. Before the Syrian civil war, European tourists regularly visited the city, as did Christian and Shiite pilgrims seeking to trace the final steps of John the Baptist or to pray at the blue-tiled Shrine of Sayyida Zeinab, the Prophet Muhammad's granddaughter. Owing to Syria's history of Arab nationalism and economic socialism, Western brands and products were almost non-existent inside the city's walls, except for the elite. The anomalies were a Four Seasons hotel and a Kentucky Fried Chicken tucked inside a diplomatic enclave.

In contrast with his father's tough but modest appearance, Bashar al-Assad and his London-born wife, Asma, cultivated the image of the Middle East's most glamorous and modern couple. His first trips after taking power in 2000 were to Western capitals, including London and Paris, where he sought to end Syria's isolation and open the country to foreign investment. Asma, meanwhile, built NGOs and hosted visiting international women's delegations at Assad's Damascus palaces, lecturing about the need for education, poverty alleviation, and the emancipation of the Palestinian people. *Vogue* famously called her "a rose in the desert" in a 2011 hagiography, which was eventually pulled from Condé Nast's website after civil war broke out in the country later that year. In that article she talked about her designer shoes and the fairy-tale life she lived.

The Assads' progressive, Western-friendly veneer, however, was belied by the presence in Damascus of key players in the Axis of Resistance. Senior members of the Qods Force and Hezbollah, who coordinated the supply of arms into Lebanon and the Palestinian territories, kept military offices in the city. The political leaderships of Hamas and Palestinian Islamic Jihad, both designated as terrorist organizations by the United States and the European Union, were based in nondescript homes in the quiet backstreets of Damascus. North Korean engineers and arms traders were active in the Syrian capital, intimately involved in developing the Assad regime's ballistic missile and chemical weapons programs. The North Koreans were also secretly building a nuclear reactor in the eastern deserts of Deir Ezzour province, behind the backs of the Western powers. The plant was a virtual carbon copy of the heavy water plant North Korea built in the city of Yongbyon to secretly produce plutonium for nuclear weapons.

Bashar al-Assad's leadership was characterized by his desire to court and bridge two distinctly different worlds. An ophthalmology student in London during the 1990s, Bashar took power at just thirty-four and fueled hopes of modernizing and opening up Syria. During the short-lived Damascus Spring of 2001, Bashar took steps to free up Syria's media and political parties, and later he allowed foreign companies to take ownership stakes in local banks and finance firms. He also flirted with pursuing a peace agreement with Israeli leaders, which would have given control of the Golan Heights back to Syria and lifted U.S. economic sanctions on the regime. In return, theoretically, Bashar would end Syria's support for Hezbollah and other militias fighting Israel and sever Damascus's ties to Iran. Israeli officials, however, were skeptical he would ever follow through.

Despite these overtures, Bashar soon proved to be as brutal as his father, and even more erratic. Many Arab leaders were stunned to see the new Syrian leader proudly photographed alongside Hezbollah's secretary-general, Hassan Nasrallah, and Hamas's political boss, Khaled Meshaal. Hafez al-Assad, they said, had viewed such militia commanders and politicians as below his status and purposely kept them at arm's length. Bashar also deepened Syria's relationship with Iran beyond what his father had desired. The presence of the Revolutionary Guard and its Qods Force grew much more pronounced in Damascus. On posters, Bashar appeared next to Ali Khamenei, Iran's supreme leader, while his father had sought to balance his relationship with Iran and Syria's Arab neighbors, maintaining his unique regional influence. The younger Assad, in contrast, appeared reliant on the members of the Resistance Axis for his security and regional influence.

The older Assad had had a clear understanding of Israel's red lines and had never sought to recklessly cross them. He was at times admired, ironically, by the international community for sticking to the commitments his government made, even as he ran one of the world's most repressive states. But Bashar, unsure of his political footing, pursued a schizophrenic policy of growing more dependent

on Iran for his security needs while concurrently trying to appear as
a reformer to attract Western support. He wanted it both ways.

A MAJOR THREAT TO Bashar al-Assad's nascent leadership and regional
power, as well as Iran's, emerged in the mid-2000s in neighboring
Lebanon under the leadership of Rafik al-Hariri, a billionaire businessman and on-and-off prime minister. A close ally of both Saudi
Arabia and France, Hariri was Beirut's richest man, having earned
billions of dollars from construction contracts in Saudi Arabia,
building hotels and office towers for the royal family. His success
made him a force across the Arab world. Hariri returned to Lebanon
in the early 1980s, entered politics, and became the leader of the
Sunni community, overseeing the rebuilding of central Beirut following the end of Lebanon's disastrous fifteen-year civil war. By
2004, the politician had redirected his energies from business to an
aggressive challenge of Syria's political and military domination of
Lebanon, which had grown suffocating to most Lebanese. Beirut's
thriving financial sector fed the Syrian economy and made Assad
uncomfortably dependent on Hariri. The mustached politician
grew to become a symbol of Lebanon's cultural and economic re-
birth, as well as its independence.

The Assad family, like virtually all of Syria's elite, never accepted
Lebanon as an independent country, thinking of it as an integral
part of a "Greater Syria" that was disbanded following the breakup
of the Ottoman Empire after World War I. Damascus believed its
writ extended to precolonial borders that included Lebanon and
parts of Turkey and Israel. The Assads saw pro-Western governments
in Beirut, Baghdad, and Jerusalem as existential threats to their
country, while Hariri saw the Europeans and the United States as
his natural allies. The two men were on a collision course.

Hariri's plan was to regain power in Beirut by winning legislative
elections scheduled for summer 2005 and pushing initiatives to
weaken Syria's hold on Lebanon. This included an international

agreement, known as the Taif Accords, which called for the withdrawal of thousands of Syrian troops stationed across Lebanon as well as Damascus's omnipresent intelligence service. To do this, he needed to block the reelection of Lebanon's pro-Syrian president, Emile Lahoud, to another three-year term. Assad saw Lahoud as Syria's de facto viceroy in Beirut; his removal would undermine Syria's entire power structure in Lebanon.

Hariri also aggressively worked to weaken Assad by plotting with his close friend Jacques Chirac, the French president, and with the Bush administration in 2004. This included passing UN Security Council Resolution 1559, which required Syria to withdraw its remaining seven thousand troops from Lebanon. Hariri sought to use the UN resolution to force Hezbollah to disarm and disband its militia, which was deployed across Lebanon and backed by Syrian and Iranian intelligence. Such moves, many American and European officials believed, would cripple Assad's ability to maintain control of Lebanon—and possibly Syria—just four years after replacing his late father. U.S. officials didn't believe Bashar al-Assad had consolidated power among the Syrian military and the ruling Baath Party and thought he could be vulnerable to a coup d'état if he lost Lebanon. The Bush administration was still in regime-change mode.

The White House also believed Syria's loss of Lebanon could cripple Iran's regional ambitions. Tehran used Lebanon as its military front against Israel and Syria and as a land bridge to move weapons to Hezbollah. Iranians viewed Syria and Lebanon as providing the Revolutionary Guard with the "strategic depth" required to pursue its campaign against Israel and the West. The pipeline of Iranian arms and influence into the Levant could be shut down if Hariri succeeded with his plan.

President Assad responded brutally to the political moves against him in Lebanon. From his presidential palace in the hills above Damascus in the summer of 2004, he told Hariri he would "break Lebanon over Hariri's" head if he continued to fight the reappointment of President Lahoud. In the months that followed, a string of car bombings targeted anti-Syrian politicians, such as the parliamentarian Marwan Hamadeh and a number of prominent journalists. No one doubted who was responsible.

Two months later, a team of Hezbollah operatives initiated a conspiracy to plot the assassination of Hariri and his political allies, according to Lebanese and UN investigators. It was an attack that could fundamentally alter the politics of the Mideast, not unlike the 1995 murder of Israeli prime minister Yitzhak Rabin. U.S. officials believed the operation was closely coordinated with both Iran and Syria.

The leader of the Hezbollah team was well known to U.S. intelligence agencies. Mustafa Badreddine had been active in terrorist plots going back to the early 1980s and was the brother-in-law of one of the United States' most wanted men, Imad Mugniyah. The FBI had placed a $5 million bounty on Mugniyah for his alleged role in overseeing the Marine Corps bombing twenty years earlier, among other terrorist acts.

Badreddine had actually been captured in Kuwait in 1984 while overseeing yet another plot to bomb the U.S. and French embassies there. He was held for nearly a decade in a Kuwaiti prison before Saddam Hussein's forces unwittingly freed him in 1991 as they emptied the country's prisons at the start of the Gulf War. The Hezbollah operative quickly returned to Beirut to team up with Mugniyah and strengthen the organization's power in Lebanon.

Both men had trained in military camps established by Iran's Revolutionary Guard and were devout followers of the Ayatollah Khomeini and Iran's revolution. Under their leadership, Hezbollah became a virtual unit of the Revolutionary Guard. Iranians named a street after Imad Mugniyah to honor his role in fighting Israel and its backers.

In December 2004, Badreddine and three other Hezbollah men began regular surveillance of Hariri as he moved between his home, Lebanon's parliament, and the offices of his political allies. Four logistical support teams were established to back up the assassins.

In January 2005, Badreddine's team purchased a Mitsubishi minivan from a showroom in the northern Lebanese city of Tripoli. They loaded it with a massive bomb and recruited a local Sunni youth and militant to publicly claim credit for the forthcoming attack and to falsely link it to al Qaeda sympathizers. Badreddine's team trained and instructed a suicide bomber to position the Mitsubishi at a key intersection on the corniche road in West Beirut. At close to 1:00 p.m. on February 14, the unidentified bomber detonated the explosives-laden Mitsubishi just as Hariri's six-car convoy passed the St. George Hotel, a Beirut landmark that had stood since the days of French colonial rule. The blast left a twenty-foot crater in the road and was estimated by Lebanese police to have contained roughly 2,200 pounds of TNT. Twenty people, in addition to Hariri, were killed instantly, and nearly three hundred were injured.

Hariri's assassination led to massive street protests across Lebanon that fomented the so-called Cedar Revolution (referring to the cedar tree on the country's national flag). Bashar al-Assad, under intense international scrutiny for his suspected role in the bombing, pulled his remaining soldiers out of Lebanon, and Rafik al-Hariri's son Saad was elected prime minister in Beirut. The UN followed by establishing a special court to investigate the attack, which ultimately led to the indictments of Mustafa Badreddine and other Hezbollah leaders. Imad Mugniyah was assassinated in 2008 outside Syrian intelligence offices in Damascus in a car bombing for which no one claimed responsibility. Badreddine was killed in Syria in 2016.

But Hezbollah and its Syrian and Iranian backers took the tumult as only a temporary loss. Hezbollah's monthlong war with Israel in the summer of 2006 solidified the militia and political party as the kingmaker in Lebanon. And Iran and Syria quickly resupplied Hezbollah with tens of thousands of rockets after the conflict with the Israelis ended. The international community, while convinced of Assad's role in the Hariri murder, never moved to indict him or his top generals.

The conflict between the United States, Iran, and their respective allies was spreading like wildfire as the Middle East quaked in the years following Saddam Hussein's removal. The Bush administration sought to remake the region into a pro-Western bulwark in response to the extremist threat. But Tehran, Damascus, and their Axis of Resistance weren't lying down, as evidenced in Lebanon. They were going to reshape the region on their own terms. As the battle in Iraq continued, the flow of jihadists and foreign fighters intensified, with the majority coming through Syria—under the close watch of the Assad regime.

IN LATE 2007, THE Pentagon captured a massive cache of al Qaeda's logistical files in the Iraqi city of Sinjar, which sits on the country's northern border with Syria. Two al Qaeda affiliate groups operating inside Iraq, called the Islamic State of Iraq and the Mujahidin Shura Council, compiled the documents. They catalogued the travels of nearly seven hundred foreign nationals who had entered Iraq to fight coalition officials between August 2006 and August 2007. Most of the men, who ranged in age from seventeen to fifty, were logged as "martyrs"—suicide bombers—in al Qaeda's files. Only a small number were categorized as regular militia fighters or men performing logistical or clerical jobs for the insurgency.

They came to fight from across the Arab world. The largest contingent—more than 40 percent—hailed from Saudi Arabia. But another 20 percent came from Libya, and others were recruited from Morocco, Yemen, Syria, and Algeria. The arrival of North Africans into Iraq particularly worried Western intelligence agencies because of their original proximity to Western Europe. There was a concern these fighters would become more radicalized in Iraq and then take their fight to France, the United Kingdom, and Germany, a fear that became all too prophetic.

The journeys of these fighters into Iraq were remarkably uniform. A seventeen-year-old Libyan national named Muhammad

Anwar Rafiia'a Yahiya was among those who made the trip to Iraq through Syria to conduct a suicide bombing mission, according to a file compiled by the Islamic State of Iraq in April 2007. The high school student came from the Libyan coastal city of Dernah, which was one of the largest recruitment centers for foreign fighters joining the Iraq jihad. The Libyan traveled to Cairo and then flew to Damascus, where he was assigned to an al Qaeda coordinator named Abu Abbas. He left home with just 700 Libyan dinars—about $508—but then deposited his funds with one of his al Qaeda handlers before heading over the border to Iraq to fight.

Almost all of the fighters flew into Damascus International Airport, where they were met by al Qaeda recruiters or coordinators, normally referred to by Arabic honorifics, such as Abu Umar or Abu Abbas, rather than formal names. The jihadists then made their way by bus to Iraq, mainly through the eastern Syrian province of Deir Ezzour. Al Qaeda and other insurgent groups preferred this route because the Arab tribes in the province had relatives on the other side of the Syrian-Iraqi border and largely sympathized with the campaign against the United States, easing the movement of the fighters. Once at the border, the fighters were forced to surrender their passports and cellphones to the al Qaeda smugglers and travel with only the equivalent of a few hundred dollars to the front.

Pentagon and counterterrorism experts who monitored the Assad regime's interactions with al Qaeda and its foreign fighters realized it was a tense and suspicious relationship at best. Unquestionably, Syrian intelligence officials sought to penetrate these groups and utilize them to bleed American forces inside Iraq. But Damascus also wanted to track the fighters and make sure they didn't stay inside Syria, where they could potentially turn against the Assad regime itself. Syrian officials knew there was latent support for Sunni fundamentalists inside their country.

"Syria has an interest in keeping the U.S.-backed regime in Iraq off balance, but it must also fear a backlash from jihadi groups, many of which despise Alawite 'apostasy' as much or more than the United

States," West Point's Combating Terrorism Center wrote in a detailed 2007 report on the Sinjar documents. "For Syria, supporting jihadi groups is at best a double-edged sword."

Al Qaeda leaders themselves detailed their conflicted attitudes toward the Syrian regime in a multitude of writings posted on jihadi websites after 9/11. Many described their accounts of the war in Iraq and their travels through Syria to the front, where they established training camps along the Syria-Iraq border. The onetime commander of al Qaeda's overall operations in Iraq, the Jordanian Abu Musab al-Zarqawi, was among those based in this border region, according to these accounts. Zarqawi and other al Qaeda leaders described their wariness about cooperating with Syrian intelligence officials, questioning their true commitment to the Islamist cause.

SYRIA'S ROLE IN PROMOTING the insurgency fueled conflicting policy responses from the Bush administration. A number of Middle East strategists in Washington continued to hold out hope that Damascus could emerge as an ally against al Qaeda and be weaned off its alliance with Iran. They cited Hafez al-Assad's decision to join the U.S.-led international coalition that drove Saddam Hussein's forces out of Kuwait in 1991, heralded by the George H. W. Bush administration as a landmark development that strengthened the Arab-Israeli peace process that had begun that same year.

And at times Syria's intelligence services even cooperated with the United States. In the year following the September 11 attacks, Damascus had provided American security forces with information on Mohammed Haydar Zammar, later identified as a key planner of the al Qaeda strikes on New York and Washington who had been taken into Syrian custody after he was extradited from Morocco. Damascus also gave information to U.S. authorities on an al Qaeda plot to bomb an American naval unit in Bahrain, which proved so useful that a senior administration official told a congressional panel in 2002 that "the cooperation the Syrians provided in their own interest saved American lives." What Washington gave Damascus in return was never clear, but when Syria was nominated that year for a rotating seat on the UN Security Council, the Bush administration did nothing to block it.

In February 2005, Damascus also secretly handed over Saddam's half brother, Sabawi Ibrahim al-Hassan al-Tikriti, to Iraqi security forces. He had been playing a major role in financing the insurgency from his safe haven inside Syria, according to U.S. officials. The Bush administration said at the time that his capture provided a windfall of intelligence on the role Iraqi Baathists and Saddam's confidants were playing in destabilizing Iraq. They hoped they could build on Damascus's help to further improve U.S.-Syrian relations.

The improving relations early in the Iraq War were short-lived, however. Just two months later, in April 2005, Syrian officials announced they were cutting off all military and intelligence cooperation with Washington. Damascus's ambassador to Washington, Imad Moustapha, privately fumed that the Bush administration had reneged on a commitment to Syria not to make public the Assad government's role in Tikriti's capture. The diplomat said this disclosure risked fueling instability inside his country because of the vast domestic opposition to the occupation of Iraq. American officials, however, believed Damascus's decision was mainly driven by Syria's anger over the White House's decision to pull its ambassador to Damascus, Margaret Scobey, in protest over the assassination of Rafik al-Hariri in Beirut.

The breakdown of cooperation in 2005 and Hariri's assassination fueled an increasingly hard-line stance toward Damascus in the White House. Elliott Abrams, one of President Bush's closest Middle East advisors on the National Security Council, privately pressed the president to order the bombing of Damascus International Airport as a means to cut off the flow of foreign fighters into Iraq, according to former U.S. officials. The U.S. Treasury also began imposing increasingly draconian financial sanctions on the Assad regime, including cutting off the country's largest financial institution, the Commercial Bank of Syria, from dealings with Western banks.

The Pentagon, meanwhile, began plotting aggressive incursions into Syria to target al Qaeda commanders and Baathist supporters of the insurgency. General Petraeus and Stanley McChrystal, head of the Pentagon's Special Operations Command, left open the possibility of direct talks with the Syrians about joint security operations, but President Bush and the White House increasingly cooled on the idea of another outreach to Damascus.

THE UNITED STATES TRIED again to woo President Assad after the election of Barack Obama in 2009. Obama campaigned on a platform of holding direct talks with many of the world's worst despots, including Iranian president Mahmoud Ahmadinejad, Venezuelan strongman Hugo Chávez, and members of the Burmese military junta. This approach was intended as a direct rebuke of the Bush administration's diplomatic tactics, which Obama considered too rigid and shaped by a black-and-white view of the world. The new president sincerely believed his outreach could significantly cool tensions in the Middle East and Asia and help end the wars in Iraq and Afghanistan.

President Assad emerged as a central target of Obama's new diplomacy, the idea being that the Syrian leader could be wooed away from his military alliance with Iran, Hezbollah, and Hamas. As Obama's election appeared more and more certain as the summer of 2008 progressed, the candidate's Mideast advisors, including Princeton professor Daniel Kurtzer and former State Department negotiator Dennis Ross, held secret meetings with Syrian officials, including foreign minister Walid al-Moallem and Bouthaina Shaaban, one of Assad's political advisors, to set the table for an improved relationship. Ambassador Imad Moustapha, meanwhile, sensing an end to Syria's diplomatic isolation, appeared at diplomatic functions in Washington's upscale Kalorama district and began attending local think tank events focused on Obama's new Mideast policy and Syria's potential role in it. In his meetings with journalists and academics, Moustapha appeared triumphant, recounting Assad's successful eight years of weathering the Bush administration's financial, diplomatic, and intelligence war on Damascus. Syria's waiting game, he said, appeared to be working. And American officials were now knocking on his door.

Within weeks of taking office, Secretary of State Hillary Clinton sent her first diplomatic mission to Syria. According to her State Department aides, she was skeptical about the United States' ability to improve relations with Assad. Her husband had spent two years trying to broker a peace agreement between Israel and Hafez al-Assad's government during his presidency, only to see the diplomacy break down in his final weeks in office. Bill Clinton blamed his advisors, Israel, and Syria for the failure, and the experience soured both Clintons on the true intentions of the Assad family.

"Be careful when you're there," Hillary Clinton told the State Department's top Mideast official, Assistant Secretary of State Jeff Feltman, shortly before sending him to Syria in March 2009. "The Syrians are notoriously compulsive liars!"

In the ensuing months, Obama emissaries, including former senator George Mitchell, the White House's special Mideast envoy, held a series of audiences with President Assad in Damascus. Their talks had a familiar focus: getting the Syrian government to seal its border with Iraq and bolster stability in Lebanon and the Palestinian territories. But the United States was now offering carrots. In a late July trip, Mitchell said the United States would ease certain sanctions on Syria, specifically the purchases of computer software and airplane parts, to promote better ties. Assad and his advisors regularly downplayed the impact of the American sanctions, but senior Syrian officials were ebullient.

"Now we can begin to pursue new projects and improve our commercial ties to the U.S.," Syria's central bank governor, Adib

Mayaleh, excitedly told me during an interview in his central Damascus office the week of Mitchell's 2009 visit. Mayaleh cited his desperate need to purchase aircraft parts for Syria's crippled fleet of Boeing jets: sixteen of Syria Air's planes had been grounded or barred from traveling to Europe due to safety concerns.

Amid this bonhomie, Senator John Kerry, chairman of the Senate Foreign Relations Committee, quietly took the lead in pressing the Obama administration's efforts to win over Assad. The future secretary of state had a long history of traveling to Middle East hotspots and developing personal friendships with such regional leaders as Jordan's King Abdullah II, Israeli president Shimon Peres, and Egypt's former dictator Hosni Mubarak. Obama had turned to the Massachusetts lawmaker shortly after taking office to carry messages to a number of important yet troublesome American allies in the Islamic world, such as Afghanistan's leader, Hamid Karzai, and Pakistani president Azif Ali Zardari. Now it was time to see if Kerry could deliver a bigger diplomatic prize.

Kerry's entrée to Assad was Ambassador Moustapha, who had already met with the senator during the starker diplomatic days of the Bush presidency to press Syria's case for engagement. Kerry strongly backed the sentiment of many Mideast experts and independent panels such as the Iraq Study Group, which concluded that the U.S. mission in Iraq could be saved only through cooperative relationships with Iran and Syria. Moustapha had also told Kerry that Assad was prepared to resume direct peace negotiations with Israel.

Back in 2006 Kerry had defied the Bush White House and traveled to Damascus for a meeting with the Syrian leader, heading a delegation that included Democratic senators Chris Dodd and Bill Nelson. The young Assad expounded on his desire for peace with Israel and rapprochement with Washington, as he had with many Western audiences. Now, four years later, Kerry was eager to build on that encounter and his relations with Moustapha, and he soon initiated an extensive dialogue with Assad that would last for two years. A March 2009 dinner in Damascus at the five-star Naranj restaurant cemented a strong working relationship and friendship between the two men, according to Syrian officials and Kerry's aides. They dined for nearly four hours just down the street from the Umayyad Mosque, along with Kerry's wife, Teresa Heinz Kerry, and Asma al-Assad. The Assads downplayed Syria's alliance with Iran as an "unnatural alliance." The two men discussed the future of Mideast peace and building stronger U.S.-Syrian relations, according to their aides. And they pledged to continue consultations as the Obama administration's foreign policy gained traction.

Kerry was emerging as the Syrian dictator's man in Washington. Although Assad was, like his father, one of the world's most repressive leaders, Kerry stressed in his meetings with U.S. lawmakers and administration officials that the Syrian leader was strictly secular and recognized the threat posed by radical Islamists such as al Qaeda to the stability of the Middle East. "He doesn't want to lead a religious-based country," Kerry told a dinner for Arab Americans in late 2009. Kerry also portrayed Assad as a progressive Arab who understood his young population's desire for jobs and access to the Internet, desires that could be satisfied only by a real rapprochement with the United States.

Kerry's description of Assad surprised a number of Lebanese Americans, who were convinced that the Syrian leader's family was behind the killing of anti-Syrian activists in Beirut. "Kerry's characterization of Assad seemed grossly exaggerated," said one attendee at the dinner. "But the senator promoted it unchecked."

By the second half of 2010, Kerry was shuttling between the Syrians and the Israelis in a push to resume direct peace talks over the status of the Golan Heights. The senator believed the talks were progressing so well that by fall he and Assad's aides had secretly drafted terms they hoped would allow for the resumption of the peace track. In particular, the plan called for Israel to agree to resume negotiations and commit to returning all Syrian lands seized during the 1967 Six-Day War. For his part, Assad would pledge to distance himself from Iran, Hezbollah, Hamas, and the Axis of Resistance. "I thought what I brought back in writing was sufficiently powerful and real that it merited any administration to follow up on it," Kerry told me.

Still, just weeks later, in early 2011, the U.S. diplomatic pursuit proved unsustainable. American officials and French president Nicolas Sarkozy had pressed Assad to use his influence with Hezbollah to end the political turmoil that had engulfed Beirut that year and raised fears of a return to civil war. They also wanted Syria to cooperate with the UN investigation into the murder of Rafik al-Hariri, even though early reports directly implicated members of Assad's family. Instead, Syria's Lebanese allies overthrew Prime Minister Saad al-Hariri, Rafik's son, in early 2011, installing a civilian government that took a pro-Damascus line. This led the White House to call off Kerry's planned 2011 trip to Damascus.

In March of that year, Syria's leader cracked down on political opponents in one of the modern Middle East's bloodiest encounters, which is still ongoing. In five years, nearly five hundred thousand Syrians would be killed. But Kerry and the Obama administration were slow to recognize what was happening in Syria. Addressing Washington's Carnegie Endowment for International Peace in March 2011, weeks after the Assad crackdown started, the senator stunned the audience by personally recognizing the presence of Ambassador Moustapha, noting the ambassador's efforts to promote U.S.-Syrian relations, and again stating his belief that Assad would emerge as a political reformer. "My judgment is that Syria will move; Syria will change, as it embraces a legitimate relationship with the United States and the West and the economic opportunity that comes with it," Kerry said.

Only later, as the violence surged, did Kerry and the Obama administration distance themselves from Assad. By August of that year, the White House had called on the Syrian leader to step down. They began placing travel bans and financial sanctions on many of the diplomats in Damascus the United States had once used as a channel to Assad, including Moallem and Shaaban. Ambassador Moustapha, meanwhile, became the focus of an FBI investigation looking into allegations that he and his staff threatened the families of Syrian American dissidents who were agitating against Assad.

Kerry, however, never gave up his belief that there was a moment when Assad could have been turned from his alliance with Iran and the Axis of Resistance. "I never argued Assad was a reformer so far as the internal political affairs of Syria," the former senator told me. "But there was an opportunity staring us in the face on foreign affairs."

Kerry's enthrallment with Assad, even as Syria devolved into war, showed a troubling lack of judgment and raised questions about his ability to read the intentions of world leaders. Kerry didn't appear capable of distinguishing between Assad's welcoming demeanor and the police state run by him and his family.

In January 2011, when Kerry and the White House were still seeking a rapprochement with Syria, I was invited on short notice by the Syrian government to interview President Assad in Damascus. Interviews with President Assad were tightly controlled by Ambassador Moustapha. The diplomat was an anomaly in Washington's post-9/11 world: although U.S. government officials had come to view him as a pariah, Moustapha was still a star on the diplomatic circuit and among the American press. He was the only foreign official in George W. Bush's Washington who could speak to what members of the Axis of Resistance thought about the war on terror, and he was sharply critical of the White House.

Moustapha engaged in a crafty diplomatic dance with Israel's supporters in Washington and with American Jews in general. He was quick to lambaste Israeli policies, claiming they were at the heart of virtually every problem in the Middle East. And he publicly espoused a belief that the "Israel lobby" and "neoconservatives" controlled everything that happened in Washington, and in the United States in general; he regularly appeared on CNN and described allegations of Syrian malfeasance—such as its alleged nuclear weapons program—as "lies" concocted by Syria's enemies and the Israel lobby. But he'd regularly meet with Jewish academics, diplomats, and journalists at the Syrian embassy in Washington, stressing that Damascus was anti-Israel, not anti-Semitic. He embodied the Assad regime's double-dealing from his mansion in the Kalorama district. On a table in his meeting room there he kept a cookbook that detailed the Syrian city of Aleppo's history of great Jewish cuisine and which, apparently, demonstrated his own admiration for the Jewish people. He also kept a blog on which he mixed his interest in Arabic poetry and Syrian art with political observations from his active Washington social life. Moustapha's diplomatic efforts were both entertaining and disturbing. On one hand, he was charming and always open for a lunch or a phone conversation. But he was such a tried-and-true regime loyalist that virtually anything he said needed to be discounted or scrutinized.

But Moustapha, who had both family and business ties to Assad, served as a conduit to the Syrian leader. And Moustapha seemed to have concluded that if Assad wanted to communicate to Washington's leaders, he might as well talk to me—a Jewish reporter from *The Wall Street Journal*, the newspaper seen as most closely aligned with American conservatives and hawkish pro-Israel interests.

I had put in for an interview with President Assad in early 2010 and had more or less forgotten about it, assuming it would never happen. So I was surprised when Moustapha called me into his Washington office on a Tuesday morning and said with a smile, "You have to be there in forty-eight hours." The interview was on.

I was picked up at Damascus International Airport by the president's handlers and dropped off at the city's premier hotel, the Four Seasons, exhausted. The hotel resembled a giant tomb near the heart of the capital's old city, with only a few guests: mostly turbaned Arab traders, European business contractors, and Indian IT specialists. U.S. senator John Kerry would have arrived at the hotel that same evening had the White House not canceled his trip.

A pre-interview was scheduled for my first morning in Damascus—January 29—with the president's chief media and foreign affairs advisor, Bouthaina Shaaban. Shaaban was from the Assad family's Alawite sect, an offshoot of Shiite Islam, and had earned a Ph.D. in English literature from a London university. She later served as a translator for President Hafez al-Assad and, under Bashar, as minister for expatriate affairs. She was a true regime insider, but with a font of Western contacts. The Assads regularly sent her to meet the foreign media.

I had heard stories of journalists who had traveled all the way to Damascus for interviews with President Assad, only to be sent back following a bad initial encounter with Shaaban. I decided I'd narrowly focus my meeting with her on the prospects for better relations between the United States and Syria, knowing this was one of Assad's main objectives in courting the Western press. We also discussed the collapse of the government in Beirut just days earlier, which had been warmly received in Syria, and the troubles facing Egyptian president Hosni Mubarak, Damascus's arch-nemesis. She seemed to like this line of questioning, chuckling during our tea about the fall of the Hariri regime and the fact that the French, Americans, and Saudis were relying on Damascus to help stabilize Lebanon. She mentioned how Syria had previously been blamed for all the chaos there. "And now they're turning to us for the solution," she said with a big smile. The pre-interview went well.

The following morning I was driven to one of the president's working offices, located in the foothills of Damascus's Qassioun Mountain. Security at the site was surprisingly minimal. There was a gate when we entered what felt like a forest reserve, and a few guards were stationed along the road to the palace. I had expected an armed fort, but in all likelihood I had been monitored around the clock since my arrival in Damascus two days earlier. Assad's intelligence service, the Mukhabarat, knew they had little to fear.

The rail-thin Syrian leader surprised my colleague Bill Spindle, the Middle East bureau chief, and me by greeting us at the door of our car upon our arrival. I had expected a long line of handlers to shuttle us through a maze of offices and security checks before seeing Bashar. His father was famous for keeping foreign ministers waiting for hours before an audience, just to establish a sense of his authority. But Bashar took us straight into his compound.

The president and Shaaban gave us a tour of his offices and their expansive view of Damascus. The meeting room was surprisingly Spartan, featuring a brown marble floor and a few modern Syrian paintings and sculptures. Bashar spoke fluent English, but with a subtle lisp that made him seem shy, if not lacking in confidence. Despite his family's reputation for brutality, his soft voice put me at ease. I sensed I could establish a rapport with this dictator. He walked with his wiry, six-foot-two frame slightly hunched. I worried, though, that it was all a ploy to lower my defenses.

Colleagues and diplomats back in Washington had warned me not to go light on Assad and stressed he was a habitual liar. The president's enemies in Washington, particularly among the Lebanese Americans, wanted me to begin the session with an abrupt question about why he had ordered Hezbollah to murder Rafik al-Hariri. They advised that I should hit him early with evidence of his government's abysmal human rights record. But I figured such an approach might force the president to go tight-lipped or to shut down the interview entirely. It was smarter, I figured, to start with general questions about the political turbulence in the Middle East and the prospects for peace between Syria and Israel. I'd often found that politicians like Assad could hang themselves answering even benign questions, if you gave them enough rope.

And Bashar wasted little time making news. I asked him if he was worried his government was susceptible to the same type of revolutions or political revolts consuming other Arab countries, because of his repressive policies and the religious imbalance in the country. (Bashar's Alawite minority lorded over a country that was around 70 percent Sunni.) I mentioned that the country's stagnating economy wasn't providing enough jobs for Syria's youthful population. But he rebuked me, saying he'd already started real reforms in his country by opening up the media, the banks, and the educational system. "If you want to go towards democracy, the first thing is to involve the people in decision making, not to make it," he said. "It is not my democracy as a person; it is our democracy as a society. So how do you start? You start with creating dialogue."

Assad then shot back that he would never be tested. He was the leader of the resistance to Israel, he proclaimed. His words made clear to me why his alliances with Iran, Hezbollah, and Hamas made sense politically in the region. They, plus Syria, were united by their hatred of the Jewish state. Indeed, he described himself as a bulwark against Zionism and the West, even while he courted the United States. He opened up the potential for peace with the Jewish state, but also stressed that his support in the Arab world rested on his opposition to Zionism.

"Syria is stable. Why?" Assad asked in one of his more animated moments. "Because you have to be very closely linked to the beliefs of the people. This is the core issue. When there is divergence . . . you will have this vacuum that creates disturbances."

Despite his fluency in English, the Syrian leader's responses to questions about the Arab revolutions used odd phraseologies about how the region's political systems had been infected by "microbes" and "stagnant waters." "What you have been seeing in this region is a kind of disease," he said. "That is how we see it." His language seemed to be informed by his years of studying ophthalmology in London and Damascus. But it also suggested a tyrannical streak. He described his desire to "cut off" the malignancies that existed in Syrian society. He portrayed himself as the father to the Syrian people — and only he knew when the time was ripe for change.

True to form, he also offered up blatant lies about Syria's roles in Iraq and Lebanon, claiming Damascus had no ability to stanch the flow of fighters crossing its borders and no involvement in fueling instability in Beirut. He also dismissed the UN's investigation into the murder of Rafik al-Hariri and said the charges of Syrian involvement were baseless. "How can you accuse anyone without having any evidence that they are involved or complicit?" he asked us. "They said they suspect some people who were close to the region, some people who used the telephone, and things like this, i.e., theories. But we do not have any concrete evidence."

Assad also said his government had never attempted to develop a nuclear program, despite the fact that UN inspectors reported finding vast amounts of uranium particles at the site in Syria's Deir Ezzour province bombed by Israel in 2007. Why would he build such a facility, he asked, when it could fuel such criticism of Syria? The facility that was destroyed had been a "conventional" military site, he said, not one used for nuclear weapons, and he suggested that Israel was trying to frame Syria. "If they believed it was nuclear, they should have done that without the attacking," Assad said of the Israelis. "If they want to create a problem for Syria, they could tell the IAEA, 'Look, we have the satellite images, go to Syria and Syria will be cornered.'"

Assad, however, clearly wanted to send a message to Washington that he was a man who could be trusted and engaged. He told me that Damascus and Washington shared common strategic interests and that American economic sanctions on Syria were only preventing it from integrating more closely with the West. He said Iran and Syria were not natural allies, as his government was avowedly secular while Tehran's was Islamist. And he stressed that peace between his government and Israel was still possible.

"We need to have normal relations. Peace for us is to have normal relations, like between Syria and any other country in the world," Assad said, sitting slightly back on his couch. Bouthaina Shaaban, who had closely tracked his every word, interjected at one point with a clarification. She noted that Syria couldn't have peace with Israel until all the Arab states did. She didn't specifically mention it, but one of the reasons Egyptian president Anwar Sadat had been assassinated in 1981 was that he had signed a peace agreement with Israel without the support of the other Arab states. "So having a peace treaty only with Syria could be only one step, but cannot be peace," Assad clarified. "That is why comprehensive peace [between Israel and the Arab states] is very important. This is the real solution."

The interview with Assad lasted for nearly ninety minutes. But after a quick handshake, he vanished. One aide told me the president "liked you" and that other meetings could be set up if he approved of the article. He suggested I could become a regular guest of the president's in the future. I frantically wrote the story over the course of an afternoon, worried about how it would be received. The spread of the Arab Spring and the protests that were gripping Tunisia and Egypt made Assad's defiant, confident words incredibly newsworthy. I would have preferred to write the article after I left the country, given the erratic nature of the Syrian regime. But the *Journal* wanted the story that day, while I was still in Damascus.

The Assad interview was closely studied by Western intelligence services and Israel after its publication on January 31. Analysts seemed to draw conflicting conclusions. Some of President Obama's Mideast advisors believed Syria's leader was signaling he was willing to make peace with Israel and distance himself from Iran, if offered the right incentives. Benjamin Netanyahu in Israel, however, drew the exact opposite lesson, according to his aides: Assad had said he was a leader of the Axis of Resistance, so therefore he could never end the war with Israel and abandon his allies in Hezbollah, Hamas, and Iran.

I felt I was being forced into the role of a diplomatic intermediary between Washington and Damascus—a position that most journalists probably coveted but also feared. A reporter's role is to build understanding between opposing sides, I believe. But with Assad and his history of dissembling, I was concerned that I was being manipulated by the dictator. I didn't want to filter his words. But I knew he had spoken untruths, and I needed to challenge them.

Just a month later, protests broke out against Assad's rule. At first, many Syria analysts thought the uprising would prove short-lived and never reach Damascus. But the Syrian security forces' heavy crackdown and the killing of teenagers fueled the much broader civil conflict that eventually fractured Syria and still threatens the future of Iran's regional alliances. Bashar al-Assad's vicious military offensive against his political opponents, using tanks, airpower, and chemical weapons, destroyed any last hopes in the West that he was a man willing to take risks for peace, either with Israel or with his own people. A colleague remarked that my meeting in Damascus was like interviewing Adolf Hitler in 1939 on the eve of World War II.

THE MEETING WITH PRESIDENT ASSAD wasn't the only time I was sought out to serve as an intermediary between the Axis of Resistance and the American public. Syria has also hosted the Palestinian militant group Hamas for much of the past two decades. The organization, like Hezbollah, closely tied its military operations to the Assad regime and Iran. But it's also used the ballot to gain political control of the Gaza Strip in the Palestinian territories. The movement's political chiefs, fearing assassination attempts, remained in Damascus and made many of Hamas's decisions remotely from their Syrian safe haven. They regularly coordinated their activities inside Gaza with Hezbollah, the Syrian intelligence services, and visiting Iranian Revolutionary Guard commanders.

But unlike Hezbollah, Hamas was a Sunni organization, essentially the Palestinian arm of the Egypt-based Muslim Brotherhood, the pan-Arab Islamist movement that was born out of the collapse of the Ottoman Empire in the 1920s and had political supporters and fundraising networks in most Middle East countries. U.S. officials believed that Iran's sponsorship of Hamas showed Tehran's willingness to reach across sectarian lines to challenge the United States and Israel. In their view, Iran's relationship with Hamas, unlike Hezbollah, was purely strategic and political, more than religious. Hamas's leadership would eventually leave Damascus after the onset of the civil war in 2011.

During one extended stay in Syria in 2009, I was granted a meeting with Hamas's political chief, Khaled Meshaal. The Palestinian was born in Kuwait and had spent much of his political career based in Jordan. In 1996, Israel's intelligence service, the Mossad, attempted to assassinate him in Amman by squirting a poisonous toxin into his ear. Meshaal survived only after Jordan's late King Hussein intervened and forced Israeli prime minister Benjamin Netanyahu to ship over the antidote, threatening to terminate Jordan's peace treaty with Israel if he didn't. The Israeli leader quickly complied. King Hussein, though no fan of Hamas, worried that Meshaal's death could spark a broad Palestinian uprising in his own kingdom.

Meshaal was charismatic and had increasingly challenged the Palestinians' secular political party Fatah for political dominance in the occupied territories. Egypt, Jordan, and Saudi Arabia all worried Meshaal could stir up internal dissent in their own countries. Arab governments equated Hamas's secrecy and cell-like structure to communist organizations during the Cold War. These governments were convinced Iran was backing Hamas to weaken them. Many European diplomats believed that as the Palestinians' secular leaders in the Palestinian Liberation Organization aged, became corrupted or discredited, or fell into obscurity, Israel and the West ultimately would have no choice but to negotiate with Meshaal.

Meshaal forged a dashing, Che Guevara–type persona revered across the Arab and developing worlds and among the American left. He had steely blue eyes and a closely cropped, salt-and-pepper beard. His secluded life in Syria and covert travels across the Middle East and Central Asia added to his shroud of mystery and invincibility.

I took a taxicab with a colleague to a quiet backstreet in a central

Damascus neighborhood for my meeting with Meshaal. The Syrian capital, despite hosting so many militant and terrorist groups, was remarkably peaceful before the civil war. There was little of the traffic and cacophony of noises that gripped most of the Middle East's capitals. Vendors and street urchins were a rarity. Cool winds blew into the city on summer nights.

This calm, though, hid shadows from history. A number of Nazi officers had found shelter in the Mideast following the end of the Second World War. They provided counsel to the Egyptians and the Syrians for their wars against Israel. One of them, Alois Brunner, settled in Damascus in the late 1950s. He was a close associate of the SS commander Adolf Eichmann and had worked with him to exterminate Europe's Jews through the Final Solution.

Brunner advised the Assad regime on the use of torture and interrogation techniques. He received round-the-clock protection from Syrian security forces, but still lost a finger and an eye after receiving a letter bomb from the Mossad. A German magazine once quoted him as saying his only real regret in life "was not killing more Jews." His home was not far from where I was interviewing Meshaal; for all I knew, he was still living there.

My colleague and I walked into a nondescript bungalow. A bodyguard gave us a cursory frisk before sending us through a metal detector. Upon entering a second-floor room, I suddenly found myself confronting Hamas's culture of martyrdom and resistance. Photos of assassinated Hamas politicians and military leaders lined the walls. In setting up the interview, I had wondered why Meshaal would meet with someone from *The Wall Street Journal*, and especially a journalist with the last name Solomon. Like the Assad regime, Hamas had intermediaries in Washington who engaged with American reporters, vetting them and providing a back channel. These included Arab diplomats, journalists, and academics at think tanks. Meshaal wanted to enhance his image in the United States, I was told. Like Ambassador Moustapha in Washington, Hamas officials stressed their movement wasn't anti-Semitic and that they were merely fighting the "Zionists" who occupied Palestinian lands—and this was a point they wanted made to the Obama administration.

Meshaal arrived in the audience room seeming every bit the consummate politician. He vigorously shook my hand and led me to two chairs that were set against a faux backdrop of Jerusalem's Old City. His underlings served Arabic tea. Meshaal understood enough English to engage in pleasantries. He wanted the interview to be conducted in Arabic, he told me. His translator, known as "Little Khalid," had lived in Texas. He spoke American-accented English impeccably.

The point Meshaal clearly wanted to make was that Hamas, despite its alliances with Iran and Syria, was willing to enter into a prolonged *hudna*, or truce, with Israel that could last for decades. He stressed that Hamas supported the creation of a Palestinian state based on its 1967 borders with Israel, a view many Western diplomats believed equated to a de facto recognition of the Jewish state by Hamas. "We along with other Palestinian factions in consensus agreed upon accepting a Palestinian state along the 1967 lines," Meshaal told me. "This is the national program. This is our program. This is the position we stand by and respect." Israeli officials believed it was all a ruse.

Still, when pressed as to whether Hamas could ever truly recognize a Jewish state, Meshaal's eyes flashed. He thundered through his translator: "I don't care about Israel—it is our enemy and our occupier, and it commits crimes against our people," he said. "Don't ask me about Israel, Israel can talk for itself."

The pace of the interview stalled as I struggled over where to lead the discussion next. The contradiction between his hopes for a *hudna* and his anger toward Israel seemed glaring. I tried to regain some momentum by turning toward Israel's continued building of settlements in the West Bank and asking if the cessation of such construction would be received as a conciliatory step. He stressed it wouldn't be enough. "If Israel doesn't accept a halt to stop building settlements, what then?" Meshaal said. "The end of the settlements is a necessary step, but it's not the solution itself."

The interview concluded with Meshaal presenting me with a large box containing a vast array of baklava from Damascus's most famous sweet shop. He also gave me a framed rendering of the Old City of Jerusalem like the one in his office. The Al-Aqsa Mosque, one of Islam's holiest, and the Church of the Holy Sepulcher, where Jesus is entombed, were depicted against the backdrop of the city. Nothing in the image referenced Jerusalem's centuries-old Jewish history.

I returned to the hotel where I was staying, Le Meridien, to write up my interview with Meshaal. When I turned on my computer it immediately crashed. I assumed that Syrian intelligence agents had hacked my hard drive while I was away, though apparently they didn't mind letting visitors know they were being watched.

I hustled over to my colleague's house down the block to make sure we could file the story by the deadline. I arrived back at the hotel around two in the morning, after the Meshaal story had hit the Web. I knew some of my friends in Washington's pro-Israel community weren't thrilled that I was giving voice to Hamas's leader. While I believed I needed to get both sides of a hopelessly complex problem, they felt that I was publicizing the views of a terrorist and that I was being used. I braced for some blowback.

I turned on my cellphone to read the emails that were starting to stream in. There were some congratulatory notes about the interview. An Israeli television network wanted to interview me. One of my good friends in Washington, however, wasn't amused: "You're a tool," he texted me. I knew he was only half joking.

My trips to Damascus underscored for me just how tightly connected this Axis of Resistance really was and how rooted these relationships were in violence. The ability of the United States to woo these countries and groups into a partnership appeared to be a long shot. Iran and its partners were accused of assassinating a former head of state, collaborating with al Qaeda, and brutally repressing their own people. The risk, in my view, was that by engaging the Axis, Washington risked being complicit in its actions.

And as a journalist, I questioned my own role. The interviews with Assad and Meshaal captivated me and fed my knowledge and my reporting. I felt I knew much better the players about whom I was writing. But I was also spreading their messages and, in Assad's case, his deceits. Did this make me complicit as well?

CHAPTER 5

The Physics Research Center

O N AUGUST 14, 2002, AN IRANIAN POLITICAL ACTIVIST NAMED ALIREZA Jafarzadeh braved the ninety-degree heat in Washington, D.C., and shuffled across Fourteenth Street into a conference room in the city's historic Willard Hotel, just blocks from the White House, to release some startling news. The journalists who greeted the bespectacled Persian in the Willard's Taft Room were a smattering of newspaper and wire reporters and cameramen from cable television. In a summer dominated by the buildup to the Iraq War, many of Washington's top-tier journalists were busy trying to confirm the latest date for the U.S. invasion, or details on Saddam's alleged ties to the al Qaeda terrorist network. Most of the major networks, meanwhile, hadn't even heard of Jafarzadeh or his organization.

Jafarzadeh appeared timid and unsure as he walked up to the lectern after being introduced by his colleague Hedayat Mostowfi. The spokesman wore owlish, professorial glasses and a pressed suit. The two men unfurled a map of Iran, with arrows pointing to two Iranian cities, Natanz and Arak, where they claimed the country was building covert nuclear facilities. They also produced a chart showing the sophisticated front companies that Iran was using to procure nuclear equipment. They described in technical terms Tehran's efforts to develop a nuclear fuel cycle. But for many of the journalists in the crowd, the cities were unfamiliar and the companies' names unpronounceable. The science of nuclear weapons wasn't a specialty for most in the Washington press corps.

"Many secretive nuclear activities are at work [in Iran], without any knowledge" of it in the United States or United Nations, Jafarzadeh announced to the world as the cameras rolled. "The very fact that Iran can be building nuclear sites without . . . monitoring is terrifying."

The dissident continued for forty minutes, detailing how Iran's secret nuclear program was under the direct guidance of Supreme Leader Khamenei. Jafarzadeh revealed that Russian nuclear experts from the former Soviet Union were based at some of the Iranian sites. And the Iranian military was pursuing a broader program of weapons of mass destruction, which included chemical and biological agents.

Jafarzadeh culminated his presentation with an appeal to the Bush administration and European governments. End any diplomatic outreach to Iran's rulers, he said, and accelerate economic sanctions on Tehran. In turn, the regime's opponents and the Iranian "resistance" would overthrow the mullahs. "If Western countries refrain from a policy of appeasement, the Iranian people will deal with this regime," Jafarzadeh said.

Jafarzadeh, in his early forties at the time, was the U.S. representative of an Iranian opposition group called the Mujahedin e-Khalq, or People's Holy Warriors, which was formally listed by the U.S. State Department as a terrorist organization. Many in Washington and Europe were wary of Jafarzadeh and the MeK, a onetime Marxist-Islamist student movement that had joined with the followers of the Ayatollah Khomeini in the 1970s to depose the shah. During the political turmoil of that time, MeK operatives killed American diplomats and military contractors who were seen as supportive of the monarchy, eventually landing the MeK on the U.S. terrorism blacklist.

Many Persian Americans didn't understand how the MeK could operate so openly in Washington and how Jafarzadeh could be holding press conferences live on C-SPAN so close to the Oval Office. But the MeK had morphed in the decades after the revolution into the most committed and militant opponent of the Islamic Republic of Iran worldwide. The leftist organization and Iran's ruling clerics competed for power and clashed in the post-shah era, culminating in the mass arrests and executions of the MeK's leaders and followers. As a result, the MeK had made some powerful friends in the United States and Israel who shared their hatred of the Iranian regime. MeK members, often using the names of front organizations, were regular visitors on Capitol Hill and attended conferences run by pro-Israel groups in Washington. They passed on their intelligence troves to analysts at the Pentagon and the CIA.

Jafarzadeh, however, didn't expose the MeK's secret collaborator in bringing to light Iran's nuclear work that afternoon. As the world prepared for the invasion of Iraq, Israel's security and intelligence services grew concerned that Iran, which was seen as the far bigger threat, would get lost in the shuffle. They not so subtly joked that the Bush administration had misinterpreted their comments and was getting ready to attack the wrong Middle East country that started with the letter *I*.

Seeking to draw attention to Iran's nuclear advances, Israeli intelligence looked for a conduit to make their information public in the summer of 2002, according to U.S. and European officials who worked on Iran. The Mossad initially sought to convey its information on Natanz and Arak via Reza Pahlavi, the Virginia-based son of the last Iranian monarch. But the "Baby Shah," as he was widely called, bristled at playing this role. He was worried that he'd be branded by Tehran as a tool of the "Zionist entity." The Pahlavi dynasty had already been criticized by Iran's mullahs for allying themselves with the Israelis in the 1960s and 1970s against the Palestinians and other Muslim causes. The MeK, however, proved a willing collaborator. U.S. and European officials said Jafarzadeh's organization emerged in the 2000s as a close ally of the Israelis, driven by their shared hatred of Tehran's theocratic leadership.

Despite Jafarzadeh's exhortations, the press conference ended in a whimper. Many of the journalists appeared uninterested and headed for lunch. A few went up to Jafarzadeh and quizzed him about his findings but in the end didn't file reports.

"They seemed to have trouble digesting this thing. They didn't know what to think," Jafarzadeh told me ten years later over tea in a downtown Washington conference room. The Iranian American had become more polished in the ensuing decade, writing books on Iran's terrorism threat and appearing regularly as a Fox News television analyst. He also led a high-cost, and eventually effective, campaign to get his organization removed from the U.S. terrorism list. A long list of influential Republicans and Democrats were recruited— and paid—to speak for the MeK. They included former presidential candidate and Vermont governor Howard Dean and the Bush administration's first homeland security czar, Tom Ridge. "Our announcement on Natanz and Arak changed the political landscape toward Iran," he went on, a small smile forming under his pencil-thin mustache.

THE MEK'S DISCLOSURE, while dismissed or misunderstood by much of the press, rocked the international diplomatic community and the Bush administration, even as they were focused on the Iraq War. The United States was building its case for Saddam's overthrow largely based on the threat allegedly posed by Iraq's nuclear program. But Iran was suddenly exposed as having nuclear facilities far more advanced than anything Iraq was believed to possess. Tehran also had far more extensive ties to terrorist organizations, such as

Hezbollah, Hamas, and Palestinian Islamic Jihad, than Baghdad did. This meant a huge risk of nuclear proliferation if Iran decided to share its capabilities with its proxies.

One of the sites disclosed by Jafarzadeh, located in the central Iranian city of Natanz, was an enrichment facility that could allow Iran to transform crushed uranium ore, widely known as yellow-cake, into a gas that through additional refinement could form the grapefruit-sized metal sphere at the heart of a nuclear warhead. The Iranians had built two large halls to house the equipment to produce this nuclear fuel, the MeK revealed, under the guise of conducting experiments in desert cultivation. Already a thousand Iranian government workers were at the site. The Atomic Energy Organization of Iran was overseeing the project, and top-level politicians were regularly flying in from Tehran to monitor developments.

A separate covert site in the city of Arak hosted a plant that was immediately suspected of being intended to produce the heavy water used in a nuclear reactor. The spent fuel from this type of reactor can be mined for the plutonium that could provide the heart of a different type of nuclear bomb. American nuclear experts called a heavy water reactor a "bomb-making factory." The heavy water plant had been under construction for nearly six years and was already 90 percent complete, the MeK concluded. It had been built near the bank of a local river in order to provide the reactor with adequate water to cool it. Iran was moving toward having the complete nuclear fuel cycle.

Indeed, Tehran was moving to develop two paths to a nuclear bomb, the evidence suggested—one based on enriched uranium and the other on plutonium. This strategy was similar to the one pursued by the Americans involved in the Manhattan Project in the 1940s. The United States hadn't been sure which was easier or quickest, so it went down both paths.

Within days of Jafarzadeh's announcement, inspectors from the UN's nuclear watchdog, the International Atomic Energy Agency in Vienna, wrote Iran's Foreign Ministry and demanded access to the

Natanz and Arak facilities. A private Washington think tank, meanwhile, acquired satellite photos that pinpointed these nuclear sites and identified Natanz as a gas centrifuge plant. After some initial stonewalling, Tehran consented to the IAEA's inspectors' visit. In a dramatic speech, President Mohammad Khatami went on television in January 2003 and admitted Iran was building the sites highlighted by Tehran's enemy, the MeK, but stressed they were strictly for peaceful purposes.

Instead of assuaging U.S. concerns, Tehran's confirmation of the sites set off a scramble inside Western intelligence services to learn just how far the country might already have gone in its pursuit of a nuclear bomb. The facilities at Arak and Natanz, rather than representing the nascent beginnings of a weapons program, could be part of a much more elaborate infrastructure already in place, they feared. U.S. intelligence services already knew that Tehran had purchased equipment from the rogue Pakistani scientist Abdul Qadeer Khan, who was caught red-handed in 2003 selling atomic weapons designs to Libyan dictator Moammar Gadhafi and centrifuge components to North Korea. Did Iran have access to the foreign-made designs as well? How many other sites were hidden in the vast expanses of the Iranian deserts?

The United States, the Europeans, and the Israelis would use everything in their arsenal over the next decade to try to stop Iran's advances on the nuclear front, including spying, computer attacks, and assassinations. As this campaign advanced, the United States and its allies increasingly focused on a small group of Iranian scientists and military officers believed to be overseeing Iran's own version of the Manhattan Project.

IN THE SUMMER OF 1989, Iran's Ministry of Defense constructed a cluster of offices in a secluded park near the hills of northern Tehran to house a top-secret program, called the Physics Research Center. The center's work was kept totally separate from the country's main nuclear bureaucracy, the Atomic Energy Organization of Iran, which was a public body and had relations with the UN's nuclear watchdog, the IAEA, and other international scientific bodies, going back to the shah's rule. Indeed, the United States provided nuclear materials, including enriched uranium and a five-megawatt research reactor, to the shah's government in the 1960s as part of the Atoms for Peace program launched by President Dwight D. Eisenhower. The United States eventually sought to reclaim the enriched uranium after Iran's Islamic revolution in a blunt lesson of the law of unintended consequences.

The Physics Research Center was initially headed by a Sharif University professor named Seyed Abbas Shahmoradi, a well-known Iranian academic who specialized in nuclear physics. But his new office had no formal listing in Iran's government registries. He was joined at the center two years later by Mohsen Fakhrizadeh, a physicist and a senior officer in the Revolutionary Guard who also occasionally taught engineering at Imam Hossein University, which is directly overseen by the IRGC. Born in 1961, Fakhrizadeh joined the military in his twenties and was immediately dispatched to the front to fight the Iraqis.

The men had had little previous contact, engaged in careers at two very distinct Iranian institutions, Sharif University and the Revolutionary Guard. But their shared expertise in nuclear physics made them standouts in postrevolutionary Iran, and together they would preside over a massive expansion of the Physics Research Center at the request of the Iranian military and the IRGC.

Shortly after it was established, the Physics Research Center began sending out a stream of telexed orders to engineering and equipment companies in the United Kingdom, France, and Germany. The content of the center's requests hinted at its interest in the technologies required for nuclear weapons, as among the orders placed were ones for magnets that could form parts for centrifuges and high-speed cameras used to map fissile detonations. Western analysts cautioned that this equipment could have dual uses—that is, it could theoretically be used for civilian purposes, such as in medicine or the mining industry, as well as for military projects. The center also requested from European universities and scientific institutes research papers and books describing the physics normally associated with the triggering of a nuclear detonation. Those were definitely not dual-use items. But at the time, there was little Western scrutiny of Iran's activities and no real knowledge of the Physics Research Center. Tensions over Israel were still relatively low. And the world had yet to expose the underground nuclear black market run by the Pakistani scientist A. Q. Khan, which sent dangerous technologies to countries ranging from North Korea to Libya. The exposure of his network would reveal just how easily sensitive technologies were being acquired by rogue states.

Furthermore, Shahmoradi and Fakhrizadeh took great care to mask the center's role in these procurements. Many of the orders were formally made by Sharif University, either through Shahmoradi's office or through other academics. This gave the appearance that the university's physics department was seeking equipment and research papers as part of normal academic work. A closer look at the paperwork, however, would have revealed that many of the orders were ultimately delivered to the center's offices, not Sharif University.

For example, in a telex sent on January 1, 1991, Sharif University's purchasing department requested catalogues and samples of magnets that could be used in developing gas centrifuges from a European engineering firm called Magnet Applications Ltd. But the return address was the post office box and fax number in Tehran of the Physics Research Center, not Sharif University. The magnets matched the specific dimensions of those used in centrifuges produced by European firms. A centrifuge enriches uranium by circulating the chemical element in a gaseous form in a cylinder that rapidly rotates like a top on a pin. The magnets help keep the cylinders stable and upright as the rotation separates a heavier isotope of uranium, called U-238, from a lighter and more fissile one, U-235.

The greater the concentration of U-235, the more powerful the fissile reaction that could be generated by detonating an atomic bomb.

The telexes also show that a "Department 70" linked to the Physics Research Center spent tens of thousands of dollars in the early 1990s purchasing technical reports from a British company, also using Sharif University as a cover. The reports covered all the scientific elements related to producing nuclear fuel, including centrifuge and laser enrichment, uranium conversion, and heavy water development.

Iranian scientists who later rose to become prominent members of the Islamic Republic's government assisted the Physics Research Center by making requests on its behalf. One of these was Ali Akbar Salehi. In the 1970s he had been one of the dozens of physicists the shah sent to the United States as part of his nuclear program, and he earned his Ph.D. from the Massachusetts Institute of Technology in 1977. It was in his role as a dean at Sharif University that Salehi made the requests linked to the Physics Research Center. Later he served as Tehran's ambassador to the IAEA during the late 1990s and became the head of the Atomic Energy Organization of Iran. He was Iran's foreign minister from 2010 to 2013 and was one of the chief negotiators involved in the nuclear agreement talks with the Obama administration. Salehi has denied any role in a weapons program but has served as one of Tehran's most public and effective defenders of its nuclear program. "We have strongly marked our opposition to weapons of mass destruction on many occasions," the scientist wrote in an opinion piece for *The Washington Post* in 2012. "Almost seven years ago, Iranian Supreme Leader Ayatollah Ali Khamenei made a binding commitment. He issued a religious edict—a fatwa—forbidding the production, stockpiling and use of nuclear weapons."

REPLACING SHAHMORADI IN THE EARLY 1990s as the head of the Physics Research Center, Fakhrizadeh built on the fruits of this initial research and acquisitions and grew its staff during the 1990s to include more than six hundred people in twelve divisions. Among them were offices focused on uranium enrichment, laser enrichment, and the science needed to convert uranium gas into the metallic spheres used in a nuclear warhead. There were also departments focused on the mining of uranium and its conversion into the powder-like form called yellowcake. Fakhrizadeh repeatedly changed the name of his organization in a bid to throw Western intelligence agencies and the IAEA off the scent. First it merged into an office inside the Defense Ministry called the AMAD Plan in 2003. This later turned into an organization called FEDAT, or the Field of Expansion and Deployment of Advanced Technologies.

Fakhrizadeh and his team placed particular focus on developing a component called a neutron initiator, which has no civilian application. The device floods neutrons into the core of an atomic weapon after the detonation of the high explosives, facilitating the chain reaction of an atomic bomb. Fakhrizadeh cast about Tehran's universities seeking greater support to develop and build this device. In one memo written in the 1990s and later acquired by Western intelligence agencies, the physicist called for cooperation between his office and scientists at Shahid Beheshti University, another government school. He made a desirable offer to the scientists and academics: permanent employment in an unstable Iranian job market. "Our [nuclear] capacities are adequate at the moment," Fakhrizadeh wrote, "but of course they are not perfect." The understated memo hinted at the clandestine life the scientists at the center would be forced to lead in order to ensure their safety, revealing Iran's obsessive focus on infiltration by U.S., Israeli, and Arab saboteurs and assassins since the 1979 revolution.

A breakthrough for Fakhrizadeh's program came in 1995 when Iranian officials made contact with a Russian nuclear weapons scientist who had worked during the 1970s and 1980s at Chelyabinsk-70, a Soviet nuclear research site in the Ural Mountains. Like many

Soviet scientists, Vyacheslav Danilenko needed to find commercial work outside the government as the communist state imploded. While at Chelyabinsk-70, Danilenko had specialized in creating small, highly precise detonators that sent powerful shock waves through the plutonium or enriched uranium that lies at the core of a nuclear weapon. These types of detonators helped the Soviets miniaturize nuclear weapons, allowing them to fit inside missiles or conventional bombs. Searching for new opportunities, Danilenko reached out to the Iranian embassy seeking joint ventures. Shahmoradi and the Physics Research Center eagerly replied.

So began a six-year relationship that became central to Tehran's development of nuclear weapons technologies, according to current and former IAEA officials. The Soviet expert made at least three visits to Tehran in this time—visits, he would tell the UN, in which he lectured on the seemingly benign science of creating nanodiamonds. These are synthetic gems created by bombarding graphite with the same sort of precision shock waves used to initiate a nuclear blast. But UN investigators concluded that Danilenko had also instructed the Physics Research Center "on explosion physics" and how to create an implosion device for a nuclear weapon. Danilenko's public research on detonators exactly matched designs produced by scientists working at the Physics Research Center, the UN noted. In a 1992 paper, Danilenko described a fiber-optic instrument that measures precisely when a shock wave strikes thousands of different points along the surface of a sphere. Iran conducted at least one major test of such an instrument. Danilenko was also an expert in building the infrastructure in which to conduct such test blasts.

The culmination of Danilenko's collaboration with Iran and the Physics Research Center took place at a military facility twenty miles southeast of Tehran. The base, known as Parchin, had been built by the late shah's father, Reza Shah Pahlavi, in the 1930s as the main garrison for troops protecting the Iranian capital. It stretched for miles in the desert. Iran developed and tested missile systems at Parchin throughout the monarchy's years. But Fakhrizadeh used

Parchin for a much more ambitious series of tests based on Danilen-ko's expertise.

In the northeast corner of the Parchin complex, Iranian military personnel stealthily constructed a large metal cylinder sometime in 2000. Inside was a test chamber that could safely mask the effects of tests involving 150 pounds of high explosives. It could also hide from foreign intelligence services the use of fissile materials such as natural or enriched uranium in those tests. The chamber was built by an Iranian company but based on a design created in Ukraine. The Soviets had used nearly identical equipment when conducting nuclear weapons tests at Chelyabinsk-70.

The test chamber took more than two years to complete. In 2002, a project team from the Physics Research Center arrived at Parchin with the specific mission of testing Fakhrizadeh's designs for a nuclear implosion device. Included in the mission were nuclear scientists believed by the IAEA to have trained under Fakhrizadeh and who worked with the center, even though the Iranian government denied the claims. One was a war veteran and university lecturer named Fereydoun Abassi-Davani. He was joined at Parchin by a nuclear engineer from Shahid Beheshti University, Majid Shahriari.

One of the devices tested was a neutron initiator. The device is described by scientists as something like the lighter inside a barbecue grill: just as the lighter kindles the fire in charcoal, neutrons initiate fission in a nuclear warhead. The resulting chain reaction releases huge amounts of energy—a flash of light and deadly heat as well as radiation. In an implosion warhead, explosives compress a spherical core of highly enriched uranium or plutonium, or a mixture of both, to the point that it triggers a fissile reaction. The neutron initiator is a golf-ball-sized sphere embedded in the center of the core and usually made out of a mix of beryllium and polonium. It's activated by the immense pressure from the converging shock wave, and its production of neutrons starts the nuclear reaction. Mastering the physics behind such an implosion bomb is highly complex and potentially dangerous given the extremely radioactive nature of the materials.

Abbasi-Davani and Shahriari were experts in analyzing the yield of both conventional and nuclear blasts, and they were tasked with simulating the detonation of an implosion bomb and the ability of a neutron initiator to stimulate a fissile reaction. The test didn't need actual nuclear explosive materials but could use stand-in materials, such as tungsten, to mimic the shock waves created by a nuclear blast. The team from the Physics Research Center set up neutron detectors and X-ray cameras just outside the test chamber to record the radiation from the explosion.

This was seen as a major advance in Tehran. But their success made Fakhrizadeh, Abbasi-Davani, Shahriari, and the rest of their team marked men.

NOT LONG AFTER JAFARZADEH's disclosure in Washington in 2002, the United States' top electronic spying agency, the National Security Agency, made a breakthrough in its surveillance of Iran's nuclear program. While sweeping up electronics intelligence that year, the American snoopers picked up phone communications between Fakhrizadeh and Iranian military personnel. The intelligence painted a confusing picture of the state of Iran's nuclear capabilities. The scientist is recorded vociferously complaining to colleagues that the Iranian government had significantly cut back funding for his work at the Physics Research Center. He said he would no longer be able to continue with his activities on anywhere near the same scale as before.

Within months of this intelligence coup, U.S. spy satellites detected bulldozers in Iran razing the offices of Fakhrizadeh's center in north Tehran. The entire compound was flattened and paved. In its place was constructed a sports facility. Iran seemed to American officials to be slowing, if not giving up, its Manhattan Project.

Some U.S. officials believed Tehran had frozen Fakhrizadeh's program because of the MeK's exposure of the facilities in Natanz and Arak. They argued that Tehran feared that the United States might follow its invasion of Iraq with an attempt to topple the Islamic Republic. In 2003, the U.S. war effort in Baghdad was progressing and not yet facing the nationwide insurgency that would kill hundreds of thousands. Some American officials were openly talking about moving on to Tehran and Damascus after Iraq. Ending Iran's weaponization work, at least temporarily, would deprive the United States of a primary rationale for starting such a conflict.

However, there were deep divisions both inside the U.S. intelligence community and in European and Israeli intelligence agencies over whether Fakhrizadeh had really stopped his work and Tehran had really ceased its development of nuclear weapons. IAEA reports documented Fakhrizadeh continuing to establish new organizations to conduct weapons studies after 2003. And some U.S. officials and lawmakers argued that Fakhrizadeh's hijacked communications were part of an elaborate Iranian ruse to confuse American spies. Tehran had historically proven to be a master of such subterfuge.

Regardless, Fakhrizadeh's communications ended up forming the core of a controversial 2007 U.S. National Intelligence Estimate that concluded Tehran had ceased its efforts to develop nuclear weapons. Much of the report remains classified. But the Bush administration's release of the NIE's executive summary—done not because they wanted to release the report, since they knew it would undercut their Iran policy, but because they assumed it would leak—created consternation in Western capitals, almost as much as the MeK's revelations had done in 2002.

Hawkish members of the U.S. administration and their allies in Israel, France, and the United Kingdom believed the report had torpedoed any possibility of the United States' launching military strikes to destroy Iran's nuclear infrastructure during Bush's final months in office. Some members of the White House even accused the U.S. intelligence agencies of purposely slanting their intelligence to undercut any moves toward military action. Ahmadinejad called the NIE a "divine victory" for Iran.

INTELLIGENCE ON IRAN'S NUCLEAR WORK continued to come into Washington and the IAEA's headquarters in Vienna from a range of countries, not just Israel. Germany emerged as a critical partner for the United States on the Iran nuclear issue. While Germany's diplomatic and business ties at times could pose a threat to the efforts to contain Tehran, the Germans were also a major source of intelligence. And they scored a real coup when one of their contacts, code-named Dolphin, provided a treasure trove of intelligence in exchange for seeking exile in the West.

The CIA found more than one thousand pages of documents on the thumb drive Dolphin provided, including Iranian correspondence relating to the conversion of uranium oxide into uranium tetrafluoride. This chemical process is crucial to creating the highly enriched uranium used in weapons. The Iranians in the files referred to this step as the "Green Salt Project" and, according to the documents on the memory stick, the program was managed under a department known as Project 5.13. Its goal was to produce a ton of the "green salt" per year.

The intelligence also indicated that Iran continued to pursue two tracks in developing its enrichment program—one through the military and one through the Atomic Energy Organization. The former was assumed to be related to Fakhrizadeh's work. And this fueled doubts within the intelligence community about whether Tehran had truly shut down its bomb work.

In February 2008 the IAEA presented an expansive report to its Board of Governors describing the suspected dealings of Fakhrizadeh's office. The report relied heavily on the information derived from the German intercept. The Iranians claimed the information had been fabricated by the Mossad.

THE NAMES AND LOCATIONS of Fakhrizadeh's core institution, the Physics Research Center, continued to morph as the focus on Iran's nuclear work intensified. In 2008, the Europeans publicly accused Iran of moving some of its nuclear weapons work to Malek Ashtar, an Iranian university located in northern Tehran, not far from the center's original offices. The CIA had begun tracking the school after it began procuring dual-use equipment that could be used in a nuclear weapons program, just as Sharif University had done in the early 1990s. Many of Fakhrizadeh's collaborators were believed to be either based at the university or associated with it.

The CIA began secretly communicating with a researcher at Malek Ashtar University named Shahram Amiri. The scientist, who was in his early thirties, wasn't a high-ranking member of Fakhrizadeh's organization, and he hadn't played a direct role in the Parchin tests. But he knew the structure of Fakhrizadeh's program and the extent of its work. As a result, Amiri became the target of a secretive CIA intelligence operation called "Brain Drain," which was specifically focused on recruiting Iranian scientists and defense officials (the program had already been successful in helping a senior member of the Revolutionary Guard to defect in 2007).

After making contact with the CIA, Amiri sent encrypted emails to the Agency, using normal Gmail and Yahoo accounts, and he sometimes spoke with his handlers via Skype. The information he provided challenged the U.S. intelligence community's earlier 2007 assessment that Tehran had halted its efforts to design a nuclear weapon.

But by April 2009 Amiri was spooked, and he worried he might be discovered by Iranian intelligence, particularly in the wake of the revelations provided by Dolphin. The CIA maintains the authority to bring as many as a hundred people into the United States each year under a government provision that allows the spy agency to bypass ordinary immigration requirements, and so Amiri arranged with his CIA handlers to take a trip to Saudi Arabia, ostensibly to perform the hajj; from there he would seek asylum in the United States. Leaving his wife and young son in Iran, Amiri traveled through the Saudi holy city of Medina, where his immigration documents to the United States were processed. The CIA paid the Iranian $5 million for his cooperation and established a residence for him in Arizona.

What transpired afterward emerged as one of the strangest episodes in modern American espionage and underscored the murkiness of the U.S.-Iran spy wars. A year after Amiri's arrival in the United States, the academic posted a video on YouTube from his new home in Tucson. In the video, an overweight Amiri, wearing a T-shirt and speaking in Persian, says he was kidnapped by the CIA after being injected with a drug while riding in a taxi in Medina.

Just days later, however, Amiri posted a second video, this time with him wearing a suit, looking more composed, and speaking in English. This one describes how he was in the United States working to further his education and earn his Ph.D. He says he had no ties to Iran's nuclear program and was free to travel around the United States. "My purpose in today's conversation is to put an end to all the rumors that have been leveled against me over the past year," he said. "I am Iranian, and I have not taken any steps against my homeland."

U.S. officials working on Amiri's case said his sharp shift was driven by Iranian threats against the scientist's family. These officials said Tehran was able to deliver its warnings into the United States through a sophisticated network of assets they maintained in immigrant communities in the country. The Iranians are believed to have exploited Amiri's growing sense of cultural alienation after being thrust into a suburban American community. Former U.S. officials said they didn't do a good job of acclimating and protecting Amiri, acknowledging that the separation from his family took a toll.

Tehran's threats eventually forced Amiri to take an almost un-heard-of step: re-defection. Exasperated by Amiri's rants on the Internet, the CIA allowed the Iranian to orchestrate his return to Tehran through Iran's lone diplomatic mission in the United States, an "interests section" that was ostensibly part of the Pakistani embassy in Washington, D.C., though not housed there. On the evening of July 10, 2010, Amiri took a taxi alone to the Iranian mission, north of downtown. He was greeted by Iranian diplomatic personnel and quickly shuffled up to the building's second floor. From there Amiri went on Iranian media to say that he was now free and that he was still a loyal defender of the revolution. He then said he hadn't divulged any information and was returning to Iran of his own free will, despite being offered $50 million to stay. "I don't think that any Iranian in my place would have sold his dignity to another country for a financial award," Amiri said. He was then whisked off to Washington's Dulles International Airport for his return trip to Iran.

Two days later, Amiri arrived to a hero's welcome in Tehran's Imam Khomeini International Airport. The Iranian officials who greeted him at the airport said he had been working as a double agent all along, providing Tehran with classified information on the workings of the U.S. spy services. "This was an intelligence war between the CIA and us, which was planned and managed by Iran," an unidentified Iranian official told state media at the airport. Amiri is seen on-screen weeping and hugging his seven-year-old son.

U.S. officials to this day say Amiri proved to be an invaluable source for the U.S. government, providing detailed information on Fakhrizadeh and his organization's operations and helping the United States uncover a secret uranium enrichment site in the Iranian holy city of Qom, a facility that the Obama administration believed was specifically designed to produce weapons-grade fuel. The plant was constructed inside a mountain and guarded by anti-aircraft missile batteries. The United States made public its discovery of the site not long before Amiri's departure for Iran in 2010. Though Amiri received a hero's welcome at first, some Americans think he may have been executed. The Iranian is believed to have paid for his espionage: Iranian media reports said he was sentenced to ten years in prison.

BETWEEN THE INFORMATION EXPOSED by Dolphin and the Amiri episode, the validity of the NIE claiming that Tehran had ceased nuclear weapons development continued to be whittled away. The spy games between the West and Iran, meanwhile, grew even more lethal, as Ahmadinejad accelerated his country's nuclear program following his reelection in 2009. From just a few centrifuges at the beginning of his tenure, the program grew to include thousands. And Iranian officials indicated they were on the cusp of producing weapons-grade uranium at its two enrichment sites, though denying that it would be used for bombs. Despite their denials, Iranian nuclear scientists quickly became the targets of an expansive assassination campaign that shook Iran's security establishment to its core.

On an early March morning in 2010, on the grounds of Tehran's infamous Evin prison, guards ushered twenty-six-year-old Majid Jamali Fashi to the gallows, where he confessed on Iranian state television to assassinating Tehran University professor Massoud Almohammadi three months earlier. The nuclear physicist had been sitting in his sedan when Fashi detonated a remote-controlled bomb attached to the car's undercarriage; Mohammadi was killed instantly, and Fashi fled into the streets of Tehran in an effort to evade capture. Some Iranian opposition groups claimed the killing was an inside job, authorized by the regime because of Mohammadi's sympathies for the political opposition. But Western intelligence services said they believed the scientist had ties to Tehran's weapons program.

Fashi, in a lengthy account of the assassination publicized in Iranian state media, said the attack had been directly ordered and overseen by the Mossad, Israel's intelligence service. At the time, Mossad and the Israeli government were pursuing a vigorous campaign to derail Iran's nuclear program. This included launching, in coordination with the United States, cyber attacks on the Natanz enrichment facility and the Bushehr nuclear reactor. Israel was also trying to slow down Iran's nuclear work by introducing faulty equipment into the program's supply chain.

Fashi was an expert in the martial arts discipline called pankration, which combines wrestling, boxing, and forms of street fighting. As a member of the Iranian national team, he frequently traveled to competitions in neighboring countries, including Azerbaijan. It was in Azerbaijan, Fashi told his interrogators, that he was recruited by Mossad agents out of the Israeli embassy in Baku, the Azeri capital. The Israelis paid him $120,000 to carry out a string of attacks. It was certainly true that Mossad had extensive intelligence assets in the country; Israel had long had close relations with Azerbaijan, a result of the two countries' mutual fear of Iran, which has historically viewed Azerbaijan as a rogue province that was part of the ancient Persian Empire and so should rightfully be under Tehran's control.

But Iranian officials briefed on the case also cited political motivations. They believed he was a member of the MeK, the dissident organization that was cooperating closely with the Mossad. The MeK was the group that had gone public with the intelligence on Natanz and Arak nearly a decade earlier in Washington. (The MeK neither confirmed nor denied its role in the assassinations.) Some Iran analysts say Fashi's confession may have been coerced, but they acknowledge that the story sounded credible because of Israel's history of operations against Iran.

Fashi said his minders instructed him on conducting surveillance and countersurveillance and on the use of munitions. He was told to study and memorize Mohammadi's daily activities. A model of the scientist's house was constructed at the Mossad training camp in Azerbaijan, along with a mock-up of his neighborhood in northern Tehran. Fashi was schooled on how to conduct assassinations while on a motorcycle.

In all, Fashi said, Mossad devised at least ten attacks for him to conduct inside Iran, targeting a number of scientists and other figures involved in the nuclear program. Israel was bent on showing Iran that its defenses were weak and that no one involved in the nuclear program was safe. The Israelis hoped to demoralize and instill fear in the country's nuclear brain trust and make them think twice before cooperating with the military or the Revolutionary Guard—or even opening their mail.

Iran made a state spectacle of Fashi's execution. The widow of the murdered scientist told the assassin on government television that he would "face the wrath of God" for his duplicity. Fashi then said from the gallows, "The end of the road has nothing except repentance—and rope." Finally hooded guards released a trap door beneath his feet.

THE TARGETING OF THE NUCLEAR scientists continued apace following Fashi's execution. The assassins appeared intent on eliminating those men who worked for the Physics Research Center. If they couldn't hit Mohsen Fakhrizadeh directly, they'd take out those close to him.

On November 29, 2010, Fereydoun Abbasi-Davani and Majid Shahriari, veterans of the center and the Parchin tests, prepared for their morning commute to work from their respective homes in the city's affluent northern suburbs, not realizing they were being watched. It was indeed the case that the United States, Israel, and other Western intelligence agencies had been covertly tracking their work for more than five years, and the United Nations had sanctioned Abbasi-Davani in 2007 for his partnership with Fakhrizadeh, who had been blacklisted a year earlier. But the scientists had bigger problems that day.

Assassins had been monitoring their movements to and from their homes and workplaces for months. On that November morning, masked men on motorcycles sped toward the two scientists. Jumping off their bikes, they attached magnetized bombs to the undersides of Abbasi-Davani's and Shahriari's sedans in an operation eerily reminiscent of Fashi's. It happened so quickly bystanders didn't realize anything was amiss. Tehran's chaotic streets quickly swallowed up the masked men as they sped off into anonymity.

Abbasi-Davani knew something was wrong when he heard a subtle click underneath his car, he told Iranian reporters. He grabbed his wife, and they dove out of their car just before the bomb detonated. They both sustained cuts and burns from the blast but walked away largely unhurt.

Majid Shahriari wasn't so lucky. The blast killed him instantly, sending a fireball high into the morning sky above Tehran. Photos of his contorted body made newspapers and television news broadcasts around the world. The Iranian government began displaying the carcass of the scientist's car at national events as a symbol of the hostile acts perpetrated by the Americans and the "Zionists," and eventually placed it on display at the Holy Defense Museum. Again Tehran accused Mossad of having the blood of Iranian scientists on its hands, though Israel never either confirmed or denied its role in the assassinations.

President Ahmadinejad displayed defiance in a nationally televised event in February 2012, shortly after one of the attacks. The ceremony was officially convened to commemorate the fueling of Tehran's research reactor, which for the first time was using uranium plates produced inside Iran. But photos of five murdered scientists were displayed behind the firebrand leader as he spoke on a dais. He fell to his knees after his oration to kiss the daughter of another murdered scientist, Darioush Rezaienejad, while Fereydoun Abbasi-Davani looked on. "We won't rest until these martyrs are avenged," Ahmadinejad said.

AT THE REVOLUTIONARY GUARD's headquarters in Tehran, General Qasem Soleimani and his fellow commanders in the Qods Force plotted their retaliation. Soleimani was dusting off an old playbook.

For decades, the Guard and its proxies had executed attacks on American, Israeli, and Arab targets overseas. These included the bombing of the U.S. Marine Corps barracks in 1983, which used a Hezbollah suicide bomber, and the 1994 attack on the Jewish community center in Buenos Aires. The strikes often utilized Iranian diplomatic missions overseas, or Persian and Arab émigrés. They targeted Tehran's exiled political rivals in European cities, including Berlin and Paris. This assassination campaign was particularly intense in the early 1990s in the wake of the Iran-Iraq War, as Tehran sought to intimidate its political opponents.

One of Soleimani's deputy generals in the Qods Force was a man named Abdul Reza Shahlai. His name was little known in Western intelligence circles. But among Shahlai's primary responsibilities was oversight of terrorist strikes against Iran's enemies, according to U.S. officials. The United States first encountered Shahlai in Iraq, when captured Shiite fighters described to their American interrogators how Shahlai had overseen the January 2007 attack on a U.S. military base in Karbala, which killed five American soldiers and was executed on the ground by members of Hezbollah and Iraqi Shiite militias.

Shahlai's reach stretched far beyond Iraq and the Middle East, including to a family member living in the United States. Shahlai's cousin Mansour Arbabsiar had moved to the United States in the 1970s after gaining entrance to a Texas university. He later went on to work as a used-car salesman in Corpus Christi. He'd had a string of failed marriages to local women. Most of Arbabsiar's neighbors viewed the balding, paunchy forty-seven-year-old as a semi-employed buffoon rather than a threat to the United States. But Arbabsiar maintained a high-level connection to Tehran that U.S. intelligence services hadn't detected. Even after three decades in America, the Texan continued to communicate with his powerful cousin. They met up on the few occasions when Arbabsiar traveled back to visit Tehran, according to U.S. intelligence officials.

In late 2011, Shahlai approached Arbabsiar with a proposition. As the murders of the Iranian scientists continued, the IRGC wanted to strike back by assassinating Saudi Arabia's ambassador to the United States, Adel al-Jubeir. One of King Abdullah's closest strategic advisors, he regularly flew back to the kingdom to personally advise the monarch on the latest developments in the United States or to outline the important events shaping the Middle East. Al-Jubeir positioned himself as a hard-liner on Iran, pressing the Obama administration to confront the country and stop its nuclear advances by any means possible. And he was something of a star in Washington as well. In the wake of 9/11, he was a regular on Larry King's talk show. He also dated Campbell Brown, a CNN news anchor, and had a high profile on Washington's diplomatic circuit.

Shahlai plotted to kill al-Jubeir while he lunched at Café Milano, a high-end Georgetown eatery known for its politically powerful clientele, according to U.S. officials briefed on the intelligence. Killing al-Jubeir in the heart of Washington would send a clear signal to the United States and its allies that Tehran could retaliate anywhere and that no one, no matter how powerful, was beyond the Qods Force's reach. In essence, it reprised the strategy Iran believed the Israelis were using by targeting its nuclear brain trust. Because Tehran viewed Saudi Arabia, Israel, and the United States as operating together in targeting its nuclear program, it considered an attack on al-Jubeir to be a strike against them all.

Arbabsiar was no seasoned terrorist. So the IRGC steered its plot in a more complex and international direction. The car dealer's home in Texas was not far from the border with Mexico, an area overrun by criminals and drug gangs. Executions and beheadings were regular occurrences over the border in cities such as Juarez. Shahlai wanted his cousin to bring in hired assassins, preferably members of an international drug cartel known as Los Zetas, to carry out the attack on al-Jubeir. This would provide Iran with deniability. While the country had historically utilized proxies, such as

Hezbollah, for its overseas attacks, and was accused of launching attacks on Israeli targets in Argentina in the 1990s using local operatives, the Mexico plot was a novel twist.

Arbabsiar began flying to Mexico to make contact with members of Los Zetas. Over a string of trips, he succeeded in conveying his cousin's overture to the narco gang. But he also inadvertently tipped off the FBI. An undercover agent began meeting with Arbabsiar, posing as a member of Los Zetas, as the plot advanced. The agent probed Arbabsiar to find out for whom he was working in Iran and how far the planning had gone for the operation.

Arbabsiar began calling a Tehran-based intermediary of his cousin's, named Ali Gholam Shakuri, to discuss the details of the plot. In conversations taped by the FBI, the two men referred to the assassination of Ambassador al-Jubeir as the "Chevrolet" they were hoping to purchase. "How are your efforts going to buy the Chevrolet?" Shakuri asked his U.S.-based interlocutor in the summer of 2011. "We're ready for the purchase," Arbabsiar responded.

Shortly thereafter, the Qods Force wired Arbabsiar more than $100,000 to execute the assassination. This fueled panic inside the FBI, as concerns mounted that the Iranian plot was imminent. FBI agents stormed Arbabsiar's home in Texas and whisked him to New York for an arraignment. He was accused of abusing the New York financial system in an attempt to conduct murder. Top U.S. officials, including Secretary of State Hillary Clinton and Attorney General Eric Holder, called the plot one of the greatest terrorist operations ever thwarted in the United States. "This was directed and approved by elements of the Iranian government and specifically senior members of the Qods Force," Holder told reporters. "High-up officials in those agencies . . . were responsible for the plot."

Some Iran experts, both inside the United States and overseas, quickly discounted the FBI's claims. They cited the spectacular, Hollywood-style nature of the plot and cast doubt on the notion that the Iranians would risk courting a direct conflict with Washington by carrying out an assassination inside the United States. For one thing, nothing like that had ever been done before. An alternative theory was that members of the Qods Force purposely wanted the plot exposed to embarrass President Ahmadinejad and weaken those in Tehran still hoping to negotiate with the United States on the nuclear issue.

Arbabsiar, though, eventually pleaded guilty, getting more than thirty years in prison. And the highest levels of the U.S. intelligence services were convinced that the plot was real. They cited the large wire transfer to Arbabsiar. They also understood the extent of the feud between Iran and the United States and feared that things were spinning out of control.

THE PLOT AGAINST THE SAUDI envoy was just one of at least a half dozen operations the Qods Force launched in retaliation for the assassinations of the nuclear scientists. They dispatched Iranian and Hezbollah operatives to Baku, Azerbaijan, in November 2011 to target American and Israeli diplomats using explosives and snipers, according to U.S. and Azeri officials who investigated the operation. Bombing plots linked to Iran were exposed in Nairobi, Mombasa, Bangkok, and New Delhi in early 2012. That July, a suicide bomber struck a bus in the Bulgarian resort of Burgas that carried forty-two Israeli tourists, mostly youths; five were killed and thirty-two injured. Bulgarian authorities charged Hezbollah with executing the strike.

As the tit-for-tat bloodletting intensified, Mohsen Fakhrizadeh continued his work in north Tehran. Once more the scientist renamed his office and moved its location. The newest incarnation of the Physics Research Center was known as the Organization of Defensive Innovation and Research or by its Persian acronym, SPND. Fakhrizadeh staffed the body with many of the same senior scientists and Revolutionary Guard officials who had worked at his center more than a decade earlier, according to IAEA staff. The SPND hosted six directorates, including research labs for metallurgy, chemistry, and explosives testing. IAEA and U.S. officials believed

Fakhrizadeh and his staff were still working on perfecting technologies applicable for developing atomic weapons. But Fakhrizadeh knew his operations were under constant scrutiny, so he was more guarded and kept SPND's operations diffuse.

Fereydoun Abbasi-Davani, the scientist who had survived the downtown Tehran assassination attempt, used his newfound national celebrity to move up the chain of the Iranian government's bureaucracy. President Ahmadinejad named him vice president of Iran in 2011 and concurrently the president of the Atomic Energy Organization. His post gave him expansive powers to oversee the direction of Tehran's nuclear fuel production and Iran's relationship with the IAEA. He'd essentially moved from being at the center of Iran's secret nuclear program to being the public face of its aspirations.

Abbasi-Davani, despite facing a UN travel ban, was afforded special diplomatic status as vice president and began traveling regularly to Vienna to meet with IAEA officials. Interestingly enough, in that role he negotiated with the agency on its demands to have unlimited access to inspect the Parchin military facility, where he had allegedly taken part in the clandestine weapons work a decade earlier and which remained at the center of Western fears about Iran's long-term intentions. But Abbasi-Davani and his diplomatic colleagues repeatedly rebuffed the IAEA's demands.

The scientist oversaw the rapid expansion of nuclear-fuel production at Iran's atomic sites, including the underground enrichment facility in the city of Qom. Faster centrifuges, which could increase the output of enriched uranium by three to five times, were installed under the scientist's watch. Abbasi-Davani told Iranian lawmakers that the country would develop nuclear submarines, a program that required Iran to produce highly enriched uranium, meaning uranium that was 90 percent pure rather than its previous level of 20 percent.

U.S. and Israeli intelligence officials doubted Tehran had the capability to produce submarines. But they saw the vice president's comments as an excuse for Iran to move to the brink of producing weapons-grade fuel. They were further unnerved when Abbasi-Davani met in 2012 with North Korean officials to sign an agreement on scientific cooperation. U.S. and Israeli officials had long believed Tehran and Pyongyang were sharing nuclear weapons data and equipment. At an event in Tehran, North Korea and Iran announced they were establishing joint laboratories, engaging in scientific transfers, and exchanging their scientists. "The Islamic Republic of Iran and North Korea have common enemies since the arrogant powers can't bear independent governments," Supreme Leader Khamenei said at the time.

Abbasi-Davani, meanwhile, railed against the West, which he accused of the attempt on his life. On a trip to Vienna in late 2011, he gathered international reporters at the IAEA's headquarters near the Danube River and told them that Israel, the United States, and Britain had plotted for more than five years to kill him. But he defiantly and triumphantly stressed that he had survived. "Six years ago the intelligence service of the U.K. began collecting information and data regarding my past," he said. They even "checked into the back door of my room in the university to see whether I had a bodyguard or not. . . . But I am still here."

CHAPTER 6

The Rial War

IRAN'S RAPID ADVANCES ON ITS NUCLEAR PROGRAM WERE SOWING panic in the Obama administration and the Israeli government. Military threats, the assassination of nuclear scientists, and diplomatic isolation weren't curbing Tehran's gains. The U.S. administration was increasingly concerned that Israeli prime minister Benjamin Netanyahu might strike Iran on his own, risking a broader Middle East war. The United States had for decades imposed various forms of trade sanctions on Tehran, but with only limited impact. The White House thus decided to ratchet up pressure on Iran where it really hurt—its bank accounts.

In the summer of 2011, U.S. intelligence services began tracking large flows of Iranian oil money that were being processed through a small bank in the United Arab Emirates' financial capital, Dubai. The firm, Noor Islamic Bank, was then transferring these funds back to Tehran through Iranian state banks the U.S. Treasury Department had already sanctioned for allegedly financing Iran's nuclear program and supporting international terrorism. The fact that Iran was using such a small banking partner showed the United

States that penalties imposed since 2006 were effective in driving the country underground and out of the global economy. But Iran was still finding loopholes. The remittances going through Noor Islamic Bank made up as much as two-thirds of Iran's total oil revenues in 2011, according to U.S. officials. The Obama administration saw an opportunity to hit the Iranians hard, as pressure from the U.S. Congress was building for the White House to try to shut down Iran's entire oil trade—the lifeblood of the country's economy.

For five years already, the Treasury Department and the U.S. Congress had pursued an intensifying financial war against Iran in a bid to force Tehran to end its nuclear program. The U.S. sanctions were targeting virtually every sector of the Iranian economy—particularly its banks, shipping companies, and insurance sector. But increasingly the heart of Washington's strategy was to dry up Iran's oil exports, which financed around 70 percent of Tehran's total budget, by crippling its ability to conduct any trade. Denying Iran this cash, U.S. officials believed, might be the only way to get Iran to capitulate on its nuclear work, short of war.

IN 2004, THE GEORGE W. BUSH administration established a new office at the Treasury Department. It was called the Office of Terrorism and Financial Intelligence, or TFI, and included units focused on intelligence collection, sanctions, and financial crime. Up until that year, successive administrations had at times used the Treasury Department to punish America's enemies with economic sanctions or to track the finances of Latin American drug kingpins and American organized crime leaders. But Treasury didn't yet have a seat at the table in the country's national security apparatus. It was a marginal player, even though Treasury's offices were situated right next door to the White House.

This dynamic changed radically after 9/11. The Bush administration quickly prioritized strategies for cutting off the financing of terrorist groups globally, with Treasury at the center of these efforts.

Spearheaded by the Patriot Act, passed in 2001, expansive new laws were rushed through Congress to combat international money laundering and terrorist financing. The legislation strengthened the government's powers to conduct surveillance on telephone communications and wire transfers. And Treasury used its subpoena power to gain access to many of the records of the Belgium-based SWIFT network, which facilitates virtually every bank-to-bank transaction around the globe. Allowing the United States this access fueled unease among European financial regulators, who cited privacy concerns. But Treasury analysts suddenly had the ability to spy on businesses or executives believed to have terrorism links.

TFI had only one financial intelligence analyst in 2004 but quickly grew to having more than a hundred and a front-row seat in prosecuting Washington's wars in Iraq and Afghanistan. And it mastered the secret game of drying up terrorist groups' finances. Treasury uncovered al Qaeda's and the Taliban's financial ties to Saudi Arabia, Pakistan, and the Gulf states. And it scored early successes in dismantling U.S.-based charities that were financing militant groups such as Hamas and Hezbollah.

The Treasury also proved adept at cutting off rogue states' funding. In the early 2000s, U.S. officials discovered that North Korea was financing its nuclear and missile programs by exporting heroin, knock-off cigarettes, and counterfeit dollars. Many of the funds raised this way, the Bush administration learned, were moving back to Pyongyang and its leadership through a small bank in the former Portuguese colony of Macau. The Treasury warned banks globally that Banco Delta Asia was engaged in money laundering and moving contraband. North Korea suddenly found itself virtually incapable of dollar transactions, and foreign banks from Singapore to Mongolia feared being targeted by Treasury if they engaged in business with the Macanese firm. Wary depositors eventually made a run on the bank, forcing the local government to take it over.

"We learned that denying access to the dollar was a crucial tool in punishing the U.S.'s enemies," said Juan Zarate, a Bush adminis-

tration official who helped lead Treasury's counterterrorism operations after 9/11. "It was emerging as a potent weapon in our national
security architecture."

Indeed, Treasury knew that major businesses simply couldn't
function without access to U.S. dollars, the world's default currency.
Treasury could force foreign firms to choose between doing business with the United States or conducting it with rogue states and
criminal enterprises. To most, the decision would be a no-brainer.

TREASURY SOON PLACED IRAN squarely in its crosshairs following the
arrival in 2004 of its first undersecretary for terrorism and financial
intelligence, Stuart Levey. Levey had no special expertise in finance
when he took the post. A public prosecutor educated at Harvard, he
served in the Justice Department of the George W. Bush administration after providing legal advice to the candidate during the 2000
campaign and recount in Florida. Levey, in his early forties at the
time, had boyish looks for a high-powered attorney; some friends
joked about his recent bar mitzvah. But he'd proved to be an aggressive prosecutor. And he knew how to work the Washington bureaucracy.

Once at Treasury, Levey used his legal mind to ruthlessly fixate
on Iran. The Iranians, having backed out of earlier commitments to
the Europeans to freeze their production of nuclear fuel, had an essentially unrestrained program under their new fanatical president,
Mahmoud Ahmadinejad, when Levey began his work. And Tehran
had paid only a small price for backing out of the European diplomatic agreements. The Bush administration needed to develop an
overarching strategy to curb Iran's capabilities, so Levey decided to
build on the tactics Treasury had developed during the first four
years after 9/11 to put in place one of the broadest campaigns of financial warfare ever launched against a single country.

On Secretary of State Condoleezza Rice's plane, Air Force III, in
the winter of 2006, as she was en route to the Middle East, Levey

gave the diplomat a menu of financial weapons for the Bush administration's new campaign against Tehran. The initial focus, he told
Rice, would be small: cutting off some of Iran's major state banks,
such as Melli, Saderat, Sepah, and Mellat, from access to the U.S.
dollar. Major international business transactions, including oil and
gas sales, are almost always priced and conducted in the U.S. currency, due to its stable rate and availability. Levey argued that the
United States was unlikely initially to get the United Nations Security Council to support sanctions on these banks, as many European, Chinese, and Russian firms still did business with Iran. But he
believed that over time unilateral U.S. actions toward these banks
would have a devastating impact on their businesses. Any reputable
foreign bank or company had to have access to U.S. dollars if it was
going to conduct international business.

"We wanted to find a way to put the Iranian regime under so
much pressure that it would be forced to choose between integra-
tion with the international community, along with the attendant
benefits, and increasing, painful financial isolation," Levey told me
in a series of interviews starting in 2007. "It was never about contain-
ment; we wanted an option short of military action that could potentially be a game-changer."

Levey went on to describe to Rice an intensifying assault on
Iran's finances, which would be tempered only if Tehran gave
ground in nuclear negotiations. Virtually all sectors of Iran's economy would be fair game: shipping firms, airlines, insurance companies, and ports. The United States also saw a particularly ripe target
in the Revolutionary Guard. The military unit was carving out a
dominant position in large sections of the Iranian economy, including the lucrative oil and gas sector. Targeting the IRGC, Levey believed, could essentially kill two birds with one stone: weakening
Iran's military and its broader economy as a whole. Regular Iranians
might even welcome the move, Levey hoped, because they were
being pushed out of business by the IRGC and its cronies.

Levey didn't explicitly state it, but his office's strategy of cascading waves of sanctions on various sectors of Iran's economy amounted to a nearly total trade embargo on Iran. Without access to banks and the dollar, and with its shipping firms and airlines blocked, Tehran would be incapable of conducting normal business. Faced with such conditions, Levey hoped, Iran would capitulate and give up its nuclear ambitions. And the campaign might also fuel broader opposition to the regime among the Iranian public, if not foment a new revolution. "We saw an escalating financial war that had virtually no end, if Iran didn't capitulate," Levey says. "And Secretary Rice was on board and fully supportive from the beginning."

CUTTING OFF IRAN'S FINANCES, Levey soon learned, would be a global game of whack-a-mole. Governments in Europe, Asia, and the Middle East were initially reluctant to go along with the United States' financial war against Iran. The UN Security Council was also wary of placing major Iranian commercial banks or companies on sanctions lists, in part because many international businesses remained deeply invested in Tehran. Unlike North Korea, Myanmar, or Zimbabwe, Iran was not yet a global pariah. And unlike those countries, Iran had oil wealth, a skilled workforce, and a youthful population that sought engagement with the West.

This dynamic forced Levey to embark on global road shows to sell Arab, Asian, and European bankers on the need to wall off Iran's economy. The Treasury official's presentation was simple: *Any business with Iran is a risk because seemingly legitimate commerce is often a front for nuclear trade or terrorist activity. If you take the chance of doing commerce with Iranian firms,* Levey said in speeches from Dubai to Istanbul and Beirut, *you could lose your own bank's or company's access to the U.S. financial system.* European and Arab diplomats privately groused when they learned Levey and Treasury officials were arriving in their towns to lecture their bankers on the threat Iran posed to their businesses. His message was clear, how-ever: they could do business with Iran or with the United States, but not both.

"As you make your business decisions, I urge you to consider whether it's wise for your company to focus its efforts on doing busi-ness with Iran," Levey told a gathering of Arab bankers and business-men at the Fifth Annual Conference on Trade, Treasury, and Financial Management in Dubai in March 2007. "I recognize that it may be tempting to step into the void that is being created by other companies pulling back their business in Iran, but they are pulling back for a reason. . . . You should worry too."

Levey's appearance belied his tough talk. His voice cracked like a teenager's when he spoke at press conferences. He often appeared shy and deferential. The fact that he was Jewish, like many senior Treasury officials, fed into the conspiracy theories that ran rampant across the Middle East. They described a U.S. and global financial system controlled by Israel and the Jews. Levey and his colleagues at Treasury were aware of these stories and felt uneasy about them. In Tehran, Levey was promoted to public enemy number one—a Zi-onist agent in Washington bent on destroying the economy of the Persian Empire. Protestors marshaled by Iran's government to chant anti-American slogans on Tehran's streets took to carrying pictures of Levey and other U.S. officials.

Levey's strategy increasingly focused on choking off Iran's oil sales, which made up roughly two-thirds of Tehran's state revenues. China, India, South Korea, Japan, and other major powers were dependent on Iran for oil supplies and therefore were unwilling to place their economies at risk by abruptly shutting off their energy purchases. Treasury knew this, but Levey and his team still began to devise ways to block oil transactions by severing Iran's access to global banks. And U.S. officials were looking to find alternative oil supplies for America's allies.

The strategy, though, was controversial. For decades, Iran had been among OPEC's top oil exporters. Economists at the Treasury, and Treasury secretaries Henry Paulson and Timothy Geithner, privately warned Levey that rapidly cutting off Tehran's oil exports could hurt the United States' own economy by shrinking the fuel supply and driving up global energy prices.

"We were concerned that . . . [if we were] so abrupt in imposing these sanctions on oil and financial institutions, and not giving us certain waiver authorities, that it could effectively crash the global economy," Ben Rhodes, Obama's deputy national security advisor, told me. "If you flip the switch a certain way, it could have negative effects or countries could simply ignore it."

LEVEY AND THE TREASURY also turned up the pressure on Iranian insurance companies, airlines, ports, and transport firms. A special emphasis was placed on the Islamic Republic of Iran Shipping Lines, or IRISL, the country's largest cargo handler. Treasury had blacklisted the company in 2009 for allegedly moving arms to Hezbollah and Hamas through the Mediterranean and for importing equipment for Iran's nuclear program. But U.S. officials knew IRISL was also a major cog in Iran's legitimate economy, shipping everything from food to automobiles. This raised a moral quandary that Levey and his staff continually faced in combating Iran: how to stop its nuclear program without unfairly damaging the lives of normal Iranian civilians.

IRISL engaged in an elaborate game of subterfuge as Treasury pressed foreign companies to stop allowing the company's ships into their ports. IRISL repainted the colors of their fleet's outside hulls. They sailed ships under the flags of Liberia, Malta, and other countries that sold flagging rights. And Tehran established hundreds of front companies in Caribbean and European cities in an effort to hide Iranian ownership. But IRISL's ships were still increasingly denied access to foreign ports, particularly when global insurance companies denied them coverage.

Treasury was also choking off Iran's ability to fly internationally.

In the wake of the Islamic Revolution in 1979, the United States had sanctioned exports of American airplane parts to Tehran as punishment for the hostage crisis. The result was that Iran's international flag carrier, Iran Air, possessed an aged and depleted fleet of Boeing aircraft that had been bought, for the most part, during the shah's era. The safety of many of the planes was in question due to the lack of regular maintenance. Tehran publicly stated that the United States should be charged with human rights violations in an international court as Iranian planes increasingly ran the risk of crashing because of maintenance-related issues.

The Treasury Department under Levey stepped up its efforts against not just Iran Air but also smaller airlines such as Yas and Mehr. All of these companies, Treasury argued, were engaged in terrorist activity due to their shipments of weapons to Hezbollah, the Assad regime, and militant groups in Iraq. International airports subsequently began denying Iran Air, the country's lone overseas carrier, landing rights because of security concerns.

BUT TEHRAN WAS STILL finding ways to exploit holes in the world's financial system. Many smaller banks and countries were eager to pick up the slack as multinational companies left Iran. They could charge higher fees or interest rates to Iranians in exchange for the risk they were taking by defying the U.S. Treasury Department.

Europäisch-Iranische Handelsbank AG, or EIH Bank, of Frankfurt, was among the small firms still willing to take the risk. German companies were the largest European traders with Iran, providing engineering expertise, specialty metals, and software, and many German firms that did business in Iran conducted all of their trade through EIH. Iran and Germany established deep political and economic ties in the 1930s, when the Nazis were aligned with Reza Shah Pahlavi. Germans and Persians both identify themselves as descendants of the Aryan race. German firms built much of Tehran's infrastructure, including its subway system. The close business relationship endured after the United States and Britain replaced Reza Shah with his son Mohammad in 1944 because of the father's Nazi sympathies, and later the relationship even survived the 1979 revolution that threw out the family altogether.

The Treasury sanctioned EIH in late 2010, banning it from using the U.S. dollar or engaging with American banks. The move sparked an outcry from German businesses and politicians. Powerful trade groups pressed the German government not to follow Washington's lead. Levey personally delivered intelligence to German finance officials to document how Iran had used EIH to finance at least two transactions aimed at procuring equipment for Iran's nuclear program. The Germans complied and blacklisted EIH, rather than risk broader U.S. penalties.

Levey believed that offering countries the choice of doing business with either Iran or the United States, but not both, was the brilliance of their Iran strategy. It assumed that most foreign governments and businesses didn't want to cooperate but that ultimately they would have to. The result was that by 2010 most of Europe had largely cut itself off from Iran because of the fear of more U.S. sanctions and fines. And while Washington's heavy hand angered European businesses, U.S. officials believed President Obama's repeated efforts to hold direct negotiations with Iran on its nuclear program made it easier for Washington to pursue sanctions, as it meant that the Europeans couldn't blame the White House for not extending a hand to Tehran. The onus of blame for the stalemate was shifting.

TEHRAN BEGAN MOVING MORE of its assets to the East. In the 1970s, with the help of the United Nations, Iran had established a little-known trading office in South Asia called the Asian Clearing Union (ACU). The ACU brought together seven of the region's poorer countries that faced trouble conducting trade due to both a lack of U.S. dollars and their fluctuating currencies. The ACU allowed these countries to essentially barter goods through its system, which in a large part was based on IOUs. The ACU's headquarters were in Tehran, and many of its senior executives were Iranians. At the time of ACU's establishment, Tehran saw the trading office as a vehicle to cement Iran's role as an economic leader in the Middle East and Central and South Asia.

Levey and other U.S. and European officials in 2010 grew alarmed by the amount of trade going through the ACU. The Treasury found it virtually impossible to detect who was conducting what type of business thanks to ACU's opaque trading system, but it believed many of the trades involved sanctioned banks, such as Saderat and Mellat, selling their oil to Asian buyers. Further, U.S. officials worried that the ACU masked Tehran's ongoing efforts to procure equipment for its nuclear program through middlemen based in India and Pakistan.

In January 2011, Treasury wreaked havoc on the Indian economy when it announced it was sanctioning the ACU, barring it from U.S. dollar transactions. Indian officials had begun conducting much of their oil trade with Iran through the ACU after Germany's EIH shut down its business. After its access to oil via the ACU was blocked, New Delhi first tried to purchase Iranian oil in rupees as a means to evade American sanctions. But India's oil purchases from Iran totally outpaced the country's ability to make payments in its own currency. So New Delhi was forced to start looking for alternative energy supplies beyond Iran where it could pay in dollars, a dynamic that was repeating all over the world as U.S. sanctions hit one bank after another.

The Treasury's action effectively shut down the ACU, which was almost completely dependent on Iran. India and others couldn't afford to cross the Treasury. Iranian financial officials and businesses were getting desperate as the global economy was closing itself off to them. Levey and his staff were successfully plugging up the holes.

Tehran established one more financial channel through the Persian Gulf in order to continue its oil trade. Noor Islamic Bank, the UAE bank headquartered in a small business complex in downtown

Dubai, was controlled by the son of the emir of Dubai, Sheikh Mohammad bin Rashid Maktoum. Its business was largely focused on providing Islamic banking services to businesses in the Gulf. For example, Islamic law prohibits the charging of interest, so the bank had rules against paying interest to clients. The practice attracted Muslim clients but prevented Noor from being a major player in international business.

By the end of 2011, as Tehran's nuclear program expanded, Treasury was tracking more than $10 billion in Iranian oil sales going through Noor Islamic Bank each month, a sum that accounted for as much as 70 percent of its global oil sales. U.S. financial intelligence was perhaps Washington's most precise form of information on Iran at this point, as large U.S.-dollar trades had to be registered at the Federal Reserve.

The United States' focus on Noor Islamic Bank set off a heated internal debate between the UAE's two major royal families, according to U.S. and Emirati officials. The al-Nahyan family of Abu Dhabi—the political capital of the UAE—took one of the hardest lines against Tehran in the Persian Gulf and viewed Iran's nuclear program as an existential threat. They also knew that some Iranian maps showed the territory of the UAE as being just another province of the Persian Empire. The al-Nahyans were prepared to go to almost any length to contain Iran's weapons program and to push back Tehran's territorial aspirations.

The al-Maktoum family in Dubai, however, was in a bind. They were heavily reliant on the Iran trade. But their ability to resist pressure from the Abu Dhabi royals had been weakened when the al-Nahyan family bailed out Dubai to the tune of tens of billions of dollars as its real estate bubble burst and its credit rating sank in 2007 and 2008.

U.S. Treasury officials flew to Dubai in late 2011 to say that the Obama administration was prepared to sanction Noor Islamic Bank, which would send out a warning sign about the UAE's entire financial system. Heated exchanges occurred between U.S. and Emirati officials, who worried that the UAE's entire economic recovery could be placed at risk. The Treasury was unmoved. "'Don't test us' was our message," said one Treasury official who took part in the meetings.

In early January 2012, Noor Islamic Bank formally notified the Treasury that it had cut off all of its Iran trade to avoid facing U.S. sanctions. The fallout was dramatic. The value of the Iranian currency, the rial, plunged by more than 30 percent against the dollar in just a few days. Tehran was virtually unable to conduct any dollar-related transactions, which were required for oil sales. Billions of dollars of Iranian oil revenues were detected sitting in offshore bank accounts, unable to be repatriated. Banks throughout the world were spooked about any ties to Tehran.

U.S. officials saw the collapse of the Iranian currency as a clear sign that Tehran's financial system was cracking. The key, the Americans learned, was to find and then block the key nodes in Iran's international financial network. These were banks or firms that were doing a disproportionately large amount of trading with Iran. Once those firms realized they could lose access to the U.S. financial system by doing business with Iran, they would cut it off.

Stuart Levey stepped down from the Treasury Department in 2011 and took a lucrative job as legal counsel at Hongkong Shanghai Banking Corp. (HSBC) in London. His first order of business was to help the bank wrestle with its own ties to illicit business, in particular drug money. HSBC would eventually pay the U.S. government $9 billion in fines for helping Mexico's Sinaloa drug cartel move money into American banks.

But Levey's successors at Treasury and TFI, first David Cohen and then Adam Szubin, continued relentlessly tracking Iran's oil money, including the operation in the UAE. They knew Iran was growing more and more isolated financially. "As their financial options get narrower and narrower, you do see heavy reliance on key, third-country intermediaries," Szubin told me about the UAE operation. "To the extent we could detect them and knock them out, the impact became bigger and bigger. We had some difficult conversations with foreign jurisdictions."

THE FINANCIAL WAR ON Iran was playing out in the United States as well as overseas. Local governments were divesting their money from companies or organizations doing business in Iran. And public prosecutors and lawyers based in Washington and New York were joining with the Treasury and the State Department to attack Iran's finances.

Perhaps no American law enforcement official took a more aggressive line than Robert Morgenthau, who served as Manhattan's district attorney for thirty-five years until his retirement in 2009 at age ninety. Morgenthau saw it as his duty to use the New York financial system and its outsized influence on the global economy to police the world's banks and punish Washington's adversaries. Iran became an obsession during his final years in office.

Morgenthau built on the work of his father, Henry Morgenthau Jr., who had served as secretary of the Treasury under President Franklin Delano Roosevelt. The elder Morgenthau established the Office of Foreign Assets Control, the Treasury unit that pioneered the use of sanctions to punish America's adversaries and was a precursor to Stuart Levey's work fifty years later. In his early years as Manhattan district attorney, Robert Morgenthau led investigations into New York banks that cycled Latin American drug money through the U.S. financial system and into funds controlled by the Mafia.

The Morgenthaus, a German family that had emigrated from Bavaria in the 1800s, were passionately committed to protecting world Jewry and the state of Israel. Henry Morgenthau was the top figure inside the Roosevelt administration calling for an aggressive American effort to save Jews in Germany, Poland, Italy, and Hungary from Hitler's war machine and to provide them with a safe haven in the United States. Morgenthau's efforts resulted in the creation in 1944 of the War Refugee Board, the top American agency seeking to safeguard Europe's Jews, though the family still bemoaned the fact that there were so many who could not be saved from the Holocaust. Henry Morgenthau also used his leadership of the Treasury to push President Roosevelt to reclaim billions of dollars in assets that had been looted by the Nazis from Europe's Jews during World War II, with much of the money salted away in leading Swiss and Austrian banks.

Robert Morgenthau, a World War II naval veteran, saw the threat posed by Iran and its nuclear program to the United States and the state of Israel as comparable in many ways to the Nazi threat. The native New Yorker believed that Tehran's nuclear work was designed to create an atomic weapon that could hold Israel hostage and would allow Iran's Middle East allies, including Syria, Hezbollah, and Hamas, to intensify conventional attacks on the Jewish state under the protection of an Iranian nuclear umbrella. In such a scenario, Morgenthau believed, the Pentagon and the United States would be able to offer only minimal support to its closest Mideast ally, as the likelihood of the United States engaging militarily would be slim. And here there was another analogy to World War II: the United States would be bystanders as Jews were targeted for extermination overseas.

Morgenthau was aware that bankers in Zurich, Vienna, Paris, and London were reprising their role as the financial underwriters for the Jewish people's enemies through their continued business with Iran. And he believed that New York's banking system could be used as a tool to hit back.

"If there is a buck to be made with the Iranians, I firmly believe they can always find a banker willing to take on the risk of doing business with them," Morgenthau told me in an interview in 2012. The walls of his office in midtown Manhattan were covered with photos of Israeli leaders ranging from Yitzhak Rabin to Ariel Sharon. In other pictures, Morgenthau appeared alongside John and Robert Kennedy during JFK's White House years. Photographs of U.S. naval destroyers were on display as well; when a Nazi torpedo hit his ship, the USS *Lansdale*, off the coast of Algiers in 1944, Mor-. genthau survived by treading water for four hours. "Our job is to stop the Iranians, and those who are abetting them," Morgenthau told me. "It's our duty."

IN 2005, ONE OF Morgenthau's top aides at the DA's office was a former Israeli military officer named Eitan Arusy. The thirty-two-year-old once served as a spokesman for the Israeli Defense Forces. But while in the military he also developed an expertise in tracking the finances of the Jewish state's enemies, including Hezbollah, Hamas, and their chief benefactor, Iran.

At the time, Morgenthau was ramping up a staff of counterterrorism experts to meet the post-9/11 threat. To support this, he developed a close working relationship with Israeli intelligence and law enforcement. Morgenthau brought Arusy—known for having an encyclopedic knowledge of terrorist groups and the ways they moved money—to New York to fortify his bond with the Israelis and to educate the New Yorkers about terrorist financing.

Arusy hit the ground running upon his arrival in the spring of 2005. He was surprised to learn that a foundation established by the shah in 1972 to promote Persian culture and heritage to Americans had survived the Iranian revolution and was still operating out of New York (although it had changed its name, first from the Pahlavi Foundation to the Mostazafan Foundation, and then to the Alavi Foundation in 1992). From the huge oil revenues Tehran had earned during the energy boom of the 1970s, Pahlavi had constructed a high-rise office tower on Fifth Avenue in midtown Manhattan to serve both as the foundation's headquarters and as a source of rent revenue. It also purchased offices in Queens and built mosques in Virginia, California, and Nevada. All of this construction was initially financed by Bank Melli, one of Iran's largest state banks. Tehran's ambassadors to the United Nations, who had offices only blocks away from the foundation's headquarters, had historically overseen the foundation's operations, which largely consisted of providing grants to American universities, religious foundations, and nongovernmental organizations. And though the Carter administration had frozen billions of dollars of the Iranian state's holdings and suspended lucrative arms deals following the revolution, U.S. financial regulators had somehow failed to detect the foundation during the sweep of Iranian assets that followed the severing of diplomatic relations between the United States and Iran in 1980.

Now Arusy and New York law enforcement agencies closely scrutinized Alavi's finances and the Iranian diplomats who oversaw the foundation. Because of the sanctions, no Iranian money at all was supposed to be in the U.S. financial system. They paid particular attention to Iran's ambassadors to the United Nations, including Javad Zarif, who had cooperated with the United States on Afghanistan, and his successor, Mohammad Khazaee, who moved to New York in 2007. Morgenthau's office learned that the diplomats regularly attended the foundation's meetings and that Khazaee was keeping a close watch on Alavi's donations and its overall finances, according to transcripts obtained by Arusy and U.S. law enforcement officials. "I have to be kept informed, and I have to be able to state my opinion in order for you to make a decision," Khazaee told Alavi's board during an October 2007 meeting at his residence on the Upper East Side. "We [in Iran] have to be kept informed regarding the general on-goings and allocations because we will be held responsible." The upshot was that the leadership of the Iranian regime was running the foundation.

Digging into the foundation's finances, Arusy discovered that in the 1980s Iran had constructed a complex financial system both to continue to fund the Alavi Foundation with donations directly from Tehran and to mask the involvement of Iranian banks that were banned from the U.S. market. Tehran had established a front company, Assa Corp., in one of Europe's most renowned tax havens, the Channel Islands, to finance Alavi. Banking records revealed that Bank Melli was the primary stakeholder in the Assa Corp. and thus controlled the Alavi Foundation—a clear violation of U.S. sanctions law. (Melli itself had been blacklisted since 2007 for its role in financing Iran's nuclear and missile programs.) And because Iran also was banned from doing any charitable work in the United States, the foundation's charitable activities were violations as well.

Arusy uncovered additional information by developing confidential sources knowledgeable about Alavi's operations, and he eventually gained access to some of the foundation's emails. This information served as the cornerstone of a broader campaign Morgenthau planned to launch against European banks. Financial records obtained by Morgenthau's office showed that two major European financial institutions, Lloyds Banking Group PLC of London and Switzerland's Credit Suisse Group AG, illegally served as the primary conduit for Bank Melli to move money in and out of New York for the Alavi Foundation. Lloyds and Credit Suisse systematically hid these transactions by removing the Iranian originating codes on the wire transfers made through SWIFT, the international electronic payment system. The banks' strategy, which is called "stripping" and is illegal inside the United States, made it virtually impossible for American financial regulators at the Treasury or in New York to detect that Iran was the original source of the money going into New York or the destination for funds leaving it. All this meant that the European banks were complicit in a massive scheme to evade sanctions.

Lloyds and Credit Suisse had established special units in their European offices to oversee the transactions coming in from Tehran, but without any mention of the Iranian ties. The processing steps were laid out in an internal document of Lloyds's, called the "Payment Services Aid Memoir," that advised its staff on how to remove any Iranian reference codes when wiring funds through the U.S. financial system. The practice made it appear that all transactions were originating from Lloyds's offices in the United Kingdom. "A member of Lloyds . . . would physically mark up the printed payment instruction to show what information should be changed, in-

cluding crossing out any reference to Iranian banks or other
sanctioned entities," Morgenthau's office wrote in a court filing describing the British bank's strategy.

Early in 2009, Morgenthau's office moved against the Alavi
Foundation, charging it with being a front for the Iranian government. FBI agents raided and seized its offices in Manhattan and
Queens and froze religious and cultural centers across the United
States funded by the foundation. These included the Imam Ali
Mosque in Queens, the Islamic Education Center of Houston, and
the Islamic Education Center in Rockville, Maryland. In response
to a complaint by a number of Islamic religious leaders that Morgenthau's action against the Alavi Foundation was part of the U.S.
government's efforts to persecute Muslims following 9/11, the district
attorney said he was simply safeguarding the U.S. financial system
and preventing Iran from illegally earning revenues from U.S. businesses, although Morgenthau's office also feared the Iranian government was using Alavi's network to conduct intelligence operations
and spread propaganda on behalf of the Tehran regime.

As part of the crackdown, FBI agents tailed the head of the Alavi
Foundation, Farshid Jahedi, as he walked the streets of New York in
December 2008. Jahedi was among a coterie of Iranian government
officials who maintained U.S. citizenship, thus presenting a test to
U.S. intelligence services. One afternoon Jahedi tried to get rid of
evidence by dumping the contents of his briefcase into a trash can,
according to the FBI. As agents rummaged through the detritus,
they found additional records directly tying the Alavi Foundation to
Bank Melli and the U.K.-based front companies in the Channel Islands. The FBI later charged Jahedi with obstructing justice, for
which he pleaded guilty and went to jail.

Lloyds and Credit Suisse agreed to pay fines of $350 million and
$536 million, respectively, for helping Iran (as well as Sudan) evade
U.S. sanctions. But Morgenthau's office learned that these banks
were just part of a much broader effort by Europe's banks to help
Tehran commit financial fraud in New York. From 2009 to 2012,

five other large European banks also admitted to sanctions-busting in plea agreements made with the Manhattan district attorney's office and other American financial regulators. These included the Netherlands' ING Bank, HSBC Holdings PLC of London, France's BNP Paribas, and the United Kingdom's Standard Chartered PLC and Barclays PLC. In all, these banks paid more than $4.4 billion in fines. "I don't think anyone realized that the Iranians could be this active in New York, essentially right in front of our eyes," Arusy told me.

The case underscored the fact that many European companies and governments, which were tacitly allowing this trade, were far more concerned about maintaining their business ties to Iran than with confronting the threat posed by Iran's nuclear program. Like Stuart Levey before him, Morgenthau believed that countries would comply in pressuring Iran only if their own finances were placed at risk. The fines in New York spurred a rapid push by Europe's biggest banks in the early 2010s to sever all their financial ties with Iran.

ROBERT MORGENTHAU WASN'T THE only U.S. lawyer seeking to punish Iran. Even some attorneys in the private sector were joining his crusade. And while corporate and family lawyers aren't always the U.S. government's natural allies—their pursuit of profits and compensation can actually place them in direct conflict with the government— Tehran's long history of supporting international terrorism, particularly against Americans, provided a convergence of interest between the U.S. government and private sector attorneys, particularly under the George W. Bush administration. It was like a one-two punch: the Treasury Department targeted bankers with sanctions for doing business with Iran, and American lawyers then enforced those sanctions in court. The message was clear: *Cross the Treasury and you'll pay.*

Lawyer Steven Perles was at the forefront of the campaign. A onetime congressional aide to Alaska senator Ted Stevens, who was the acting Senate minority leader in 1979, Perles had staffed a special Senate committee set up in that year to monitor the Iran hostage crisis. Perles, a transplanted Alaskan, was impacted by his experience facing Tehran's revolutionaries and morphed into a modern-day Simon Wiesenthal, dedicated to hunting down the assets of Iran and its allies. Perles worked on international trade issues while on Capitol Hill before shifting into private practice in the 1980s. Thrust into prominence by his investigative work, he regularly lectured at prominent law schools, from Harvard University to the Sophia International University School of Business in Tokyo. He was also active in Jewish affairs, receiving awards from the American Jewish Congress and the Rabbinical Alliance of America. But Perles's true calling emerged in the 1990s as Hezbollah and Hamas, with Iran's purported blessing, launched a campaign of suicide bombings against the state of Israel.

Perles was an expert on a U.S. law known as the Sovereign Immunity Act, which held that assets owned by foreign governments inside the United States should be protected from seizure or litigation. The statute was designed to preserve the United States' position as the world's preeminent financial safe haven. Perles, however, saw cracks emerge in this law in the late 1990s. President Bill Clinton endorsed legislation that allowed U.S. citizens to sue foreign governments that were on the State Department's list of state sponsors of terrorism. This included Iran as well as Syria, North Korea, Iraq, and Libya. For decades, attempts by Americans to win compensation from these countries for direct acts of violence or material support of terrorists had been blocked by the Sovereign Immunity Act. But the Clinton law empowered these Americans and opened a thick new legal vein for lawyers to mine.

An early landmark victory for Perles in his campaign for victims' rights was a judgment of nearly $250 million he won against the Islamic Republic of Iran in 1999 on behalf of the family of Alisa Flatow. The twenty-year-old American had been killed three years earlier when a bomb planted by the militant group Palestinian Islamic Jihad blew up on a bus she was riding during a holiday stay in Jerusalem. The attack was part of a wave of bombings by Islamic Jihad and Hamas following the 1993 Oslo Accords, which attempted to set a framework and timetable for a formal peace agreement between Israel and Palestine. Iran, using these militant groups, hoped to sabotage the accords.

Perles would argue in the Flatow case, and in future litigations, that these terrorist attacks weren't the work of non-state actors or lone-wolf organizations; rather, Iran was the ultimate culprit. In court, he'd present the depositions of Israeli defense officials, American intelligence agencies, and Iranian dissidents that documented how Tehran trained, armed, and funded these militant groups who killed not just Americans but citizens from allied countries. Iran, with its vast oil wealth, should be forced to pay, Perles concluded.

The verdict in the Flatow case sparked a furious hunt by Perles and his legal team to find assets linked to Iran that could be seized and used to cover the judgment, which Tehran would never pay voluntarily. (Iran's lawyers didn't even offer a legal defense during the trial, saying Tehran didn't recognize American law.) Perles initially tried, unsuccessfully, to seize diplomatic properties in the District of Columbia that at one time had been owned by the shah's government. A beautiful embassy with a turquoise-colored dome sat on Massachusetts Avenue, just on the outskirts of downtown Washington. But it hadn't been occupied since the early 1980s, and so Perles's claim was denied. The Sovereign Immunity Act, it turned out, still held sway among many U.S. courts and judges. The Flatows ultimately received compensation from a frozen $400 million fund that the shah's government had established in the Pentagon just weeks before the 1979 revolution, in order to purchase new American military equipment.

Perles, however, won a much larger series of judgments against the Islamic Republic—more than $4.2 billion—when he represented the families of 241 Marines killed by a Hezbollah suicide bomber in Lebanon in 1983. Perles's team successfully argued that the Islamic Revolutionary Guard Corps created, armed, and financed Hezbollah, and that the suicide bomber was trained at a camp run by the IRGC in Lebanon's remote Bekaa Valley. Iran and Hezbollah both denied any role in the attack, but again, neither sent defense attorneys to the trial, which was held in a D.C. federal court.

As with the case of the Flatows, Perles needed to find Iranian assets to cover this huge judgment. Many lawyers and bankers in New York scoffed that this amount of money could be found, even calling Perles an ambulance chaser who was unfairly raising the expectations of the victims' families. Any properties previously controlled by the shah in the United States had already been seized by the U.S. government, critics argued, and the withdrawal of most U.S. oil companies from Iran after the 1979 revolution undercut Perles's strategy of trying to seize the U.S. assets of some major energy conglomerates with revenues tied to Iran.

Perles looked into ways of gaining control of the U.S.-based holdings of Chinese, South Korean, and Japanese companies that derived revenues from businesses in Iran. But such efforts were again opposed by many American financial regulators, who cited the Sovereign Immunity Act. The United States wasn't Switzerland, allowing countries and individuals to hide assets behind layers of complex secrecy laws. But the vibrancy of American stock and debt markets, these U.S. officials argued, was based on confidence that assets deposited in New York and elsewhere would be protected.

In 2008, more out of desperation than confidence, Perles subpoenaed the U.S. Treasury Department to force it to provide any details it had on Iranian assets. By now Perles's relationships with U.S. administrations were rocky; his numerous lawsuits had at times run afoul of U.S. diplomatic efforts, particularly in the Middle East. President Clinton's State Department complained that the suits against Iran threatened American efforts in the late 1990s to improve diplomatic relations with Tehran after the election of the reform-minded President Khatami. Similar arguments were made that such cases undercut efforts to forge an Israeli-Palestinian peace agreement.

It wasn't until Stuart Levey came to the Treasury that Perles found an ally in the U.S. government. In early 2009, Levey surprised Perles and the families of the Marine Corps barracks bombing when his team notified the D.C. federal court that the U.S. government had traced roughly $2.25 billion of Iranian funds to a Citibank account in New York. Levey's office believed the monies, which were largely held in the form of government bonds, were the property of Iran's central bank, Bank Markazi. Tehran had initially placed these holdings in an account with a secretive European financial services company called Clearstream Banking SA, which is based in the Duchy of Luxembourg. The tiny landlocked country's stringent bank secrecy laws had made it a rising European financial center but an adversary of the U.S. government in the post-9/11 era. Clearstream in mid-2009 shifted Iran's holdings to New York, apparently to facilitate illicit trade, even though they ran the risk of being seized. Citibank's filters missed Tehran's links to the money because it was hidden inside other Clearstream accounts, U.S. officials concluded.

Perles wasted little time in jumping on Levey's intelligence. He petitioned the federal court in Manhattan to freeze the Citibank account and award the money to the victims' families to partially cover the multibillion-dollar judgment. Perles also gained clearance to submit to the court Treasury's information detailing Bank Markazi's ownership of the bonds.

The size of the Iranian holdings stunned both Perles and Treasury officials because it represented by far the largest single seizure of Iranian money since the Islamic Revolution. They puzzled how Iran and a sophisticated company such as Clearstream had erred by sending the funds into the U.S. banking system. It was either incompetence or arrogance, he thought. "We couldn't believe, in many ways, what we had stumbled onto," Perles told me. "Even in our wildest dreams, we didn't imagine that Iran could have this amount of money sloshing around New York."

The Iranian government's and Clearstream's response to the Citibank case at times seemed to run at cross-purposes. At first Clearstream's lawyers denied that the money at Citibank was Iran's, though they said that, as a Luxembourg-based company, Clearstream was prevented from disclosing the true owner. At the same time, Iran had succeeded in transferring $250 million out of Citibank just weeks before Levey disclosed his intelligence to the U.S. court. This raised concerns inside Perles's team that Tehran might have been tipped off by European banks about the New York action.

A Manhattan judge ultimately ruled in favor of freezing the $2 billion at Citibank. Iran subsequently hired New York lawyers to challenge the decision, marking a U-turn from its previous position that it didn't recognize American law. Citing the Sovereign Immunity Act, Bank Markazi's lawyers argued that American courts didn't have the legal rights to freeze the funds of foreign governments.

In late 2011, however, President Barack Obama rendered this debate moot by formally sanctioning Bank Markazi for its alleged role in funding Iran's nuclear program and support of terrorism. This ruling ordered the freezing of any assets held by Iran's central bank inside the United States. Bank Markazi's admission that it owned the bonds at Citibank, Perles mused, had made his job far easier. For him, the ruling provided some light at the end of the tunnel for the families of the 241 Marines killed in Beirut. The U.S. Supreme Court ultimately ruled the money belonged to the families of the victims. And Perles believes that the case spooked Iran, showing that its assets were being tracked everywhere. "The case [made] it clear to Iran that its money isn't safe even in secretive European accounts," Perles said.

THE U.S. SANCTIONS CAMPAIGN against Iran had created a chain reaction across the globe, reinforcing itself on many levels. Treasury's warnings to banks and businesses forced them to sever ties with Iran or risk their access to the world's largest market. U.S. courts were vigorously enforcing the Treasury's regulations. And people such as Robert Morgenthau and Steve Perles were punishing banks and companies that weren't complying. Altogether, the United States was driving Iran out of the global economy.

Treasury's financial war against Iran proved singularly lethal, thanks to the canny use of American influence. Indeed, it proved an effective tool in combating a mercurial foe who didn't play by the rules. Its effects were immediate and harsh, more so than Treasury officials had even anticipated. Red lines had been established to curb Iran's activities, and unlike so many others, they were rigorously enforced.

CHAPTER 7

The Clenched Fist

THE UNITED STATES WAS BEGINNING TO ENFORCE WHAT WOULD BE-
come a crippling war on Iran's economy. But at the same time,
Obama was clear that he wanted a diplomatic channel to Iran, and
in particular to its paramount political figure, Supreme Leader Ayatollah Ali Khamenei. The U.S. leader called it his two-track policy
toward Iran: increase financial pressure while giving its leaders a
diplomatic opening to reach a deal on the nuclear issue, which
since the revelations of 2002 was the paramount national security
issue of the United States.

In the winter and spring of 2009, just months after taking office,
Obama sent two secret letters to Khamenei. These were born out of
a painstaking back-and-forth between the new president's closest advisors. To their surprise, Iran's most powerful politician and cleric
actually responded. It was the first time that an Iranian supreme
leader had ever communicated directly with the United States.

President Obama aimed at setting a new tone with Iran's leadership. He had campaigned on breaking sharply with the Bush Doctrine of promoting regime change overseas and utilizing military

force, saying that he would reach out to the United States' staunchest enemies, whether the Castro family in Cuba or Myanmar's generals. The outreach to Iran, in a U.S. bid to end Tehran's nuclear program, was the beginning of Obama's hallmark foreign policy initiative during his presidency. The White House believed ending Iran's nuclear threat could open up a pathway for Washington and Tehran to cooperate on stabilizing combustible countries in the Mideast, including Iraq, Afghanistan, and later Syria. Rapprochement could also help build bridges to the wider Muslim world.

The letters, which were described to me by officials who helped draft them, were addressed directly to Khamenei. This marked a major shift from previous U.S. overtures to Iran, which consisted of attempts to seek out "moderates" in Tehran's Islamist government in a bid to forge a rapprochement. They had hoped to work around the rabid anti-Americanism espoused by both Khamenei and Khomeini. But Washington could never be certain about how much sway the moderates really had in Tehran. Bill Clinton's administration had thought it had a partner in Iran's president at the time, Mohammad Khatami, who openly talked about establishing a "dialogue" between civilizations and promoted an opening of Iran's political system and press. But Khamenei steadily weakened Khatami during his second term, to the point where Khatami couldn't make good on most of his promises of reform. Successive U.S. administrations seemed to underestimate the power of the supreme leader's office, something Obama and his advisors sought to correct.

Obama's letters amplified a key platform of the new Obama administration's foreign policy: Washington wasn't seeking to promote "regime change" in Tehran. Khamenei regularly ranted about the West's efforts to promote a soft revolution in his country. The invasions of Iraq and Afghanistan reaffirmed his fears that the United States was seeking to encircle Iran. Obama, almost immediately after taking office, attempted to reassure Tehran's leadership that the United States was prepared to live with and recognize the Islamic Republic, provided that it addressed the West's concerns.

"In particular, I would like to speak directly to the people and leaders of the Islamic Republic of Iran," Obama said in a message beamed into Iran in March 2009 to commemorate Nowruz, the Persian New Year. The speech preceded the letters Obama would send Khamenei a few months later, and it marked the first time a sitting U.S. president had ever addressed Iran as the "Islamic Republic," a signal from Obama that he wasn't seeking to promote a conflict.

"In this season of new beginnings," Obama said in his video address, "I would like to speak clearly to Iran's leaders. We have serious differences that have grown over time. My administration is now committed to diplomacy that addresses the full range of issues before us, and to pursuing constructive ties among the United States, Iran, and the international community. This process will not be advanced by threats. We seek instead engagement that is honest and grounded in mutual respect."

In his speeches and letters, Obama stressed to Khamenei that his overture wasn't open-ended, according to the U.S. officials who helped draft the communications. Iran's nuclear program was advancing rapidly, the president believed, and the point when Tehran's program would reach "breakout"—the capability of producing enough fissile material for an atomic weapon—was fast approaching. At that point, Obama said, a dialogue between the long-standing enemies might no longer be possible. Tehran's nuclear program would be too advanced and the purpose of any negotiation eclipsed. Obama had publicly not ruled out taking military action. Indeed, U.S. officials said the administration was pushing forward with the development of the cyber weapons it used to attack Iran's facilities. It was also developing a bomb called the Massive Ordnance Penetrator, which could wipe out Iran's underground atomic facilities.

Khamenei closely scrutinized the new president's messages, according to UN diplomats who met with the Iranian leader. He was intensely skeptical of any U.S. administration, believing that entrenched interests in Washington would upend the initiatives of leaders with even the best intentions. Khamenei believed U.S. policy was squarely under the thumb of the Israeli government and the Sunni Arab states, all of whom opposed any rapprochement between Washington and Tehran. "They chant the slogan of change, but no change is seen in practice," Khamenei told a gathering of tens of thousands of Iranians in the holy city of Mashhad in his first public response to Obama's Nowruz speech. "We haven't seen any change."

But as Obama's personal letters arrived at Khamenei's offices in Tehran in the ensuing months, the supreme leader became more intrigued, according to Western diplomats who met with him around that time. In May he personally wrote Obama, delivering his communication through the Swiss embassy in Tehran, which was the United States' formal diplomatic representative in Iran, since there was no American embassy. Khamenei's letter outlined the litany of abuses the supreme leader believed the United States had committed against the Iranian people over the past sixty years. He mentioned Washington's military alliance with the shah and the human rights abuses the shah had committed against his people. Khamenei also cited U.S. intelligence support for Saddam Hussein during the Iran-Iraq War, which Iranians argue enabled Baghdad to eventually launch chemical attacks against Iranian forces. Khamenei also griped about U.S. support for the 1953 coup against President Mohammad Mossadegh.

But the supreme leader didn't rule out some sort of accommodation with Washington on the nuclear issue. He stressed his theme of "mutual respect" between the two countries as possibly opening up a pathway. "He left the door open," said an American diplomat who read the letter at the time. This fed sentiments in the White House that the diplomacy should proceed.

IRAN WAS PERHAPS THE MOST contentious foreign policy issue debated during the 2008 presidential campaign. The conflicts in Iraq and Afghanistan had created war fatigue among many voters, which

Barack Obama seized on during the Democratic primaries and then his run against the Arizona conservative John McCain. Unlike George W. Bush with his overtly confrontational policies, Obama said, he would restore America's image and prestige overseas by offering to talk with Iran, along with Syria, North Korea, Cuba, and Venezuela.

Obama's position placed first Hillary Clinton and then John McCain in a strategic bind. Clinton had voted for the Iraq War, so she was determined to distance herself from its failures. She criticized the management of the Bush administration's campaigns in Iraq and Afghanistan. And she stressed that if elected she would focus on restoring the American economy over the next decade. But she viewed Obama's position on Iran as vulnerable. In one of the more contentious debates during the campaign, she called her Democratic challenger "naive" for thinking he had the charisma and personal charm to wipe away decades of enmity with Tehran by personally embracing its leaders. She said Obama risked elevating the Islamic Republic's international status by dealing directly with Khamenei, tarnishing the White House in the process. "I think I would closely coordinate with my advisors before approving any direct talks with Iran," she said during the debate. "This isn't something that should be taken lightly, as my opponent suggests."

Obama and his aides in turn jumped on Clinton's position, seeing it as a vehicle to clearly differentiate him from the senator and former First Lady and to feed off the post–Iraq War sentiment. Though he had spent just two years in the Senate, Obama understood that the growing tensions with Iran could define his presidency and that he needed to stake out his position early on. "He decided that instead of backing off it, we should double down on it and say, 'No. This is actually the core contrast,'" said Ben Rhodes, who served as a close campaign aide to Obama in 2008. "The same mind-set that led people to follow a herd momentum into a conflict with Iraq was not being tested on Iran."

Clinton's position on Iran marked her as perhaps the most hawkish on the issue among the Democratic Party's leadership. She embraced the need for military force if Tehran didn't roll back its nuclear program, something Obama was reluctant to do. Differences on Iran would affect their working relationship going forward. Jewish voters and pro-Israel lawmakers on Capitol Hill, who deeply opposed any engagement with Iran, embraced her. Clinton's position also dampened some criticism of her from the right. Many Republicans, who hated her social platforms, suddenly viewed her as among the most pragmatic of the Democrats seeking to succeed George W. Bush. This sentiment held throughout Obama's first term, when Clinton served as his secretary of state. It would also split the pro-Israel community in the Democratic Party and Washington's foreign policy establishment.

McCain's criticism of Obama's Iran stance was even sharper. The Arizona Republican argued that, counter to Obama's semantics, every American president from Jimmy Carter through George W. Bush had in fact already sought to engage Tehran. The results had been either tragedies, such as the 1979 American hostage crisis and Iran-Contra, or failures, such as the ambassador-level talks in Baghdad in 2007 that had been aimed at reducing the sectarian violence in Iraq but which, the Pentagon concluded, did nothing to reduce Tehran's training of Shiite militias or its shipments of IEDs and other munitions into Iraq.

McCain charged that Obama was set to run straight into Iran's tried-and-trusted practice of engaging Western countries but then dragging them into months of tedious negotiations without, in the end, giving any ground. McCain argued this dynamic had afflicted the French, German, and British diplomats who met with Iranian nuclear officials for five straight years, without the involvement of the Bush administration, in the early 2000s. The talks achieved a short-term freeze of Iran's nuclear work, but then Tehran accelerated its activities under President Ahmadinejad. McCain argued that Barack Obama was going to play right into this Iranian strategy if he won the White House, providing Tehran with months, if not years, of political cover to push ahead with its nuclear and military programs.

"Senator Obama wants to sit down, without any precondition, across the table and negotiate with this individual," McCain said of Ahmadinejad during a July campaign stop in Louisiana. "My friends, that's not right and that's naive and that shows a lack of experience and a lack of judgment."

Obama, however, was unbowed, as his march to the White House appeared certain. Even before the election, members of his campaign team met with Syrian leaders, including President Assad, to notify them of the new American approach Obama would take once in office. Among these envoys were Jewish advisors, such as the Princeton professor Daniel Kurtzer and the Middle East negotiator Dennis Ross. Obama personally telegraphed to many in Washington's most hawkish organizations that he was going to engage the Islamic Republic, in effect warning them of a major policy shift. If Tehran responded with a "clenched fist," he argued, Washington's ability to gain international support to exert even more financial pressure on Iran down the road—or even take military action—would only be enhanced. Obama argued that international opposition to the Bush administration's Mideast policies had undercut U.S. efforts to impose multilateral sanctions on Tehran—a point that had merit.

In June 2008, Obama, along with McCain and Clinton, addressed Washington's powerful pro-Israel lobby, the American Israel Public Affairs Committee (AIPAC), at its annual policy conference in Washington. Despite facing a potentially hostile audience, the young candidate sought to woo the Jewish voters at AIPAC to support his new position. "Our willingness to pursue diplomacy will make it easier to mobilize others to join our cause," Obama told thousands of AIPAC members at Washington's cavernous convention center, occasionally earning applause. Some in the audience said they were concerned about alienating the man most people believed would be the next president of the United States. "If Iran fails to change course when presented with this choice by the United

States, it will be clear . . . that the Iranian regime is the author of its own isolation," Obama told the AIPAC audience.

Once in office, Obama quickly moved forward with his strategy, delivering the Persian New Year message to the Iranian people and sending letters to Khamenei. Within months of taking office, Obama was awarded the Nobel Peace Prize for his positions on stopping the spread of nuclear weapons globally. Iran was the central focus in this strategy. "What was interesting about Iran is that lots of things inter- sected: nonproliferation, Israel, the Middle East, and the Iraq War," Rhodes said. "All of these different currents of American foreign policy converged in Iran in a way that made it not just a big issue in its own right, but a battleground in terms of American foreign pol- icy."

OBAMA HAD LITTLE TIME to pursue his outreach to Khamenei before the first major foreign policy crisis of his administration emerged. Just six months after Obama took office, Tehran held presidential elections. Mahmoud Ahmadinejad was seeking a second four-year term. The politician had emerged as a star among the Islamic and developing nations after his 2005 election, due to his confronta- tional polices toward the West. His calls for Israel's destruction even rallied many Arab populations behind the Persian leader's rhetoric. And Ahmadinejad's unbending position on Iran's right to produce nuclear fuel was widely backed by the Non-Aligned Movement (NAM), a Cold War–era coalition that was made up of countries from most of the developing world. White House officials believed the vote would provide a gauge as to whether Tehran might soften its stance toward the West on the nuclear question.

Even before the Iranian elections, Obama's outreach to Khame- nei was facing skepticism from Israel, the Arab states, and even some members of the U.S. president's own cabinet. Israeli prime minister Benjamin Netanyahu, channeling much of John McCain's angst, pressed Obama to set a clear timeline for his diplomatic outreach to

Iran. The Israeli leader argued that the diplomacy should not extend beyond the end of 2009, when the United States and Europe should start putting in place "crippling" new sanctions on Iran. (The U.S. Congress, with the support of pro-Israel lobbyists, was already drafting legislation on this front.) Netanyahu and his advisors particularly pushed for a formal oil embargo on Iran to dry up Tehran's largest source of revenue, rather than pursuing the Treasury's stepped-up approach. And they wanted the United States to be prepared to take military action to knock out Iran's nuclear sites, possibly in collaboration with the Jewish state, if Tehran didn't capitulate.

The oil-rich monarchies in the Persian Gulf were also worried about Obama's diplomacy. Countries such as the United Arab Emirates, Bahrain, and Saudi Arabia had grown rich in part because of the isolation of Iran after the Islamic revolution, becoming major energy and service providers after Tehran was forced to pull back from the global economy. The UAE port of Dubai supplied many of the shipping, financial, and trade services that Iranian companies might have performed if there had been no American sanctions. Saudi Arabia, the UAE, Qatar, and Bahrain had all scored major arms deals as the United States beefed up its military capabilities, as well as those of its allies, along Iran's borders and in the Persian Gulf. Many of these Arab leaders feared that Obama would cut off the gravy train of military and oil deals that had made Iran's regional neighbors rich.

In March 2009, Hillary Clinton—by now Obama's secretary of state—met with the UAE's foreign minister, Sheikh Abdullah bin Zayed al-Nahyan, on the sidelines of an international conference on the Palestinian territories, held in the Egyptian resort of Sharm el-Sheikh on the Red Sea. The placid azure waters of the resort town contrasted sharply with the contentious issues discussed inside its conference rooms. During this meeting, Sheikh Abdullah, an Emirati prince, pressed Clinton to keep his country briefed on any diplomatic overtures to Tehran and how this might impact the UAE and the other Gulf states, according to U.S. officials who took part in the meeting. The secretary of state and her husband had strong relations with the UAE going back to Bill Clinton's White House years. The former president regularly gave paid speeches in the country. The Emiratis, like the Israelis, saw Hillary Clinton as a potential ally in an administration that might be hostile to their security interests.

Clinton stressed to the British-schooled diplomat—who wasn't yet forty and was known by the acronym ABZ—that she would keep his country up to date on any developments concerning Iran. But she also voiced a skepticism, shared by others inside Obama's cabinet, about the prospects for success. "Our eyes are wide open" when it comes to Iran, Clinton told her Emirati counterpart. She said she was "doubtful Iran would respond" to the calls for international dialogue that President Obama was promoting, or that Tehran would scale back its nuclear program in any meaningful way.

Clinton's comments weren't well received at the White House. Obama's aides believed she was undermining a signature foreign policy initiative of the new U.S. president in the eyes of one of Washington's closest Arab allies. White House officials always knew that policy differences with Clinton, going back to the campaign, risked undercutting Obama's international objectives. But they still calculated that it was better to keep Clinton inside the tent than outside, where she could publicly criticize White House initiatives.

The American diplomat who briefed reporters on Clinton's meeting at Sharm el-Sheikh was quickly removed and sent to a new posting in Vienna. And Clinton's advisors became increasingly cautious about briefing journalists on the secretary's private meetings, worried about offending the White House. They didn't want the bad blood from the campaign drifting into foreign policy.

As Iran's June 2009 elections grew closer, the Obama administration further toned down the anti-Iranian rhetoric that had defined the later years of the Bush administration. U.S. officials said they didn't want to allow Khamenei or Ahmadinejad to make the United States an issue during the campaign, which could give political ammunition to Iran's conservative and hard-line political players. The White House was intent on opening nuclear diplomacy but viewed any diplomacy with Tehran as frozen until its election cycle was completed. The Obama administration needed to know who they would be dealing with.

In the months leading up to the vote, the State Department also rolled back some of the democracy-promotion initiatives that the Bush administration had championed to spur change in Tehran, such as funding to train Iranian journalists and opposition websites. Khamenei had publicly denounced these programs as attempts to stir a "color revolution" inside Iran, along the lines of those that had broken out in former Soviet states such as Georgia and Ukraine during the Bush administration. Obama's advisors voiced skepticism that such programs even worked; furthermore, they didn't see a need to antagonize Khamenei. The Obama administration, for example, cut funding for the Iran Human Rights Documentation Center, based in New Haven, Connecticut, which catalogued the abuses committed by the Islamic Republic dating back to its founding in 1979. The State Department denied Freedom House, the Washington-based organization focused on global human rights, $3 million in new grants for a Farsi website that sought to promote democracy.

Critics of the Obama administration's moves said it was coddling the Iranian regime in a bid to promote a deal on the nuclear program at any cost. "Because Iranians seem willing to take risks, we should be willing to provide them with help when requested," said Jennifer Windsor, then executive director of Freedom House, after her organization's funding request was declined in 2009. "The White House clearly didn't want to rock the boat," said Karim Sadjadpour of the Carnegie Endowment. "They were fixated on the nuclear issue."

U.S. officials predicted an uneventful election in 2009 and believed none of the candidates opposing Ahmadinejad offered much hope for dramatic change. Mohsen Rezaei was a former Revolutionary Guard commander whom the Argentine government was seeking to arrest for his alleged role in orchestrating the 1994 bombing of the Jewish community center in Buenos Aires. The other two main candidates, Mir Hossein Mousavi and Mehdi Karroubi, were also longtime supporters of the Iranian revolution. Mousavi had served as Iran's prime minister in the 1980s, during which time he had been just as committed to pursuing Iran's nuclear program as any other Iranian official, and Karroubi had twice been president of the Iranian parliament. Both men were creatures of the Islamic Republic; while opposed to Ahmadinejad, they didn't want to fundamentally change the structure of Iran's theocratic government or the power of the ayatollahs.

American officials' assumptions about the Iranian election meant the Obama administration was caught flat-footed when a wave of young, middle-class voters rallied that June behind Mousavi to protest Ahmadinejad and his hard-line supporters in the military and the supreme leader's office. The campaign spurred a vigorous and heated debate between the two men on issues ranging from economics to Iran's place in the world. Mousavi chastised Ahmadinejad for mismanaging Tehran's finances and needlessly agitating the West through his threats against Israel and denial of the Holocaust. Ahmadinejad countered that Mousavi and Karroubi were representatives of Iran's corrupt elite class and were denying Iran's poor the fruits of the country's oil wealth. In a nationally televised debate, Ahmadinejad took the rare step for an Iranian politician of attacking Mousavi's wife, claiming she had fraudulently obtained her Ph.D.

Support for Mousavi and Karroubi quickly cascaded into what became known as Iran's Green Movement. It took its name from a green sash given to Mousavi by former president Khatami, the reform movement's standard-bearer. Campaigners wore green shirts and scarves, or painted their faces green, to demonstrate their opposition to the regime. On Election Day, June 12, parts of Tehran were bathed in green as Iranians stood in long lines to cast their votes. The sheer size of the outpouring of support for Mousavi caused many in the White House and State Department to believe that Ahmadinejad would lose the election, though U.S. officials were skeptical that this political change would fundamentally change Iranian policy.

Within hours of the voting booths closing, Iranian state television announced that Ahmadinejad had won the election, with 64 percent of the ballots cast. Mousavi's office immediately cried foul, arguing it was impossible to call the election so quickly after voting ended. Opposition news sites claimed that Mousavi was well ahead in the election. But the Iranian state was adamant that the incumbent had won with a healthy majority. Election returns even showed that Ahmadinejad had won handily in Mousavi's home province of East Azerbaijan, according to state media, prompting even more protests from the Green Movement.

The seeds for a major conflict were sown in Tehran's streets. Over the next two days, first tens of thousands and then hundreds of thousands of Iranians started taking to the streets to protest the results. Many started chanting "Where's my vote?" in Farsi or carrying placards emblazoned with the same mantra. The large numbers of foreign media who had been allowed into Iran to report on the election were giving twenty-four-hour coverage to the political crisis and the state's response. Iranian security forces responded by shutting down the Internet and confining the opposition candidates, Mousavi and Karroubi, as well as their families and staffs, to their homes. The government also started to expel foreign reporters.

By the third day, as many as three million Iranians massed at the center of Tehran, according to media reports and opposition leaders. Their target was Azadi (Freedom) Square, a national monument that had served as the center for political protests in Tehran going back to before the shah. The Iranian security forces appeared incapable of suppressing the popular outrage about the vote. And for the first time in more than a decade, Khamenei and the Revolutionary

Guard seemed genuinely confused over how to respond to a political threat.

But the Green Movement, despite a pro-Western position, found almost no support in the White House. In fact, it had thrown Barack Obama's Iran policy into chaos. This White House wasn't seeking to spread democracy in the Middle East, or to aggressively intervene in the affairs of other states. That was the doctrine of his predecessor. Obama's mantra had been to wind down the U.S. wars in Iraq and Afghanistan and cast the United States as a benign superpower, more interested in stability than in stoking democratic change. But all of a sudden the potential for major change emerged in Iran.

President Obama held emergency meetings in the Oval Office as the numbers of people on the streets of Tehran swelled. Some administration officials argued the political revolt offered the United States the most important opportunity to promote democratic change in Tehran since 1979. At the very least, they said, the president should provide moral support for the protestors in a public statement. Over at the CIA, many also believed Washington should be doing more, such as enhancing the ability of the protestors to communicate with one another.

Administration officials who took part in the debates said they were getting mixed messages from the Green Movement. Some supporters, particularly within the Iranian diaspora, pressed for President Obama to publicly endorse their cause. They felt it could protect them from an anticipated government crackdown. However, many inside the movement in Iran felt that American support, even if it was just rhetorical, would give Khamenei an excuse to brand them as American lackeys.

President Obama ultimately decided to remain silent in the crucial early days of the revolt. Furthermore, he ordered the CIA to sever any contacts it had developed with Green Movement supporters. The Agency has contingency plans for supporting democratic uprisings anywhere in the world. This includes providing dissidents with communications, money, and in extreme cases even arms. But in this case the White House ordered it to stand down. "'Let's give it a few days' was the answer," said a senior U.S. official present at some of the White House meetings in 2009. "It was made clear: 'We should monitor, but do nothing.'" Other Obama advisors said it was clear that the president didn't want to take any steps that might jeopardize the direct diplomacy with Khamenei. "If you were working on the nuclear deal, you were saying, 'Don't do too much,'" said Michael McFaul, who served as a senior National Security Council official at the White House before becoming ambassador to Russia in 2012.

Obama went further, though, and publicly sought to squelch the perception that Iran was about to experience major change or move closer to the West. In a June 16 interview with MSNBC he cast Mousavi as a regime insider and a fundamental player in developing the Islamic Republic's hostile policies toward the West. "Although there is amazing ferment taking place in Iran, the difference between Ahmadinejad and Mousavi in terms of their actual policies may not be as great as has been advertised," Obama said. "I think it's important to understand that either way, we are going to be dealing with a regime in Iran that is hostile to the U.S."

Obama also lagged behind European leaders, such as French president Nicolas Sarkozy, in forcefully questioning the legitimacy of the results. U.S. officials said they didn't have enough of their own independent information to gauge the level of fraud in the vote. But this only fed the perception that the Obama White House didn't want to stir the pot in Iran. The president's desire to pursue a nuclear agreement trumped all other issues. "It is up to Iranians to make decisions about who Iran's leaders will be. We respect Iranian sovereignty and want to avoid the United States being the issue inside Iran," Obama said at the White House, also on June 16. "What I would say to those people who put so much hope and energy and optimism into the political process, I would say to them that the world is watching and inspired by their participation, regardless of what the ultimate outcome of the election was."

There was some dissent within Obama's administration over this soft approach, largely from Hillary Clinton's State Department; the internal conflict mirrored the differences exposed during the campaign. On June 17, as the Iranian regime moved to cut off Internet access, an office at Foggy Bottom communicated with the social media site Facebook to take steps to ensure that Iranians could continue communicating using its Web pages. The move by two young American diplomats, Jared Cohen and Alec Ross, was initially reprimanded by their higher-ups, according to former U.S. officials, fearful that it strayed from the president's line of staying out of the Iranian controversy. But the State Department then reversed itself and publicized the two officials' intervention with Facebook, a sign, these officials said, that Clinton was sensitive to criticisms that the United States wasn't doing enough to support the Green Movement. It wouldn't be the last time Clinton appeared to break from Obama on the issue of how directly to challenge Tehran. After leaving the Obama administration, Clinton said the failure to support the Iranian opposition—at the time of the uprising—was one of her greatest regrets during her time as secretary of state.

Khamenei and Iran's government forces utilized the general lack of international outrage, and the Green Movement's own tactical errors, to regroup following the opposition's takeover of Azadi Square. The movement's leaders were divided, and Mousavi appeared reluctant to publicly challenge Khamenei. Inexplicably to some in the Green Movement, their own leaders called for protestors to return home after their massive show of force on June 17. They felt that momentum was on their side and that they needed time to recalibrate their strategy. They also believed that even some of Iran's traditional revolutionary leaders, such as former president Akbar Hashemi Rafsanjani, would rally to their cause. There were clear fractures between Khamenei and many of the other leaders who had founded the Islamic Republic but wanted a more open system.

However, the Green Movement had underestimated the skill

and ruthlessness of Khamenei and, in particular, the Revolutionary Guard. Over the ensuing two months, it unleashed its paramilitary arm, the Basij, against the Green Movement's leaders and its supporters across Iran. Iran's security forces placed Mousavi and Karroubi under permanent house arrest, and they arrested thousands, incarcerating many in Tehran's notorious Evin prison. Even members of the Iranian elite, such as Rafsanjani's daughter and Mousavi's son, were detained in what quickly became the broadest crackdown in Iran since the revolution.

The Iranian government's selective use of terror and brutality also unnerved the world. A video on YouTube documenting the shooting and death on a Tehran street of a Green Movement protestor, a woman named Neda Agha-Soltan, shocked the opposition and served as a signal to the international community of the extent the regime would go to in order to push back its political challengers. Wide-scale use of rape and torture of men and women, particularly in prisons and hospitals where protestors were being held and treated, were reported, stunning the White House and other Western powers.

Obama was finally forced to make a tactical shift and publicly condemn the regime in late June, after the crackdown was in full force. "In 2009, no iron fist is strong enough to shut off the world from bearing witness to the peaceful pursuit of justice," the president said in a prepared statement ahead of a White House press conference. "The United States and the international community have been appalled and outraged by the threats, the beatings, and the imprisonments of the last few days."

But the White House's moves were too late. The IRGC and its Basij continued their roundup of the Green Movement's leaders and the suppression of its supporters. Through the end of summer and early fall, Iranian state television aired show trials of opposition leaders confessing to being agents of the United States, Israel, and the West. Thousands of political activists fled to Turkey, France, Australia, or the United States to evade Khamenei's security forces.

Obama had bet that minimizing U.S. involvement in the Iranian crisis might soften Tehran's response, or even win its gratitude. But in the end, the opposite was true. "There were a few days where the opposition held the streets and real change was possible," said Karim Sadjadpour of the Carnegie Endowment, who regularly met with Obama administration officials. "But Obama didn't realize that, regardless of his actions, Khamenei would paint the uprising as a Western plot."

The unexpected uprising was snuffed out nearly as fast as it started. At the time, U.S. officials downplayed that they had missed a major opportunity. But as Ahmadinejad consolidated his power and the nuclear negotiations stalled, criticism of the White House grew. Many Iranians said the biggest window to effect change in decades had closed.

Even as the crackdown on the Green Movement continued, the Obama administration pressed forward with the pursuit of nuclear negotiations. Critics said engaging with Tehran so soon after the crackdown only legitimized Ahmadinejad's reelection. It would also serve as a green light to Khamenei and his security forces that they could repress their population without any serious consequences. But Ahmadinejad's government, possibly because it sought international acceptance, was declaring its willingness to engage in its first direct high-level contacts with the United States and other Western powers since Obama's inauguration. And this came as Tehran's nuclear capacity continued to grow.

ON THE OUTSKIRTS OF Geneva in late October 2009, in a town called Genthod, American diplomats joined with representatives of the P5+1—the UN Security Council members plus Germany—in a plush European villa to outline a plan to deter Iran's nuclear ambitions. Just weeks earlier, the U.S., French, and U.K. governments had jointly announced that their intelligence sources had uncovered a new Iranian uranium enrichment facility buried in a mountain outside the holy Iranian city of Qom. U.S. officials believed that had the site been left undetected, Tehran planned to use the facility to produce the highly enriched uranium used in building a nuclear weapon. Iran admitted to hiding the construction of the site from inspectors at the IAEA, but stressed it wasn't for weapons use. Tehran said it needed to keep the Qom site secret and underground in order to protect it from an Israeli or American military strike. The West believed this was a ruse.

The U.S. and Iranian delegations to the Swiss negotiations were led by two mild-mannered and unassuming negotiators, William Burns on the American side and Saeed Jalili on Tehran's. Jalili was the head of Iran's Supreme National Security Council and the personal representative of Ayatollah Khamenei. A veteran of the Iran-Iraq War, he, like most of Iran's senior leaders, spouted anti-American catchphrases and railed against the double standards of the West. But the diplomat, with his trim beard, spiky silver hair, and collarless shirts, had the appearance of a religious scholar. He peppered his speeches with calls for world peace and "harmony" among the world's religions and ethnic groups. Jalili's press conferences could stretch on for more than an hour without making any headlines.

Burns was a rare State Department diplomat who rose to the top of the Foggy Bottom bureaucracy without displaying any particular political leanings. Burns had served as the ambassador to Jordan and Russia under George W. Bush and was assistant secretary of state for Near Eastern affairs. His regional experience and apolitical nature placed him in a strong position to engage with Jalili and to break down Iran's paranoia toward the United States, according to American and Iranian officials. His non-ideological diplomacy also appealed to the Russian and Chinese delegations at Geneva.

Jalili entered the talks at Genthod maintaining the same line that Iran had expressed in its earlier negotiations with the Europeans: that Tehran had the right under the United Nations' Nuclear Nonproliferation Treaty to enrich uranium and produce its own nuclear fuel. Iran also wouldn't negotiate unless the United States first began unwinding the expansive economic sanctions imposed on the Islamic Republic. The penalties were already starting to cut off Iran's banks from the global economy, though they would become much worse. The United States, France, and the United Kingdom had been expecting Iran to take this unbending position, so Jalili's comments were no surprise.

But the United States, Russia, and other European countries had come to Switzerland with a highly technical offer that was designed to both test Tehran's willingness to engage and significantly diminish its ability to build a nuclear weapon in the short term. Nuclear experts inside the U.S., French, and Russian governments, backed by advisors from the IAEA, devised the concept, called a "fuel swap." It basically sought to call Iran's bluff on its claims that it only sought civilian nuclear power by providing it with fuel that was sufficient to power a nuclear reactor but not of the quality and quantity needed to produce a bomb. For the White House, this marked the ideal first step toward a rapprochement with Tehran, if Jalili would accept the proposal. If not, the administration said, it was prepared to put in place more economic sanctions on Iran.

Sitting at a conference table at the old Swiss villa, Burns and his partners detailed to Jalili the outlines of the plan. Iran would need to ship out two-thirds of its uranium stockpile, which had been enriched to 3.5 percent purity, to Russia, where it would be converted into the fuel plates used to power Tehran's research reactor. French nuclear power companies would play a role in fabricating the fuel plates, which in that form couldn't be used for nuclear weapons. In return, the P5+1 would lift sanctions on Iran's airline industry, provide greater support to Iran's civilian nuclear program, and support Tehran's bid to join the World Trade Organization.

Burns and other Western diplomats reveled in the plan, because they believed it would keep Iran from acquiring enough fissionable material to produce a nuclear bomb for at least another year. Negotiators believed this would give the United States enough time to launch military strikes on Iran if it decided to break out and try to assemble a bomb. If the first stage succeeded, more negotiations could be held to permanently scale back Iran's program. At the time, Iran had 1,800 kilograms of uranium that had been enriched to 3.5 percent purity. Tehran was estimated to need an additional 1,200 kilograms to construct one bomb, if it was processed further into weapons-grade material.

Burns personally laid out the importance of the deal in a forty-five-minute one-on-one meeting with Jalili in Genthod. The American also raised issues such as Iran's human rights record and the June elections, and Jalili responded that Iran wanted to broaden its dialogue with the United States to include the topics of Iraq, Afghanistan, and the Persian Gulf. This illustrated the delicate balance of the diplomacy: the United States wanted a deal focused on the nuclear question but found it difficult to exclude other security issues. Still, to the Americans' surprise, Jalili tentatively accepted the fuel swap arrangement, stirring a collective sigh of relief in Washington and European capitals. "This limits Iran's ability to have the breakout ability needed to have nuclear weapons," an aide to Burns told reporters in Geneva at the time. The diplomats in Switzerland decided to hold follow-up discussions at the IAEA's headquarters in Vienna to finalize the technical details of the plan.

But, as with much of the West's diplomacy with Iran since 1979, this initial euphoria over the Geneva agreement quickly turned into confusion and then heartbreak. Just a day after Jalili's agreement with the P5+1, senior Iranian officials were quoted by state media denying they had struck an accord on the fuel swap. Senior Iranian officials and politicians then began publicly attacking the deal, arguing that Western countries such as France couldn't be trusted to deliver the nuclear fuel to Tehran on time. They wanted a simultaneous exchange of Iran's stockpile of enriched uranium for the fuel plates, and they wanted it to take place in a matter of weeks, something the IAEA said wasn't technically possible. American officials were again confused about who was calling the shots in Iran, and if Khamenei had even blessed the talks to begin with.

A major internal battle inside Iran ensued, according to Iranian and European officials, and exposed major cleavages inside the country's political system. Ahmadinejad had initially told Jalili to accept the agreement—in part, these officials said, to enhance the president's political standing, both internationally and inside Iran, in the wake of the disputed June vote. The president's critics in Tehran, particularly those close to Khamenei and the Revolutionary Guard, began attacking the deal and charging that the president was selling out to the United States and Israel, a tactic designed as much to weaken Ahmadinejad as to satisfy substantive opposition to the agreement.

Ultimately, Ayatollah Khamenei ruled against the agreement, according to Iranian and European officials, fearful of losing leverage internationally if Tehran shipped out the majority of its fissile material. Some people involved in the diplomacy said they believed Ahmadinejad never consulted with the supreme leader before instructing Jalili to accept the deal. This was a maneuver that ultimately doomed the original agreement and created significant distrust between the two Iranian leaders for the remaining four years of Ahmadinejad's second term. The fallout from the failed deal also rekindled fears inside the White House that the United States couldn't reach a sustainable deal with an Iranian government that was so fractured internally. "The failure of the Geneva agreement really marked a shift to a more confrontational stance towards Iran," said Dennis Ross, who closely advised Obama on Iran at this time. "Hopes for a successful engagement with Khamenei began to fade."

IN THE WAKE OF the failure in Geneva, the Obama administration and its European allies began preparing to implement the "crippling" sanctions that the White House had promised if diplomacy failed. And the Obama administration seemed correct in its assessment that seeking engagement with Tehran, even if unsuccessful, would force the Europeans, Russians, and Chinese to support sanctions. The responsibility for the failure of the diplomatic approach clearly fell on Tehran.

This latest push for sanctions focused on implementing a fourth round of economic penalties on Iran through the UN Security Council. It also included unilateral sanctions by Washington and the European Union that were being developed by the U.S. Treasury Department and the Congress and which would increasingly target Iran's oil revenues.

A last-ditch diplomatic effort spearheaded by two developing economic powers, Turkey and Brazil, emerged in the spring of 2010 to head off this call for more economic penalties on Iran. The initiative, pursued by Turkish prime minister Recep Tayyip Erdogan and Brazilian president Luiz Inácio Lula da Silva, illustrated how the Iranian nuclear crisis was increasingly dividing the Western powers from the developing nations, many of whom supported Tehran's position on uranium enrichment. The Brazilians and the Turks said they coordinated their diplomacy with Washington, but many U.S. officials viewed it as an affront to their efforts to isolate Tehran. Erdogan and Lula both saw their countries as emerging powers and together presented an alternative to U.S. hegemony.

At a triumphant press conference in Tehran that May, Erdogan and Lula announced that they had succeeded where the West had failed. Ahmadinejad, allegedly with Khamenei's backing, had agreed to a revised version of the fuel swap deal with only marginal differences, they said. Iran would ship out 1,200 kilograms of enriched uranium to Turkey in exchange for fuel rods. Iran would also allow increased monitoring by the IAEA. In return, the push for new sanctions against Iran at the United Nations would be halted, the leaders argued.

"America is angry over the proximity of independent countries like Iran and Brazil. . . . That is why they made a fuss ahead of your trip to Iran," Khamenei told Lula after the marathon negotiating session, according to Iranian press reports.

The United States and the Europeans, however, didn't support the initiative, viewing it as a ploy to ward off more economic pain for Iran. Furthermore, the new agreement's terms no longer carried the weight the earlier plan's would have. The country's fuel stockpile had grown by over 1,000 kilograms in the six months since the Geneva meetings. This meant that the transfer of 1,200 kilograms of fissile material to a third country no longer had the value it once did, since Iran would retain enough nuclear fuel to make an atomic weapon. And the Turkish and Brazilian initiative didn't require Iran to stop enriching uranium to a level of purity that, as previously noted, the United States viewed as near weapons grade.

"The confidence that the original . . . deal would have done is greatly diminished," said a senior U.S. official who discussed the latest agreement with Turkish and Brazilian diplomats. "This is, in essence, grasping at straws that somehow this would help resolve the issue. But this is an area . . . we don't agree with them on."

The Turks and Brazilians were incensed by the West's rejection of their diplomacy. They said they had only implemented what the Obama administration had required, and that a huge potential breakthrough was being missed. However, they didn't address U.S. concerns that Iran's capabilities had greatly increased during the six months between the two sets of negotiations.

The promised fourth round of economic sanctions was approved by the UN Security Council in June, essentially ending the Obama administration's initial outreach to Iran. Even before the sanctions were imposed, Obama signaled that his initial strategy to woo Tehran and Khamenei had so far failed. In March 2010, speaking to the Iranian people in another speech marking the Persian New Year, Nowruz, he voiced frustration with Khamenei's unwillingness so far to respond to his overtures. "For reasons known only to them, the leaders of Iran have shown themselves unable to answer that question. You have refused good faith proposals from the international community," Obama said. "They have turned their backs on a pathway that would bring more opportunity to all Iranians, and allow a great civilization to take its rightful place in the community of nations. Faced with an extended hand, Iran's leaders have shown only a clenched fist."

Chapter 8

Black Gold

THE TREASURY DEPARTMENT'S FINANCIAL WAR WAS BEARING FRUIT AS President Obama prepared to launch his reelection campaign in 2012. Iran's major banks were all blacklisted by the United States and Europe. Its shipping firms and airlines were being cut off from the global economy. And major corporations were severing their Iranian ties, believing the threat of losing access to the U.S. economy far outweighed whatever profits they could still reap from the Iranian market. Tehran, meanwhile, was offering few signs to the international community that it was serious about engaging in diplomacy to curb its nuclear program.

Despite the radical measures already in place, Iran was exporting more than two million barrels of oil per day to Europe and Asia. This kept Tehran's coffers relatively flush, as crude was then selling at well over $100 per barrel. Tehran, meanwhile, was expanding its nuclear program at a rapid pace. The country had installed thousands of new centrifuges at its nuclear fuel production plant at Natanz and had secretly opened the third facility in Qom. These advances were allowing Tehran to amass large stockpiles of uranium enriched to 20 percent purity levels, dangerously close to weapons grade. Iran was on the verge of having enough fissile material for an atomic bomb.

Frustrated with Iran's advances, Congress began to maneuver on its own to force the Obama White House to impose a total embargo on Iran's oil exports, the plan Stuart Levey had hinted at for years. Congressional and Treasury officials privately referred to this as the "nuclear option" in any financial war against Iran's economy. The United States hadn't taken such measures against an enemy's economy since the 1940s, when the Roosevelt administration imposed an embargo on all Japanese oil imports. The Imperial Japanese Navy responded by attacking Pearl Harbor in 1941, dragging the United States into World War II.

But there remained fears inside the U.S. government that such a radical step could drive up oil prices, hurting the United States' own economic recovery from the recession that had begun in 2008. Healing the U.S. economy had been President Obama's primary focus during his first term, and he wouldn't do anything that placed the recovery at risk, White House officials said.

The United States' main tool to enforce such an embargo would be to sanction Iran's central bank, Bank Markazi, through which all of Iran's oil sales flowed. Treasury officials believed countries couldn't buy Iranian oil without financial ties to Bank Markazi. Emerging economic powers such as China and India, however, had opposed most U.S. sanctions against Iran and might reject U.S. demands to cut off their imports, even though they would place themselves at risk of being sanctioned. Their refusal to comply with a U.S. policy demand could expose Washington as an emperor with no clothes, administration officials feared.

"If you sanctioned the Iranian central bank, you had to really think about whether the policy could be implemented," Levey told me in 2010, as the policy debate about Bank Markazi was beginning to gather pace. "To take the step and have China and India not comply, you could see a real challenge to American power and prestige."

Indeed, China, India, and other developing nations had been discussing developing a global currency that could stand beside the dollar. A public fight over Iranian oil sanctions could accelerate this debate, American officials believed. And China and India could simply have continued buying Iranian oil in U.S. dollars in a direct rebuke of Washington. Successive U.S. administrations feared that an overreliance on sanctions could hurt the country's status as the world's economic safe haven and Wall Street's preeminence as the globe's leading financial center.

THE U.S. OIL WAR on Iran started quietly in the spring of 2009, early in Obama's presidency. The White House dispatched its point man on Iran policy, Ambassador Dennis Ross, to the Persian Gulf and Asia to discuss Iran's energy trade and emerging nuclear program. Ross and the White House began conceptualizing what was essentially an oil-offset strategy: the major Arab oil producers, Saudi Arabia, Kuwait, and the UAE, would increase their exports to the Asian powerhouses, China, Japan, South Korea, and India. In return, these countries would cut back their purchases of Iranian oil. The plan, in theory, would keep Asia's economies humming without driving up oil prices. And the loss of oil sales would place enormous pressure on Tehran's bottom line.

Many of the Arab leaders were wary of welcoming Ross and distrusted him because of his close relationships with successive Israeli governments. Some Arab leaders derisively referred to Ross as the White House representative of Likud, the hawkish Israeli political party headed by Benjamin Netanyahu. In private discussions they described Ross as pursuing Israel's interests above those of the United States. And Ross's significant involvement in the Mideast peace processes under both Presidents George H. W. Bush and Bill Clinton was why Washington hadn't pushed Israel harder to make concessions to the Palestinians during those negotiations, they argued, leading to the failure of those efforts.

Despite this bad blood, there were a few exceptions. In the royal courts of Riyadh, Kuwait, and Abu Dhabi, Ross found audiences surprisingly receptive to his emerging energy scheme, according to U.S. and Arab diplomats. Officially, neither the Saudis nor the Emiratis wanted to publicly commit to pressuring Iran through the energy markets. This would break from their official policy, which went back decades, not to use oil as a geopolitical weapon. But in private they communicated to Ross their willingness to increase their production capacity as a means to punish Tehran.

The U.S. envoy heard an increasingly hawkish line on Iran from the Saudi and Emirati royal families during his stops—positions similar to the one espoused by the Israeli government. This private convergence of Israeli and Arab positions on Iran bolstered Washington's hopes of pressuring Tehran. Give sanctions a chance to alter Tehran's stance on its nuclear program, Arab and Israeli officials told Ross, but also plan for military action if they failed.

Another U.S. envoy, General David Petraeus, visited Saudi Arabia shortly before Ross and was stunned by King Abdullah's tone. Destroy Iran's nuclear program, the general was told, and roll back Iranian influence in the region. "Cut off the head of the snake," the monarch demanded.

In talks with the Chinese, Ross and other U.S. officials played up the possibility of Israel launching unilateral military strikes against Iran to stop its nuclear program. Beijing was worried that such an attack would destabilize the broader Middle East and threaten China's ability to import oil not just from Iran but from all the regional producers. Ross's response to the Chinese was that the best way to prevent such an apocalyptic scenario was to help Washington increase financial pressure on Tehran; such a move would convince the Israelis that military action wasn't necessary.

In the months after Ross's trip, major Arab oil exporters began replacing Iranian energy exports in Asian markets. The UAE's Crown Prince Mohammed bin Zayed al-Nahyan, on a private mission to Beijing in 2010, communicated his government's willingness to quadruple its oil exports to China to offset any reduction of purchases from Iran. Saudi Arabia, meanwhile, which was already exporting 700,000 barrels of oil per day to China, told Chinese officials Riyadh was willing to ramp up its production even more to assuage China's supply concerns.

Saudi officials and members of the royal families started publicly threatening an oil war against Iran if it didn't back off on its nuclear program. This kind of acrimonious talk, coming out of the Saudi palaces, was revelatory. "Iran is very vulnerable in the oil sector, and it is there that more could be done to squeeze the current government," Prince Turki al-Faisal, a former head of Saudi intelligence, told a private gathering of American and British servicemen at an airbase outside London in the spring of 2011. "To put this into perspective, Saudi Arabia has so much [spare] production capacity—nearly 4 million barrels [per] day—that we could almost instantly replace all of Iran's oil production," the prince said.

President Obama and Secretary Clinton personally raised the issues of sanctions on Iran and the scaling back of Tehran's oil sales with a string of foreign leaders throughout 2011. White House officials said sanctions on Iran were Obama's number one issue in conversations he had with world leaders that year, particularly in China and Russia. "In 2011, every bilateral meeting that the president had with an important country, Iran sanctions were the top issue. This was extraordinary," Ben Rhodes said. "These countries, especially the Chinese, they pay close attention to how you rank your asks. We told them: 'This is our biggest issue. This is our core interest.'" The tools to break Tehran's oil economy were falling into place. But the question remained: would the White House employ them?

In the meantime, there were fears inside the Obama administration that they were running out of time. In late 2011 and continuing into 2012, U.S. intelligence agencies detected stepped-up activity by the Israeli military that presaged a possible strike against Iran's nuclear facilities. The White House was particularly alarmed when Israeli aircraft flew into and out of Iranian airspace, ostensibly as a dry run for a commando raid. President Obama responded by dispatching a string of aides to Israel, including national security advisor Thomas Donilon, to walk Benjamin Netanyahu back. "We spent many hours in these consultations with them that had the purpose of essentially dissuading that strike," said a senior U.S. official who took part.

LATER IN 2011 THE U.S. CONGRESS stepped up its pressure on the White House to take out Iran's oil exports, even as the Treasury's financial campaign was ramping up. The need to stop Iran's nuclear program was one foreign policy issue that generated nearly uniform bipartisan support on Capitol Hill, largely because of the threat Tehran posed to Israel. Legislation targeting Iran was framed, in part, through the lens of the Jewish state's security concerns.

A coalition of U.S. lawmakers had been repeatedly challenging the Obama administration and the Treasury Department to impose ever more draconian measures on Tehran. In 2010 Congress had rammed through legislation that carried "extraterritorial power," meaning that other countries would need to abide by U.S. law. This broke sharply from previous American sanctions regimes. The new law, the Comprehensive Iran Sanctions, Accountability, and Divestment Act (CISADA), not only required the United States to blacklist Iranian companies and individuals alleged to be involved in Tehran's nuclear program and support for terrorism, but also required the United States to sanction entities anywhere in the world—be they Chinese, Russian, or Emirati—if they were doing business with blacklisted Iranian firms. U.S. sanctions law was increasingly becoming international law.

The White House resisted CISADA, fearing that its secondary sanctions would alienate U.S. allies and place the administration on a collision course with key investors in the American financial system, such as China and Japan, who saw the financial war on Iran as a direct threat to their economies. Still, Congress unanimously passed the legislation. The State Department and Treasury established units to enforce the laws. Billions of dollars in fines on foreign companies, mostly European, followed for their violations of U.S. sanctions laws. Many were tied to the cases exposed by Robert Morgenthau and the New York prosecutors.

The same coalition of American lawmakers assembled again in 2011 to press the Obama White House to target Bank Markazi, the Iranian central bank. The initiative was overseen in the Senate by a Democrat, Robert Menendez of New Jersey, and a Republican, Mark Kirk of Illinois. It was supported by AIPAC, the powerful pro-Israel lobby. This coalition had been privately arguing for years that the blacklisting of Bank Markazi was possibly the only financial tool that could force Iran to rein in its nuclear program.

Arab governments had for decades complained that AIPAC essentially dictated U.S. foreign policy in the Middle East, particularly with regard to the Israeli-Palestinian peace process. But Iran's neighbors, including the UAE, had also recently shown a willingness to target Iran's finances. In November 2011, AIPAC circulated a letter to Congress calling for sanctions on Bank Markazi. Ninety-seven out of one hundred U.S. senators supported the letter, placing major pressure on the White House to act.

The administration's economic planners pushed back. Treasury secretary Timothy Geithner took the lead in pleading the administration's case to Congress. He argued that the law, while well intentioned, could cause a destabilizing spike in global energy prices that could kill the United States' economic recovery. Chinese leaders had already been murmuring about reducing Beijing's holdings of American debt, and passage of the law could further raise economic tensions between Washington and Beijing at a time when the United States could ill afford it.

The White House called for a more measured implementation, stressing that China, India, and other major buyers of Iranian oil wouldn't pull out of the market overnight. They needed time to slowly reduce their dependency on Tehran, a process that would take months if not years. "There's not an issue we worked on as intensively diplomatically as getting cooperation on those sanctions. It took lots of work to cut the Iranians off, essentially," said Rhodes.

The confrontation peaked in late 2011 and fed into the U.S. presidential campaign. Republicans accused President Obama of not wanting to confront Tehran during an election year. Menendez and other Democrats accused the administration of attempting to deceive Congress by promising "crippling" sanctions against Iran but then refusing to implement the one measure that could tip the balance.

A tense standoff played out in the Senate that month as Democrats and Republicans attacked top administration officials. "You have rebuffed [sanctions on Bank Markazi] every step of the way even though it is the sanctions law that we have given you that has allowed you to achieve some limited progress," Senator Menendez told the Treasury's David Cohen and the State Department's number three diplomat, Wendy Sherman. "I find it pretty outrageous that while the clock is ticking and you ask us to engage in a more reasoned effort, . . . you come here and say what you say, which really undermines your relationship with me for the future." Geithner fired back, telling Congress it didn't fully understand the economic and diplomatic ramifications of sanctioning Iran's central bank, which some foreign diplomats and U.S. lawmakers argued was an act of war. "I am writing to express the administration's strong opposition to this amendment because, in its current form, it threatens to undermine the effective, carefully phased, and sustainable approach we have undertaken to build strong international pressure against Iran," Geithner wrote in a December 1, 2011, letter to Senate leaders.

To no avail. The Senate passed the law 100 to 0, forcing the administration to blacklist Bank Markazi in July 2012. The European Union, fortifying the congressional action, joined the United States in imposing its own ban on any purchases of Iranian oil by its twenty-eight member states. Even the most hawkish U.S. officials said they were stunned by the pace at which Iran's energy exports fell. In less than a year, Iran's crude exports dipped to as low as 750,000 barrels a day from levels close to 3 million. South Korea and Japan cut their imports to zero, which meant they had to scramble to find new suppliers. China and India pared back their own imports even while they continued to gripe to the Obama administration.

"That was the statistic I found most surprising," the Treasury's Adam Szubin told me about the plunge in Iranian oil exports. "We began at a time of $90-a-barrel oil and China growing. We brought their exports down so low that they had to limit production, which in turn harmed their infrastructure. That's what really surprised me."

EVEN AS THE OIL EMBARGO went into effect in 2012, Congress wasn't finished pursuing its own financial war on Iran. Powerful lawmakers such as Menendez and Kirk believed it was primarily their legislation that had pushed Tehran toward a financial cliff and had compelled Treasury to act as forcefully as it did. Congressional staffers, partnered with largely conservative Washington think tanks, were looking at ever newer ways to squeeze Iran's oil profits and ability to conduct financial transactions. Iran had emerged as a laboratory for concocting innovative ways to inflict economic damage.

A lethal weapon came from an unlikely source: the Foundation for Defense of Democracies (FDD), a little-known think tank based near Dupont Circle. The FDD is a small operation that focuses on combating Middle East extremism and, in particular, promoting the security of the United States, Israel, and other democracies threatened by radical Islam. Among its benefactors was Sheldon Adelson, the Las Vegas casino magnate who's been among Israel's most powerful financial supporters in the United States. Adelson once publicly called for the United States to detonate a nuclear device in an Iranian desert to prove to Khamenei the United States was serious about stopping Tehran's nuclear program. But the FDD wasn't hardline enough for the mogul, and he cut off his funding in 2013.

The FDD's executive director, Mark Dubowitz, was South African–born and Canadian-raised, and his Farsi-speaking research team fixated on the Iranian nuclear threat. They provided a constant stream of reports to U.S. lawmakers on Iranian companies and individuals that they believed should be sanctioned for their roles in developing Tehran's nuclear program. These targets ranged from units of the Revolutionary Guard to obscure Iranian trading firms in Dubai and Hong Kong. Dubowitz and his FDD colleagues were convinced that the financial pressure on Tehran wasn't extreme enough to force the Iranians to capitulate. They were looking for a new financial bomb to drop.

They found it in a Belgium-based financial firm called SWIFT, which hosts the international computer network that facilitates virtually every banking transaction in the world through an extensive messaging and financial tracking system. Without access to SWIFT, companies and countries would be reduced to a primitive form of barter trade. Few Americans had ever heard of it, despite its critical importance to businesses everywhere.

In late 2011, Dubowitz turned his efforts toward kicking Tehran off the SWIFT network. He was joined in this by Richard Goldberg, then the deputy chief of staff to Senator Kirk, the Illinois conservative. Goldberg, in his late twenties and a naval intelligence officer like his boss, was an aggressive congressional staffer who had no problem ruffling feathers on the Hill. Dubowitz and Goldberg worked as a one-two punch. At times the pair appeared to be driving U.S. sanctions policy on Capitol Hill by themselves after Senator Kirk suffered a stroke in early 2012; Goldberg was even nicknamed "Home Alone" due to the perception that he was acting without supervision.

Dubowitz called Goldberg and pointed him to the SWIFT website. Despite international sanctions, Iran had been using SWIFT to continue conducting oil trades and to procure energy-related equipment and technology. Nineteen Iranian banks and twenty-five Iranian entities used SWIFT more than two million times in 2010, sending 1,160,000 messages and receiving 1,105,000. These messages and transactions allowed Iran to conduct $35 billion in trade with Europe alone that year, Dubowitz and the FDD concluded. In Dubowitz's mind, Iran was exploiting a legal loophole in the international financial system.

By 2012, SWIFT represented one of Tehran's last entry points into the global financial system. But as Dubowitz and Goldberg had discovered, the company's bylaws required that its services not be used to facilitate illegal activities. SWIFT's own rules obliged it to prohibit access to users if they were facing international sanctions. Senior executives of the global financial institutions that formed the board of SWIFT in Brussels had the power to expel a user who "has adversely affected . . . SWIFT's reputation, brand, or goodwill."

Goldberg drafted legislation to target SWIFT's board of directors through the Senate Banking Committee. Treasury was initially hesitant about the idea of using SWIFT as a tool of economic warfare, U.S. officials said. The Obama administration was sensitive to the perception that SWIFT was being politicized in the dispute over Iran's nuclear program. Treasury did not want to further complicate Washington's relationship with SWIFT and threaten access to the financial data it used for counterterrorism operations. The agreement Stuart Levey had reached with the organization during the George W. Bush administration to gain access to this data remained controversial in Europe. There may also have been hesitation because of a concern within the U.S. government about the loss of financial intelligence into Iranian activities that SWIFT provided.

The Obama administration sought to persuade key legislators that it was better positioned to pursue this matter quietly rather than having Congress adopt punitive measures against a critical global financial actor such as SWIFT. But Congress once again overrode the White House's concerns and unanimously passed the SWIFT legislation in February 2012. The European Council soon followed suit and announced that "no specialized financial messaging shall be provided to those persons and entities subject to an asset freeze." Dubowitz and Goldberg joked that Iran had been "de-SWIFTed."

Once again, the threat of congressional sanctions, passed over the objections of the Obama administration, played a critical role in persuading foreign governments, in this case the EU, to comply with U.S.-led pressure on Iran. Tehran, meanwhile, saw one of its final entry points into the global economy shut off. All of its major banks were sanctioned, as was its central bank. And the SWIFT network, which Iranian banks had still been able to use, was closed to it now. A complicated trade based on barter and smuggling would emerge as Tehran's only means to do international business.

THE SANCTIONS WERE HITTING Iran's economic managers in Tehran hard, particularly the central bank. I visited its gleaming blue-and-black headquarters, which stared up at the snow-capped Alborz Mountains, in the spring of 2014. The sleek office tower, more than twenty stories tall, didn't appear to be an institution under siege. Construction cranes and tree-lined streets stretched out below the modern building. But inside its offices, bureaucrats were feverishly working to fend off financial collapse. Many acknowledged they had underestimated the power of the U.S. Treasury.

My primary interlocutor at Bank Markazi was its number two official, deputy central bank governor Akbar Komijani. He, like a large number of senior figures in the Iranian government, had studied in the United States. In Komijani's case, he received a Ph.D. in economics from the University of Wisconsin in the 1970s. He spoke fondly of the frigid winters in Wisconsin and the radical campus politics of the time. His English was fluent even though he hadn't visited the United States in decades.

Komijani had been a senior Bank Markazi official under the administration of the reformist president Mohammad Khatami in the late 1990s and early 2000s. Like many in the leader's administration,

Komijani was purged from government after the election of Mahmoud Ahmadinejad in 2005. He returned to academia for nearly a decade, while a surge in global oil prices filled Iran's coffers. Komijani and other Iranian economists, though, became horrified by Ahmadinejad's financial policies and rampant spending on populist programs—as just one example, the president had lost billions on a program for subsidized housing for the poor.

Komijani was one of a team of economists who were called in by President Hassan Rouhani after his election in 2013. Many of them said that while they had known the financial situation in Iran was bad, they were stunned by what they saw on the books. The government's balance sheet had a black hole of more than $200 billion, much of the money assumed to have been lost due to corruption. Bank Markazi also had incurred huge debts to the country's banks and state-owned companies, in part due to the low-income-housing scheme.

The only solution to Iran's financial woes, Komijani and Rouhani's economic planners concluded, was accessing the more than $100 billion of Iranian oil revenues frozen in overseas banking accounts because of the U.S. sanctions. To get the funds, the Rouhani team knew, they needed to quickly enter into negotiations with the Obama administration to end the standoff over the nuclear crisis. "The sanctions were a catalyzer that exposed many other problems in our economy," said Komijani in between cups of Persian tea. "If the negotiating process is speeded up, the country can have access to increased oil revenues and better access to overseas assets. . . . We will have the opportunity to import the necessary inputs for our industrial capacity."

EVEN AS KOMIJANI AND OTHERS tried to right their country's economic ship, the impact of the U.S. financial war was being felt across Iran. Oil exports had fallen to below 1 million barrels a day from more than 2.5 million before the U.S.-EU embargo went into effect. The value of the rial had fallen by 30 percent against the dollar in one trading day. And Iran was being forced to engage in a medieval form of barter to import key commodities and everyday household goods, selling its oil in exchange for wheat and tea from India, rice from Uruguay, and zippers and bricks from China.

Industry in the country seized up. A *Wall Street Journal* reporter traveling through Iran after the sanctions hit home saw factories and plants firing employees by the hundreds of thousands and taking radical cost-cutting measures to deal with the twin evils of a spiraling cost of imports and slackening demand for their products at home or abroad. At the Alborz industrial complex near the city of Qazvin, not far from the Caspian Sea, factory owners were eliminating paid holidays, reducing the numbers of free meals given to employees, and cutting the workweek by a day. Dairy companies wrote Supreme Leader Khamenei and said that if the economic siege didn't end, they would all go out of business. Iran's car industry, the largest in the Middle East, was posting production declines of 60 to 80 percent; some producers of spare parts were working at only 40 percent capacity because of a shortage of cash and a lack of raw materials.

Visiting the Iranian city of Delijan, three hours south of Tehran, our Iranian reporter saw an industrial area with 160 factories grinding to a halt. Once a model for economic growth, the city and its fifty thousand inhabitants had been producing everything from paint to industrial textiles. A university outpost had opened and offered advanced vocational training. Services businesses, such as catering and cargo transportation, had taken root. Delijan firms had been selling to Afghanistan, Iraq, and Turkmenistan. But once the sanctions hit in 2012 and the currency plunged, the cost of maintaining the factories snowballed. Many smaller factories shut down. Dozens of the bigger ones were fighting bankruptcy. At Bam Shargh Isogam, a manufacturer of insulation sheets in Delijan, a manager told the *Journal* reporter that he had fired more than half of his 350 employees and didn't pay the remaining workers for months. "From the owner to the line worker, no one is safe," the manager, who called himself Bijan, said. "Our country is facing an economic disaster."

A DECADE EARLIER, Stuart Levey and other Treasury officials had initiated a campaign to gradually wall off Iran from the global economy. Now the wall was nearly complete.

CHAPTER 9

The Arab Spring

I RAN MAY HAVE BEEN FACING ECONOMIC DISASTER, BUT IT WASN'T going to shrink from defending itself or its allies from the revolutions that swept the Middle East in 2011. Tehran's Green Revolution of two years earlier had to some extent created the climate for these democracy movements, which eventually posed a major threat to Iran's closest Arab ally, Bashar al-Assad of Syria. A collapse of the Assad regime, Iranian officials knew, would threaten Tehran's regional influence and its ability to send arms and funds to Hezbollah in Lebanon and to Hamas and Palestinian Islamic Jihad in the Palestinian territories. Whatever gains Tehran had made in its struggle against the United States and its allies since the Iraq War would be undermined by regime change in Damascus.

For the Obama administration, the political tumult raised the prospect of vastly reshaping the Middle East but also posed limitless quandaries for U.S. policy. Close American allies in Egypt and Bahrain were under threat, as were their governments' repressive rules. Should the White House support change and risk greater regional instability? Or should it back its partners at the cost of lives and human rights? A long-standing U.S. adversary turned partner, Moammar Gadhafi, was also facing a revolt in Libya. Would the United States back its red lines and prevent the killing of innocents there?

Behind the headlines, the Obama White House remained fixated on engaging Iran on the nuclear issue. To challenge Tehran's role in the shifting Middle East placed the diplomacy at risk. But if the United States stood back, Iran could grow even more powerful and feed into the region's spiraling violence.

IN FEBRUARY 2012, U.S. spy satellites tracked the beginning of a massive Iranian airlift of weapons, supplies, and soldiers into Syria to support the Assad regime. The planes were largely Russian Ilyushin jets owned by Iranian airlines such as Iran Air, Yas, and Mahan, which the Revolutionary Guard had turned to in order to make up for the aging Boeing aircraft grounded by lack of maintenance. The planes flew west over Iraqi airspace into Syria, sometimes picking up supplies in the holy city of Najaf. Commercial cargo such as cement and electronics components was intermixed with small arms, artillery, and Iranian military advisors, to confuse surveillance or Iraqi inspectors.

As the year progressed, the Obama administration had gained remarkable insight into the Syria strategy of General Qasem Soleimani, the United States' old nemesis from the war in Iraq, and the senior leadership of the Revolutionary Guard. Washington used the National Security Agency to tap into the communications between Assad's senior leadership and the Revolutionary Guard, and the CIA worked with the Israelis to develop a surprisingly effective human spy network. Many of Washington's closest allies in Baghdad's Shiite and Kurdish leaderships were close to Soleimani, giving Washington and Tehran a revolving door of intelligence.

The Iranians had concluded President Assad hadn't been prepared or equipped for the political rebellion that had gripped his country a year earlier. The Syrian military was heavy-handed and fueled what were initially peaceful political protests by torturing and murdering not only its political opponents but also young children. Damascus's authoritarian regime ran a police state, but it had never developed a sophisticated capability to control crowds or to disperse large-scale political protests. A largely hidebound military also didn't have an advanced ability to use the Internet and telecommunications to do surveillance on its enemies. Assad and his clique only understood one language in confronting dissent: brute force.

General Soleimani and his staff concluded that Syria's growing civil war risked dooming Iran's closest ally in the Arab world, according to American intelligence. The collapse of the Assad regime would choke off Tehran's ability to use the land bridge in Syria to funnel arms and money to its allies in Lebanon and the Palestinian territories—the front lines in Iran's war against Israel. Syria was the linchpin in Iran's overseas network, which projected the Revolutionary Guard's power from the Caspian Sea to the Mediterranean. Soleimani wasn't going to lose Syria without a fight.

The turning point for the Iranians came in July 2012, when Syrian rebels assassinated Assad's brother-in-law and number two intelligence chief Assef Shawkat, a close ally of Tehran's. Two other top Syrian security officials were killed in the blast in Damascus. Soleimani and his cohorts concluded that Assad's regime had been increasingly penetrated by the Sunni rebels, who were receiving growing financial and military support from Saudi Arabia, Qatar, Turkey, and the United Arab Emirates. The rebels were also closing in on Syria's largest city, Aleppo, which would give them strategic control of Syria's north and a greater ability to launch strikes on the Assad family's stronghold on the Syrian coast and on Damascus. The fall of Assad and his government could be days or weeks away, some officials in the United States concluded.

The Iranians dispatched top military advisors to Damascus to help Assad push back the rebels' gains. The Revolutionary Guard started transferring telecommunications equipment to Assad to allow him to better track the movements and communications of his enemies. And the IRGC began mobilizing its closest Shiite allies, Hezbollah from Lebanon and a slew of Iraqi and Afghan militias, to fortify Assad's defenses. "Some countries might have concluded that defending Assad at that point was useless, a lost cause," said a U.S. defense official who tracked the intelligence out of Syria in the summer of 2012. "But Soleimani concluded the opposite. They had no choice but to go to the mat for the Syrians."

It was unclear, though, if the Obama administration would take up the challenge.

THE POLITICAL REBELLIONS THAT broke out across North Africa and the Middle East beginning in late 2010—a revolutionary surge known as the Arab Spring—had caught the Obama administration and nearly every Mideast government off guard. The revolts were fueled by economic stagnation, a youth bulge in the Arab world, and charges of corruption levied against the strongmen and dictators who had ruled Egypt, Tunisia, Libya, and Bahrain for decades. The advent of the Internet and Arabic-language satellite channels such as Qatar's Al Jazeera helped spread word of the revolutions rapidly from Tunis to Tripoli and Cairo. There were political rumblings as far away as Yemen, Lebanon, and Iraq.

The early days of the revolutions appeared to mark a strategic setback for the United States, Europe, and their Mideast allies. Many of the leaders who were under threat or deposed, including Egyptian president Hosni Mubarak, Bahrain's ruling Khalifa family, and Tunisian leader Zine El Abidine Ben Ali, were close U.S. allies who helped Washington ensure security in the Middle East and promote the peace process between Israel and the Palestinians. And Bahrain hosted the headquarters of the U.S. Navy's Fifth Fleet, a key platform for the Pentagon to police the shipping lanes of the Persian Gulf and guard the West's oil supplies.

The weakening of America's allies provided a major opportunity for Iran and the Axis of Resistance to spread their influence. Iran, Syria, Hezbollah, and Hamas seized on the political revolts as proof of the crumbling U.S. presence in their region. Supreme Leader Ayatollah Khamenei cited the uprisings as another step forward in the Islamist wave that had gripped the Mideast since Iran's 1979 revolution, even though many of the protestors on the Arab street were secular and touting Western democratic ideals. The popular movements in the region "indicate a fundamental change in Arab and Islamic countries," Khamenei told his supporters in a March 2011 speech commemorating the Persian New Year. "The presence of the people on the streets and their religious orientation are two characteristics of these popular movements."

The Assad regime also rejoiced in the fall of Mubarak, who the Syrians believed had betrayed the Arabs by promoting Egypt's peace treaty with Israel in 1980. Hamas saw Egypt's revolution as an opening for its parent organization, the Islamist Muslim Brotherhood, to seize power in Cairo and support the Palestinian group's political and military campaign against the Jewish state. Russian and Chinese officials, though concerned the political unrest could hurt their own economic interests, also gloated that the Arab Spring represented blowback against the United States' foreign policies, and they predicted that it would have ripple effects across the globe.

President Assad, just days before Mubarak's fall in February 2011, spoke confidently about his hold on power, telling me the U.S.-backed order in the region was crumbling. Members of his Axis of Resistance, he argued, were on the ascent. "From the outside, what is the role of the West? It's now been twenty years since we started the [Arab-Israeli] peace process in 1991. What have we achieved?" he said in fluent English from his office atop Damascus's Mount Qasioun. "The simple way to answer this question is to say is it better or worse? We can for example say that it is five percent better than before we started the peace process. I can tell you, frankly, that it is much worse."

———

INSIDE THE WHITE HOUSE and State Department, the Arab Spring was initially treated as an opportunity to spread democracy. But what originally looked like an opportunity for hope would prove far thornier. And U.S. foreign policy would be pulled by currents it couldn't control or predict.

In Cairo's Tahrir Square, scenes of young political activists (some organized by high-tech executives and Western-educated lawyers) taking on Egyptian security forces fueled hopes in Washington that the Middle East was awakening from decades of political slumber that had created sclerotic ruling classes and moribund economies. Tunisian mobs overran the loot-filled palaces of President Ben Ali, revealing the extraordinary level of corruption that had infected the region's monarchies. Hillary Clinton condemned the abuses of the region's old order. "In too many places, in too many ways, the region's foundations are sinking into the sand," she told an audience of foreign ministers, businesspeople, and rights groups in Qatar in January 2011. "The new and dynamic Middle East that I have seen needs firmer ground if it is to take root and grow everywhere."

A few months later, the Obama administration told the Egyptian strongman Hosni Mubarak to stand down, abandoning a U.S. ally of more than thirty years over the objections of countries such as Israel and Saudi Arabia, who feared an Islamist government would follow. President Obama and his young foreign policy aides also pressed Bahrain's Sunni royal family, the Khalifas, to open up their political system to a disadvantaged population that was at least 60 percent Shiite. The White House called for the leaders of Yemen, Libya, and Iraq to embrace reform, hoping that Western-inspired activists would prevail against Islamist groups or political parties with close ties to Iran, though the United States knew this would be a struggle. In Yemen and Libya in particular, militant Islamists, some with links to al Qaeda, were seeking to exploit the upheaval to further their aims, U.S. and Arab intelligence officials concluded.

The United States' Arab allies were unnerved by what they viewed as an imbalance in Obama's response toward democracy movements in their region. The White House largely remained quiet when Iranians rose up against Tehran's Islamist regime in 2009. But the U.S. administration, conversely, pressed for the removal of Sunni Arab leaders.

The United States' closest allies in the Mideast, particularly Israel, Saudi Arabia, and the UAE, pushed back hard against U.S. efforts to promote regime change in the Arab countries. They believed Obama and his aides were playing right into the hands of not just Iran but also Sunni Islamist groups such as the Muslim Brotherhood. Israeli prime minister Benjamin Netanyahu, during a string of phone calls and meetings in early 2011, cautioned the White House against pulling its support for Mubarak without knowing who or what would replace him. The Egypt-Israeli peace agreement, the bedrock of the U.S. security framework for the Mideast, would be at risk if Mubarak was deposed, Netanyahu argued. He and his aides warned that the Muslim Brotherhood was almost certain to gain power in Cairo.

The Saudis, Emiratis, and Jordanians, meanwhile, cast the Arab Spring largely as a proxy battle between their Arab allies and Iran. King Abdullah of Saudi Arabia was adamant the United States should continue to back the Khalifas in Bahrain, arguing that Iran's proxies would come to power if any political transition took place in Manama. Iran and its Islamist allies in Egypt were also angling for influence once Mubarak fell, the Saudis argued. And the Iranians were increasingly active in Yemen through the Revolutionary Guard's backing of a Shiite militia and ethnic group called the Houthis.

The Saudis made it clear to the United States that they would act unilaterally to protect the kingdom's interests and push back against what they viewed as Iran's regional advances. In March 2011, the State Department's top Mideast official, Jeffrey Feltman, traveled to Manama to broker a political agreement between the Khalifas and the mostly Shiite political parties who had taken to the streets of Bahrain to demand more political rights. Thousands of them had been arrested and dozens killed. Scenes from a Manama hospital of young Shiite activists dying increased the pressure on the United States to find a political compromise. The Khalifas' decision to arrest some of the doctors treating the patients only hardened criticism of the Bahraini government in the West.

Feltman believed he had negotiated a political formula between the two sides that would address many of the Shiite parties' basic demands, but without mortally threatening the future of the Bahraini monarchy, according to U.S. officials. The deal included more seats in the parliament for the Shiite parties, a more inclusive government, and an advisory council that would directly communicate their grievances to Bahrain's crown prince, a Westernized monarch who had studied at American University in Washington and the University of Cambridge. But the deal wouldn't require the Khalifas to accept the protestors' most extreme demand: a quick move to the formation of a constitutional monarchy.

Feltman left Manama after three days of talks believing he had clinched a deal. But in the early hours of March 14, the Saudis, supported by a grouping of Arab states known as the Gulf Cooperation Council, sent thousands of troops over Saudi Arabia's causeway into Bahrain, backed by tanks and mechanized units. The officially stated mission of the Saudi-led force was to help Bahrain's military restore order and guard the country's key infrastructure. But the broader impact was that the political reconciliation process Feltman had promoted ground to a halt. Saudi officials were adamant that they wouldn't agree to any political process in their tiny neighbor that could open the door even a little for greater Shiite, and possibly Iranian, influence. "We were straightforward with the Americans from the beginning," said a senior aide to the Saudi royal family. "We had to protect Bahrain from Iranian influence, even if the Americans didn't seem committed as well. The risks were too high for us."

U.S. officials, used to some level of compliance from their long-standing ally, were incensed by the Saudis' move. But the position of Washington's Mideast allies increasingly recast how the Obama administration framed the Arab Spring. After Saudi forces entered Bahrain, the United States significantly muted its calls for political reforms in the country and didn't pursue any major new initiatives to promote a power-sharing agreement with the Shiites. U.S. officials also increasingly viewed Yemen and Syria as proxy battles with Iran.

As senior U.S. officials deliberated over the possible use of force against Gadhafi in the fall of 2011, Tehran and its nuclear program were strongly on their minds. President Obama had set a clear red line for Iran: Tehran risked facing U.S. military action if it took clear steps to develop nuclear weapons, such as the production of highly enriched uranium. But he'd also set one for the Libyan strongman, warning that the United States wouldn't allow Gadhafi's military to slaughter his political opponents as the world watched. When Gadhafi began moving his troops and militias into the eastern Libyan city of Benghazi and threatened to kill his rivals like "stray dogs," the Obama administration concluded it had to act, as much as a warning sign to Tehran that U.S. red lines would be enforced as out of concern for Libya's internal security. "We needed to send a clear signal to the Iranians," said a senior White House official who took part in the discussions at the time. "We knew they were testing our resolve. We knew they were watching to see if we'd act."

The United States would go on to remove Gadhafi in late 2011 by backing a NATO air campaign targeting his troops.

CONDITIONS IN SYRIA WOULD provide the Obama administration with its greatest opportunity to challenge, if not roll back, Iran's regional power. After taking office in 2009, the Obama administration faced the grim reality that U.S. policies in the Mideast over the past decade had significantly strengthened Tehran by eliminating its two biggest regional rivals, the Taliban and Saddam Hussein. Growing U.S. sanctions on Iran were hurting Tehran's finances, but had done little to constrain Iran's regional actions or subdue its efforts to destabilize Washington's allies. American officials marveled at how Iran could fund its proxies on a shoestring budget.

"I was amazed at what I saw that Iran had done throughout the region," said a senior Pentagon official tracking the Revolutionary Guard at the time. "Their effort through the Gaza Strip, Syria, Lebanon, in which Hezbollah had become a virtual partner . . . all of this was going on around the Iraq situation."

Early in 2011, U.S. officials said they saw little chance of a major uprising breaking out against Assad, even while Egypt, Tunisia, and Libya were fully subsumed by revolutions. Diplomats based in Damascus said Assad and his family ran a system so dominated by fear that they were skeptical many Syrians would risk torture or prison to try to upend his family's four-decade rule. U.S. officials also believed Assad still possessed a significant measure of support inside Syria, especially among the country's Alawite, Christian, and Druze communities, who viewed him as their protector against a potentially hostile Sunni majority, but also among the Sunni middle class and elites, who saw him as a youthful modernizer. Israeli officials, meanwhile, were cautious about supporting any uprising against the Syrian regime, thinking Assad's possible successors might pose an even greater security threat to the Jewish state. Realizing the risk of direct escalation, first Hafez al-Assad and then his son Bashar had kept the Syrian-Israeli border almost totally quiet since the 1973 war.

Small protests in Damascus and some provincial Syrian capitals did break out in the weeks following Hosni Mubarak's fall. But the Obama administration didn't try to quickly capitalize on the unrest and deal a blow against Assad and Iran. Instead, Hillary Clinton and other U.S. officials, aping John Kerry's beliefs, said Bashar al-Assad could still emerge as a political reformer and had the ability to douse the flames of any broader rebellion. The United States didn't initially offer any encouragement to Assad's political rivals or signal they wanted him to stand down. "There's a different leader in Syria now. Many of the members of Congress of both parties who have gone to Syria in recent months have said they believe he's a reformer," Clinton said during a March 2011 television appearance on *Face the Nation*. "What's been happening there the last weeks is deeply concerning. But there's a difference between calling out aircraft and indiscriminately strafing and bombing your own cities [in Libya] than police actions which, frankly, have exceeded the use of force that any of us would want to see."

IN THE SPRING OF 2011, more than a dozen small children were detained in the southern Syrian province of Deraa for allegedly scrawling graffiti on a Baath Party school. After a month, some of the children were released bearing signs of torture. But when family members demanded the release of the others, Assad and his generals dispatched troops to the province to put down what was then a peaceful protest movement.

In late April, Syrian security forces entered Deraa on a day its residents cited as the beginning of the war in their country, according to an account in *The Wall Street Journal*. What ensued was a nearly two-week siege that saw the residents of the province's capital cut off from food, water, and baby formula. Funerals for the dead became rallying cries for the largely Sunni population. At least three hundred people died, and the government arrested hundreds more across Deraa. Videos and photos from the assault fueled protests in many other parts of Syria.

U.S. officials believed Assad's heavy hand was resulting in the very type of armed insurrection he said he wanted to avoid. As the regime's crackdown intensified, arms from Libya and other Arab states started to flow to Syrian rebels. Militias began to form; some were made up of military officers who had defected from the state plus ordinary men, but others had ties to Islamist groups to Washington's chagrin. Assad's main financial and military backers in Iran and Russia, however, joined the Syrian regime in deflecting calls for political reforms. Moscow made it clear it would block any censure of Damascus in the United Nations Security Council.

Empowered, Assad repudiated growing calls from the West and the Arab states for him to negotiate with his political opponents. In speeches and interviews, he described the protests as being stoked by "terrorists" bent on destroying Syria's secular government. He accused the United States and its Sunni allies in Saudi Arabia, the UAE, and Qatar of conspiring against Damascus in a plot aimed at advancing Israel's interests. Protestors were using calls for reform "to fragment Syria, to bring down Syria as a nation, to enforce an Israeli agenda," he said in a widely watched speech before the country's parliament. Assad's supporters in the legislature responded with lyrical poems and chants, including "The people want Bashar al-Assad" and "Allah, Syria, and Bashar."

By July, Secretary of State Hillary Clinton, echoing comments she had made about Hosni Mubarak, said Assad had lost his "legitimacy" by resisting his people's calls for reform. It was a sign that the White House had exhausted its patience with the Syrian leader. U.S. ambassador Robert Ford, who had arrived in Damascus with instructions to engage Assad, began to agitate against him. The diplomat made an unsanctioned trip to the central Syrian city of Hama that month in an effort to prevent the regime from using force against unarmed protestors there. The diplomatic mission set in motion a yearlong conflict between Ford and Assad, who repeatedly used armed gangs to attack the ambassador's motorcade and embassy compound. The White House ultimately recalled Ford, worried that the Syrian regime might attempt to assassinate him.

By mid-August 2012 President Obama and his European and Arab allies had all announced their outright intent to assist in the ouster of Assad. Significant gains by the Syrian rebels in the country's northwest and northeast fueled confidence in the White House that Assad could be only months from falling, as rebel militias were getting closer to Damascus. In an action similar to the one taken against Iran, the White House and the Europeans announced a co-ordinated embargo on Syria's oil exports, cutting Damascus's revenues by as much as two-thirds, and they jointly moved to freeze Assad and his cronies out of the Western banking system. "We have consistently said that President Assad must lead a democratic transition or get out of the way," Obama said at the White House. "He has not led. For the sake of the Syrian people, the time has come for President Assad to step aside."

ASSAD'S BARBARITY AND STEADFASTNESS forced the United States and its allies to increasingly engage in a covert proxy war with Assad and his Iranian backers for control of Syria, despite President Obama's worry that the United States would be dragged into another Middle East conflict. The battle lines that formed included the United States, Saudi Arabia, Turkey, and numerous oil-rich Gulf states backing a ragtag group of anti-regime militias and political parties. Supporting Assad, meanwhile, were Iran, Russia, and Tehran's network of Shiite militant groups, which included Hezbollah in Lebanon, a rash of Iraqi militias, and Shiite fighters whom the Revolutionary Guard recruited from as far away as Afghanistan and Yemen for this battle. The stakes were exceptionally high. The winners would control Syria and from there might dictate events across the region, from Israel to Iraq. The battle also risked fueling radical Islam across the Middle East even more, as militias with links to al Qaeda increasingly streamed into Syria to join the insurgency against Assad. The United States hoped moderate rebels could stanch the tide.

From the early stages of the conflict, though, the outside powers' commitment to the battle was lopsided. For its part, the United States had imposed sanctions, but trained only small numbers of militiamen to take part in the fight. Iran, seeing its closest ally on the brink of collapse, committed vast financial and military resources to prop up Assad, and in many ways it was the Iranians who ended up running the Syrian regime's war, according to Arab and U.S. intelligence officials. Russian president Vladimir Putin, meanwhile, who was committed to challenging Washington's power in the Mideast, continued arms and energy shipments to Syria despite international opprobrium. His diplomats also provided Assad unflinching diplomatic cover to continue with his military crackdown by vetoing multiple UN Security Council resolutions aimed at censuring and sanctioning the Syrian regime. U.S. and Israeli intelligence officials believed the IRGC had deployed hundreds of advisors to oversee thousands of fighters from Hezbollah and other Shiite groups by 2013.

The Obama administration and its allies never agreed on a coherent strategy to topple Assad or on whom to support as his successor. The White House was deeply skeptical about providing arms to the secular Syrian militias, which fought under the banner of the Free Syrian Army (FSA). Washington feared weapons shipments could be diverted to more radical elements fighting Assad inside Syria. But at the same time, the United States largely turned a blind eye as Saudi Arabia, Kuwait, Qatar, and Turkey sent in arms and funds to Syrian fighters with only limited oversight. Significant amounts of these resources went to groups with ties to al Qaeda, including the Al Nusra Front and the Islamic State of Iraq and Syria (ISIS), both of which marginalized Washington's chosen allies in Syria. Their empowerment then fueled the spread of violent Islamist militias back into Iraq, Lebanon, Turkey, and Jordan as the war ground on. The fact that the United States never acted strengthened the very radical groups it had pledged to fight.

GENERAL SOLEIMANI, COMMANDER OF the Qods Force, increasingly visited Damascus to liaise with Syria's security chiefs. He personally dispatched one of the IRGC's top commanders, General Hossein Hamedani, to be his emissary in Damascus. Hamedani was among the top Iranian generals who had overseen the crackdown on pro-democracy demonstrators in Tehran in 2009, expertly using social media and the Internet to track the regime's political opponents, both within Iran and outside it. Soleimani saw Hamedani's experience and skills as directly applicable to the task of putting down Assad's insurrection.

Iran's widening military presence inside Syria revealed itself publicly in August 2012, just a month after U.S. officials were predicting Assad's fall was imminent. That month, Free Syrian Army rebels kidnapped forty-eight IRGC commanders and personnel in Damascus. Iran's government first called the men Shiite pilgrims, but then later described them as "retired" Revolutionary Guard officers who had made the trip to Syria through an Iranian travel agency that was owned by the Guard, and said that they had been captured en route to the Damascus airport. Assad, under intense pressure from Tehran, eventually agreed to swap more than two thousand Free Syrian Army soldiers in order to get the IRGC staff back home.

Later that summer, the Guard began deploying soldiers in Syria for the first time, according to Iranian military officials and Syrian rebels. The majority didn't fight, but rather were used to repair equipment and guard military installations, though many filled in for Syrian officers who had defected. FSA commanders obtained identification cards and dog tags of Iranian soldiers they said had been captured or killed in battle. "Assad asked for them to be on the ground," the head of the FSA's intelligence operations, General Yahya Bittar, said in an interview at the time. "The Iranians are now part of Syria's command-and-control structure."

The Revolutionary Guard and its allies deployed soldiers on a wider scale in the spring of 2013 as Arab states such as Saudi Arabia and Qatar increased their shipments of arms and cash to Syrian rebels, according to Syrian government officials and Hezbollah. The United States believed many of the opposition's militias had ties to al Qaeda, which further eroded any desire in the White House to arm them. Tehran particularly focused on fortifying western and central Syria, regions that controlled access into Lebanon and the

Hezbollah militiamen stationed there. That May, Hezbollah sent thousands of its elite fighters into the central Syrian city of Qusayr and almost single-handedly pushed out the rebels threatening their supply lines.

The Guard and General Soleimani directly coordinated with Hezbollah in prosecuting this fight, sending military advisors to the city, according to rebel fighters and a journalist who saw them there. Hezbollah moved to take over the governance of Qusayr, and its commanders were charged with maintaining discipline among Assad's forces. A Hezbollah commander who identified himself as Abu Ahmed spoke with Sam Dagher of *The Wall Street Journal* on a spring 2013 afternoon and appeared in complete control of the city. Driving in a pickup truck with Hezbollah fighters, he said only regime loyalists were allowed back into the city, and that they must be vetted by him personally.

Much of the city was deserted and badly damaged. Dueling Sunni-Shiite graffiti covered many walls, sometimes referencing epic battles dating from the seventh century. Christians who lived in the town praised Hezbollah for restoring order and preventing the Sunni rebels from slaughtering Syria's religious minorities. "We feel safe, we don't want them to leave," said a Christian resident of Qusayr, referring to Hezbollah.

Commander Ahmed praised the discipline of Hezbollah fighters and their ability to make up for the strategic missteps of the Syrian military. He noted that one Syrian army officer rushed to capture two villages near Qusayr during the battle and proclaimed victory even before the territory was secured. Subsequently the Syrian units were besieged when the rebels reinforced their positions. Hezbollah initiated a "superb surgical procedure" to free the Syrian soldiers from the rebels, he said. "We could have butchered them all, but we did not, we let the wounded go," Commander Ahmed said. He noted that Hezbollah's chief, Sheikh Hassan Nasrallah, ordered that "mercy" be shown to the captured rebels, and added, "I would have not done it."

Hezbollah, and Syrian militias under its command, also led the Assad regime's campaign to retake Homs, a strategic province bisecting the country. In coordinated strikes in the spring and summer of 2013, they pushed out rebels from most of the capital, Homs city. The Assad regime's fighter jets and tanks pounded rebel-held sections of the city, while Hezbollah-led units fought street battles to push back the rebels, according to fighters who took part. "We did the heavy lifting," said a nineteen-year-old Syrian militiaman, identified as Abdullah, who fought under a Hezbollah commander in a district called Khalidiya, that August. "If we take back all of Homs, the revolution is going to be completely finished."

The battle left many areas of Homs nearly destroyed. The domes and minarets of the city's main mosque were riddled with bullet holes and marks left by mortar fire. Piles of debris and the twisted carcasses of cars lined the streets. An eight-story building was flattened, and mattresses, pieces of furniture, and people's personal belongings protruded from the heap of rubble.

THE REVOLUTIONARY GUARD CONTINUED to supply the Assad regime with Shiite fighters from across the Mideast. Among the centers for Iran's resupply was a training camp the IRGC established on the outskirts of Tehran, called Amir al-Momenin. The facility, kept secret from the Iranian public for years because of security concerns, had been used by the IRGC to train Iraqi militias fighting the American forces after the overthrow of Saddam Hussein. Now, every night dozens of buses with tinted windows carried recruits from Yemen, Saudi Arabia, and Afghanistan into the base, which was surrounded by quiet farmlands. Many entered Iran under the pretext of being religious pilgrims and later were sent to Syria via Iraq. The training at Amir al-Momenin focused on small arms fire, munitions, and religious doctrine. "They are told that the war in Syria is akin to Imam Hussein's epic battle for Shiite Islam in Karbala, and if they die, they will be martyrs of the highest rank," said a Revolutionary Guard officer briefed on the running of the training camp. The Battle of Karbala, fought fourteen hundred years earlier, had been a rallying call for the Iranian regime and its Shiite allies across the Middle East, and now it was being used again.

Members of two Iraqi militias, Kata'ib Hezbollah and Asaib Ahl al-Haq, said in interviews near Damascus that they had been deployed into Syria in greater numbers throughout 2013 to help stabilize Assad's rule and protect Shiite mosques and shrines. Their members were seen patrolling sites near Damascus. Both groups were formed by the IRGC during the Iraq War and carried out some of the most sophisticated and lethal attacks on U.S. troops there. "Syria is the front line of resistance. We will support Syria until the end," General Soleimani told Iranian state media in the summer of 2013.

Soleimani's presence in Syria showed that the Iranian regime would do almost anything to save the Assad regime and to maintain regional power.

As the Obama administration tracked the increase of Iranian support for Syria during 2013, the pressure on the White House to provide significant amounts of arms and training to the Free Syrian Army intensified. Washington's key Mideast allies, particularly Saudi Arabia, Turkey, Jordan, and the UAE, believed President Obama was essentially sitting on his hands while Iran secured another major strategic victory in the Middle East. In saving Assad, the Revolutionary Guard was holding on to a land bridge linking Iran's borders to the Mediterranean via Iraq and Syria, Arab officials believed. Iran also continued to provide weapons and money to militias and political parties in Afghanistan, Yemen, and Bahrain, giving Tehran greater sway over the Persian Gulf and Central Asia. "They're trying to reconstitute the Persian Empire in just a few years," said a senior Jordanian official who tracked Tehran's regional activities after 9/11. "And the U.S. policies are only helping the Iranians."

For the United States, matching the Iranians gun for gun was never really an option because of Obama's aversion to being dragged into the conflict. The atrocities committed against civilians inside Syria were the worst the West had faced since the Balkan wars of the 1990s. And the Assad regime's systematic killing of its opposition was reminiscent of Nazi war crimes. Political opponents were tortured inside government camps or medical facilities and tracked using numbers instead of their names. Sixty thousand people were estimated to be killed in the camps alone.

Human rights groups increasingly charged the Assad regime with committing genocide against its own people. Some of President Obama's closest aides, including National Security Advisor Susan Rice, who served in the Clinton administration's State Department in the 1990s, and UN ambassador Samantha Power, were particularly sensitive to such accusations. Both had been critical of the Clinton administration's refusal to intervene in Rwanda in 1994 to stop tribal killings that left between eight hundred thousand and one million people dead in a little over a hundred days.

In 2012, the CIA established a small training facility for Syrian rebel fighters in Jordan in a bid to strengthen the performance of the opposition on the ground. The scale of the operation, however, was so minuscule that it was viewed as largely irrelevant by the Arab governments and Syrian rebel commanders who were briefed on it. The facility operated almost solely as a vetting house to ensure that the arms the Saudis and the Qataris were sending into Syria ended up in the hands of moderate Syrian fighters and not al Qaeda or ISIS. Washington's refusal to use the training base to send significant arms to the Free Syrian Army, specifically shoulder-fired missiles aimed at taking down Syrian aircraft, meant that Assad and his Iranian backers were able to maintain their military superiority on the battlefield. Washington's passivity left many Arab governments convinced the United States was secretly in league with Tehran. "We've seen almost nothing in terms of help from the Americans," General Yahya, the FSA intelligence chief, told me in the summer of 2013. "The Iranians are the only ones who are really active in the war."

A major shift in American strategy appeared to be taking shape after the United States and other Western powers accused President Assad and his generals of using nerve gas on Syrian civilians in late August 2013. For months Israel, Syria's rebel groups, and Arab governments had been amassing intelligence showing how the Syrian regime was using small amounts of weaponized gas to clear out rebel-controlled areas. The deaths associated with these attacks were low in number, but Assad's opponents believed he was increasingly testing the international community's resolve. Israel had traced around a half dozen of these small attacks in late 2012 and early 2013. President Obama had publicly stated that Damascus would be crossing a "red line" if it used weapons of mass destruction on its population, and could possibly face outside military retaliation. But the White House was largely silent about the deployment of these weapons, even as evidence of their use increased.

The mood shifted early on the morning of August 21, 2013, when Western intelligence agencies and Syrian rebels tracked the regime's bombardment of an opposition stronghold in the Damascus suburb of East Ghouta. The onslaught resulted in tons of mustard gas being dispersed on the local population within minutes, eventually leading to the deaths of nearly seventeen hundred Syrians. Videos of the victims captured on cellphones and video cameras showed women and children retching and gasping for air as the chemical agents seared their lungs. Very few of those afflicted—as few as fifty—were believed to be rebel fighters, according to the United Nations. The pressure on President Obama to enforce his red lines against Assad grew.

The following two weeks marked the most important deliberations on foreign policy during President Obama's first five years in office, according to U.S. and Arab officials who took part in them. The White House initially gave strong assurances to its Mideast allies and the rebels that the United States would strike Syria's air force and missile batteries as part of a limited campaign to cripple Assad's war machine. The White House believed the international community needed to send a strong warning to Syria and other rogue regimes that the use of chemical weapons wouldn't go unpunished in the modern era. Israeli and Arab officials said they hoped the strikes would also send a signal to Iran that the United States was serious about the potential of using force to prevent Iran's development of nuclear technologies.

Senior Saudi and Emirati officials said they received assurances from the Americans during those two weeks that the strikes on Assad were imminent. Commanders of the Free Syrian Army, meanwhile, prepared to launch a much broader military operation in parallel with the U.S. attack in the hope of quickly overthrowing the Assad regime. Syria's neighbors anticipated the U.S. onslaught with the hope it would put an end to the flood of refugees streaming across their borders, which was straining their resources.

On a trip I conducted along the Turkish-Syrian border in August 2013, senior FSA commanders were frantically and excitedly sending bombing targets and coordinates to the Pentagon from their bases in Turkish cities such as Gaziantep and Reyhanli. They identified key regime air bases and munitions factories they argued should be hit, as well as Syrian command-and-control centers. They planned to sequence their attacks with the U.S. air war. "We are getting ready and mobilized for the strikes," Abu Mohammad al-Attar, a Free Syrian Army commander, told me during a nighttime meeting at a hotel coffee shop in Gaziantep. He and other rebel leaders expressed concern that the Obama administration was more interested in punishing Assad for using chemical weapons than in seeking to topple his regime. But they remained optimistic that a major change in U.S. policy was at hand. "If the objective of the strikes is to collapse the regime, then there must be greater military and intelligence cooperation with the FSA," he said.

But just when Obama appeared ready to strike, the president reversed course. The White House officially cited the need for the administration to get congressional approval to launch military operations against the Syrian regime. They said such a legislative process could take weeks. Senior U.S. officials, however, privately said the president was never 100 percent committed to hitting Assad because of his continuing worry about dragging the United States into another Middle East war. The president and his senior staff were also still wary of allying too closely with Syria's rebels, given the presence of al Qaeda and other Sunni extremist groups within their ranks.

At the eleventh hour, the administration inexplicably made a U-turn and used the Syrian conflict to increase its engagement with Iran and Russia, Assad's principal backers. Even as the White House planned for military operations, the Obama administration was secretly holding talks with both Tehran and Moscow. U.S. and Iranian officials had already initiated the clandestine diplomacy on Tehran's nuclear program through Oman when the chemical weapons attacks occurred. President Obama and Secretary Kerry also had separately begun discussing with Vladimir Putin and his top aides a diplomatic process aimed at peacefully dismantling Assad's chemical weapons arsenal. The White House and Kremlin eventually agreed on such a deal. But it came at a significant cost—providing Assad a lease on life by giving him new legitimacy on the international stage. Iran's closest Arab ally had in essence been saved by Obama's reversal.

Iranian officials briefed on the talks with the United States in the summer of 2013 said Tehran made it clear to the American delegation that the nuclear negotiations would be halted if the United States went ahead with its attack on Assad. Iran's military and clerics would view such strikes as equivalent to the United States' declaring war on Iran. "The Iranian diplomats said it wouldn't be their decision to end the dialogue, but that support in Tehran for the negotiations would evaporate," said a senior Iranian official briefed on the

U.S.-Iranian diplomacy that August. "The Revolutionary Guard and the leader's office would view this as another sign of the U.S.'s efforts to weaken the regime. They couldn't lose Syria."

The Obama administration denied it was talked out of attacking Syria by either Iran or Russia. President Obama also hailed the agreement on dismantling Assad's chemical weapons arsenal as one of his greatest diplomatic achievements. But the president's decision not to bomb Syria permanently sucked the air out of Syria's moderate opposition and gave life to the more radical elements fighting the Assad regime, including ISIS. The White House's deal with Putin and the secret talks with Iran also fanned fears within the Sunni Arab states that the White House was shifting its strategic position in the region and entering into an informal alliance with Iran. Such a convergence posed an existential threat to the interests of Saudi Arabia, the UAE, Jordan, and the other major Sunni states, according to diplomats from these governments. This unease over Tehran's rapprochement with Washington led to a growing flow of financial support for Sunni militant groups, such as al Qaeda and ISIS, which were challenging Shiite-dominated Iran, according to U.S. officials.

"The U.S. gave us the impression that they were going to do things in Syria that they finally didn't," the Saudi prince Turki al-Faisal, a brother of foreign minister Saud al-Faisal, told me in a late December 2013 interview in Monaco. "The aid they're giving to the Free Syrian Army is irrelevant. Now they say they're going to stop the aid. OK, stop it. It's not doing anything anyway." On Iran, Prince Turki said his government felt betrayed. "What was surprising was that the talks that were going forward were kept from us," the Saudi royal said. "How can you build trust when you keep secrets from what are supposed to be your closest allies?"

SYRIA'S CIVIL WAR FED into the virus of fanatical Sunni extremism that first raised its head in the 1990s with the rise of al Qaeda. But unlike Osama bin Laden's global operations, which yielded little in terms of territorial gains, Syria bred a much more lethal monster. The Islamic State used Syria's violence and lawlessness to raise recruits from across the Arab world and funding from Persian Gulf Arab citizens eager to push back against Iran's territorial gains through its alliances with the Assad regime and Iraqi government. ISIS eventually gained control of large swaths of northern and eastern Syria and expanded its presence into much of western Iraq. The organization's gains served as a rallying call for global Islamist extremists, many of whom had appeared to be defeated or on the wane after the United States and its allies dismantled much of al Qaeda's senior leadership in the years following 9/11.

Even though ISIS declared itself at war with the Syrian government, Iran, and the broader Shiite world, the Islamist movement actually benefited from the policies of Damascus and Tehran. Syrian rebel leaders and Obama administration officials claimed the two governments knowingly abetted the rise of the terrorist organization in a bid to safeguard Assad's hold on power by portraying him as the lesser of two evils. Indeed, both Syria's security services and the Revolutionary Guard have displayed a willingness in recent decades to work with Sunni militant groups, even elements of al Qaeda, if they were in conflict with the United States and its allies. The old axiom "The enemy of my enemy is my friend" appeared to rule their foreign policy.

"Is there a symbiotic relationship between Iran and ISIS? It doesn't seem like ISIS is coming under direct attack by the IRGC or the Qods Force," said a retired Pentagon official who plotted operations against Iran. He said Iran appeared to use the presence of ISIS in Syria and Iraq as "an excuse" to deploy troops in these countries without necessarily targeting them.

ISIS's ideology was so radical that its war against rival Syrian militias was just as fearsome as its war against Damascus. Assad and his top advisors purposely didn't attack ISIS positions in northern Syria during some stages of the civil war, according to Syrian and Iraqi officials, as the Damascus regime viewed the militia as capable of weakening the Free Syrian Army and other moderate or secular opposition groups. Some Arab officials allied with Assad publicly admitted that Syria's leader ordered his military to stand down in order to gauge just how much damage ISIS could inflict on the FSA. "When the Syrian army is not fighting the Islamic State, this makes the group [ISIS] stronger," Izzat Shahbandar, a top aide to Iraqi prime minister Nouri al-Maliki, told *The Wall Street Journal* in a mid-2014 interview after meeting Assad in Damascus. "Sometimes, the army gives [ISIS] a safe path to allow the Islamic State to attack the FSA and seize their weapons."

While the Obama administration didn't see any direct operational coordination between the Assad regime and ISIS, they did see financial ties. ISIS gained control of the oil-rich provinces in central and eastern Syria, such as Deir Ezzour and Hassaekh, and began selling some of its energy to the regime. The funds allowed ISIS to finance its rapid growth. "We have seen what appear to be credible reports . . . about deals between the regime and al-Qaeda linked terrorist groups in Syria concerning the sale of petroleum products," said a senior U.S. official who closely tracked ISIS in early 2014. "It is a known fact that the regime has declined to hit the headquarters of the al-Qaeda linked Islamic State group . . . but they've hit plenty of other targets belonging to other armed groups in Raqqah."

Iran too played a double game with al Qaeda and other Sunni militants operating in Syria. While Tehran publicly cited these terrorist groups as existential threats to Iran, U.S. intelligence officials began to note that the regime was facilitating the flow of al Qaeda fighters into Syria beginning in 2013 and continuing into 2014. Some of the al Qaeda leaders whom the Iranians allowed to establish bases in and around Tehran were key moneymen and logisticians for the organization. The Revolutionary Guard and Iran's intelligence services closely monitored these men to make sure their operations were only targeting the West and Assad's enemies, but otherwise allowed them free rein.

The Treasury sanctioned Jafar al-Uzbeki, a member of the Islamic Jihad Union, in early 2014 for using Iran to move fighters into Syria. The United States said Uzbeki was part of an al Qaeda network operating from Iran that has also brought fighters into Pakistan and Afghanistan, and which operated in Tehran with the knowledge of Iranian authorities. "The network . . . uses Iran as a transit point for moving funding and foreign fighters through Turkey to support al-Qa'ida-affiliated elements inside Syria," the Treasury said, freezing any money the Uzbek warlord held in U.S. dollars.

ISIS's growth across Syria and Iraq and its decimation of the FSA and other secular Syrian militias eventually posed a major territorial and political threat both to the Assad regime and to the Iranian government. The shift again provided the opportunity for the United States and Iran to cooperate in facing the challenge of Sunni extremism, as they had in Afghanistan more than a decade earlier. But it remained to be seen if the IRGC and Khamenei would work with the United States to contest a threat so close to Iran's borders.

Meanwhile, ISIS's growth was posing a much broader threat to the wider world and Europe. Millions of Syrian refugees flooded into Turkey, Jordan, and Lebanon to get away from the terrorist group's genocidal wrath. And many of the displaced then traveled on to European countries such as Germany, France, and Austria in the hopes of finding a permanent safe haven. Europeans gripe that U.S. inaction in Syria was a primary reason behind the greatest refugee crisis in their region since World War II. And critics of the Obama administration said its hesitancy to act was driven by the White House's desire to reach a rapprochement with Iran. A nuclear deal would be an achievement, but at what cost? Was it worth the hundreds of thousands dead in Syria?

Joseph Bahout, a French academic and diplomat who specializes in Syria and the Levant, said, "U.S. policies in Iraq and Syria were subjected to the pursuit of the Iran deal and not antagonizing Iran." Even so, France was just one of many U.S. allies who didn't realize how far Obama had gone in reaching out to Tehran.

CHAPTER 10

The Road to Vienna

G LOBAL POWERS COULDN'T HAVE KNOWN IT AT THE TIME, BUT AN unlikely Arab monarchy was creating an opening to Tehran, even as Iran and the United States were mired in Syria. Salem ben Nasser al-Ismaily was hardly a high-profile player on the global stage when President Barack Obama entered office. But the Omani businessman, academic, and diplomat found himself and his country in a unique position to be able to repair Washington's thirty-five-year rift with Tehran.

Just months after Obama's election, Ismaily traveled to Washington in 2009 as an emissary for Oman's long-serving monarch, Sultan Qaboos bin Said al Said. The American-educated envoy had a proposition for the White House and one of the Obama administration's top Middle East hands, Dennis Ross: Oman could serve as an intermediary between Tehran and Washington in an effort to heal their disagreements over the nuclear issue and other outstanding issues. The sultan had received the blessing of Iran's top leaders to pursue this mission. The sultan saw it as his religious and sovereign duty to preempt a military confrontation between Iran and the United

States that could destroy his region. Situated 150 miles from the Iranian coast, Oman would suffer both economically and strategically from a conflict.

But Ismaily conveyed to Ross and the White House that if they wanted to pursue this Omani channel to Tehran, there was a list of steps the Americans needed to take to show Tehran their goodwill. These included releasing Iranian prisoners held in U.S. jails, increasing the quota for Iranian students allowed to study in American universities, and targeting Iranian militias and organizations viewed as hostile to the Iranian regime. These steps could be the start of a conversation between Washington and Tehran, Ismaily told Ross. The ball was in Obama's court.

Ismaily's official title was executive director of the sultanate's investment authority, the Omani Centre for Investment Promotion and Export Development. The fifty-eight-year-old was among the closest aides of the sultan, and held an assortment of degrees from U.S. and British universities in everything from telecommunications and engineering to business administration. Ismaily sought to advance the sultan's vision of making his tiny kingdom on the Persian Gulf a modern economic state that promoted religious tolerance and peace in a tumultuous Middle East. Ismaily normally appeared in traditional Omani dress, even with Westerners. This included a long, flowing white gown, called the *dishdasha*, and a colorful aqua turban that spoke to Oman's pristine tropical waters. He wanted Oman integrated into the global economy, hopes he iterated in his American-accented English at World Economic Forum conferences and through books such as *A Cup of Coffee: A Westerner's Guide to Business Culture in the Gulf States* and *Messengers of Monotheism: A Common Heritage of Christians, Jews and Muslims*. He was an Arab Renaissance man.

"The policy of peace is good for everyone," Ismaily told a gathering of the World Economic Forum in Jordan in 2011. "You cannot lose [with] a policy of peace. It's very important to create an environment that is conducive for doing business."

Ismaily also played a unique diplomatic role in Sultan Qaboos's royal court: special envoy to Oman's powerful neighbor, Iran. This role was a sensitive one for Ismaily but also a testament to his abilities, and to Muscat's historically close ties to both Tehran and Washington. Now seventy-five years old, Qaboos was indebted to Iran for his long rule, which was a result of the military support the shah provided in the 1970s. Communist insurgents had spilled over from Yemen and were close to taking Muscat in 1976 when the Iranian ruler sent in helicopter gunships and tens of thousands of his troops to push back the rebels. The military operation allowed Sultan Qaboos to survive and become the longest-reigning ruler among the Persian Gulf's monarchs. Even after the shah was deposed, the sultan sought to keep cordial relations with Tehran's Islamist rulers, despite their inherent hostility toward Arabs and monarchies. Iran's revolutionary government was founded on the premise of overthrowing the regional order as well as expelling U.S. forces. Qaboos's willingness to engage Tehran placed him regularly at odds with Arab leaders on a range of regional issues.

The United States, however, was also central to Oman's security in a region where very few of the Arab emirs and sultans trusted one another, and none of them wanted to be entirely beholden to regional heavyweights Saudi Arabia and Iran. Uniquely, U.S.-Omani relations stretched all the way back to the early years after the American Revolution. In 1833, in a bid to secure its global shipping routes from pirates and hostile colonial powers, Washington and Muscat signed a treaty of friendship and navigation, the first of its kind between the United States and an Arab state. Oman, abutting the Straits of Hormuz, was crucial to securing the flow of U.S. energy exports heading across the Atlantic. In 1980, after the Iranian revolution, Sultan Qaboos agreed to allow U.S. warships and aircraft to use Omani military facilities. The deal was a hedge against any Iranian attempt to spread its revolution into Oman or disrupt the flow of oil through the strategic Straits of Hormuz, off Oman's coastline. The sultan trusted Iran's ayatollahs only so far.

"We always must walk a cautious line between Iran and the U.S.," Ismaily told me in a May 2015 interview at a Dead Sea resort in Jordan. "For us, it's best if relations between the two countries are stable. We want to serve as a bridge between the two sides."

For a decade, Ismaily used his position on the investment board to promote business between Oman and Iran. The sultan was interested in building a gas pipeline from the Iranian coast to Oman, both to fuel his country's economy and to develop an export platform for Tehran's energy products. In 2010, Ismaily attempted to set up a $50 million joint venture with Iran to promote the sale of Omani goods and services inside Iran. The move piqued the interest of the American embassy in Muscat because of its potential to break U.S. sanctions laws on Tehran. Still, U.S. diplomats appeared sympathetic to Ismaily's ambitions, even if they couldn't support them. "Iran is a logical export destination as an historic trading partner and the inexpensive shipping costs given the proximity," a U.S. diplomat in Muscat wrote back to the State Department about Ismaily's trips. "It makes economic sense to pursue these ties."

Ismaily, however, emerged as much more than a businessman, author, and would-be theologian as relations between the United States and Iran spiraled downward and fears of war grew during the Bush and early Obama administrations. Oman and Sultan Qaboos had long served as a back channel among Washington, Tehran, and the Arab countries. The ruler tried to mediate the release of the American hostages held in Tehran in 1980, according to U.S. officials. Qaboos had also served as a bridge between Israel and the Arabs at a time when most Muslim countries wouldn't have any contacts with the Jewish state. In 1994, Qaboos hosted Israeli prime minister Yitzhak Rabin in a successful bid to forge limited diplomatic and trade ties, which focused on medicine, irrigation technologies, and agricultural products—an agreement that chagrined many of Oman's neighbors. Muscat also helped gain the release of

European and American sailors captured by the IRGC in disputed waters of the Persian Gulf in recent decades.

ISMAILY'S ROLE AS PEACEMAKER took center stage just months after his first 2009 discussions with the White House. His emergence wasn't initially tied to Iran's nuclear program or the steady buildup of U.S. naval forces in the Persian Gulf. It was a humanitarian gesture focused on gaining the release of kidnapped American citizens.

Far off in the remote mountains of Iraqi Kurdistan in July 2009, three American hikers, Sarah Shourd, Joshua Fattal, and Shane Bauer, unintentionally crossed into Iranian territory. Shourd and Bauer had been living in Damascus, Syria, and using the country as a base for development work, journalism, and Arabic study when their friend Fattal visited. The three UC Berkeley graduates decided to take a vacation in Kurdistan that summer and make the hike to the famous Ahmed Awa waterfalls near the Iranian border.

Bauer, Fattal, and Shourd said they believed they were still on the Iraqi side when Revolutionary Guards beckoned them through a megaphone to come to an Iranian military base. The Americans were uncertain about the location, and the Iranians quickly arrested them. They were then transferred to Tehran's maximum-security Evin prison—which holds most of the country's top imprisoned political activists and dissidents—where they were charged with espionage. Iran's security services said the three Americans were working for the CIA and had secretly crossed into Iran to conduct surveillance activities and attempt to incite unrest among Iran's minority Arab and Kurdish populations. The Americans and the U.S. government repeatedly denied the charges.

The Americans' arrests came at a particularly delicate time in relations between the United States and Iran. Nationwide protests against Ahmadinejad's reelection were in full swing in the summer of 2009, and Iran's rulers accused the Obama administration of instigating the unrest, despite criticism back in Washington that the

White House wasn't doing anything to support Iran's democracy movement. U.S. officials worried that Tehran might try to use the three hikers as bargaining chips to guard against Washington's providing significant political or material support to the opposition Green Movement. Tehran had already arrested a number of Iranian Americans during Ahmadinejad's tenure and charged them with espionage, though most would be released.

World leaders and celebrities, including UN secretary-general Ban Ki Moon, boxer Muhammad Ali, and singer Yusuf Islam (formerly Cat Stevens), all publicly called for the release of Bauer, Fattal, and Shourd. But Tehran failed to respond, providing Ismaily with an opening to prove his and the sultan's bona fides to both the Americans and the Iranians. Ismaily's years of cultivating relationships in Washington and Tehran were about to bear fruit, but he'd need to reach out to the highest echelons of the Iranian supreme leader's office and the Revolutionary Guard to achieve his goal. He'd be in regular contact with the White House and State Department to coordinate his efforts.

Beginning in 2010, Ismaily began shuttling between Muscat and Tehran to secure the Americans' release. His mission was made urgent by growing concerns about the captives' health in prison. All three had been held for various periods of time in solitary confinement and told their parents they were enduring self-imposed fasts and bouts of depression and weight loss. Sarah Shourd discovered a lump on her breast and was worried she might be suffering from early-stage cancer. Senior U.S. officials, including Secretary of State Hillary Clinton, maintained a constant drumbeat of calls demanding the Americans' release. But there were no signs the Iranians were close to capitulating.

Ismaily, though, unbeknownst to the Western media, was seeking to make the Americans deliver on the Iranian wish list he had already delivered to the White House a year earlier. Dozens of Iranian prisoners were detained in the United States and Europe on charges of arms smuggling and violating the draconian sanctions the West had imposed on Iran over the past decade. Many, like the American hikers, had become cause célèbres in their home country, and Tehran's leadership saw political gains to be made in securing their release. A former Iranian ambassador to Jordan, Nosratollah Tajik, was under house arrest in London for allegedly smuggling night-vision equipment back to Iran. An Iranian mother of two, Shahrzad Mir Gholikan, was serving a five-year sentence in Minnesota for shipping the same equipment. Her daughters tearfully took to Iranian television to call for her release.

Ismaily secretly worked out a plan that would gain the release of the Iranians in exchange for the return of the hikers. It would be a sequenced exchange playing out over three years, according to U.S. and Omani officials who took part in it. But it would allow both Washington and Tehran to claim political victories at home while building a bridge to pursue the nuclear negotiations. Ismaily also persuaded the Obama administration to eventually double the number of Iranian students allowed to enter the United States. And the State Department imposed sanctions on a Pakistan-based militant group that had been launching terrorist attacks against the Revolutionary Guard in eastern Iran.

In September 2010, Ismaily got approval from the Iranian government to bring a payment to Tehran to secure Sarah Shourd's release. The amount was $500,000, but neither the United States nor Oman would say whether the families, Sultan Qaboos, or another party provided the funds. Ismaily personally flew to Tehran in September 2010 to accompany the thirty-one-year-old back to Muscat, where she was reunited with her family. Tehran made it clear the espionage charges against Shourd stood, while she said she wouldn't stop campaigning until her two friends returned.

It took Ismaily another year to gain the release of Bauer and Fattal, which took place in September 2011. Again, the price was $500,000 each—fueling criticism in Congress that the U.S. government was essentially paying ransom to Tehran for the hikers' return.

But for the Obama administration, Ismaily's ability to deliver the Americans made it clear to the White House that Oman was a country the United States could use in its sensitive dealings with Iran. It was a channel President Obama and other U.S. officials would repeatedly rely on in the ensuing years.

"The Omanis came to us indicating that, 'Hey, if you ever want to have a conversation [with Iran], keep us in mind,'" Deputy National Security Advisor Ben Rhodes said. "So we always knew that was there. Then we negotiated the hikers through the Omanis, and that worked out well."

Out of the spotlight of the American media, Ismaily quietly brought back to Tehran four Iranians held in the United States and the United Kingdom. These included Tajik and Gholikan. They were photographed at Oman's international airport, essentially making the same trip as the hikers had, but in reverse. In a few of the photos, Ismaily can be seen standing quietly in the background on the tarmac with a wide smile. He'd taken a key step in his plans to build a bridge between Washington and Tehran.

JOHN KERRY WAS AMONG the most keen to take the Omanis up on their offer to facilitate a dialogue with Iran. The Massachusetts politician was chairman of the Senate Foreign Relations Committee in late 2011 and was pursuing an aggressive diplomatic agenda from his office in Congress, sometimes in league with the White House, but not always. The former presidential candidate had established his own connections with Salem Ismaily and saw an opportunity in the Oman channel. He began communicating to the Iranians via Muscat months before he assumed the leadership at Foggy Bottom.

Kerry crisscrossed the globe during Obama's first term to advance Washington's (and his own) foreign policy agenda. He repeatedly met with Afghan president Hamid Karzai to keep the mercurial leader behind the U.S. war against al Qaeda and the Taliban. Kerry's efforts to woo Syrian president Bashar al-Assad into the American camp ultimately failed, but they also solidified the U.S. politician's reputation as a man who would take great risks to advance a diplomatic cause. Kerry even plotted to fly to Tehran in a bid to become the first senior American to hold a dialogue with Iranian officials in their capital since the 1979 revolution. The White House publicly backed such a trip by Kerry in late 2009, despite concerns that it could lend legitimacy to President Ahmadinejad, whose reelection was still being challenged by a nationwide protest movement. The Iranians, however, never came through with an invitation.

Following Oman's successful effort to broker the three American hikers' release, Kerry saw his opening to establish a U.S. channel to Iran. On December 8, 2011, the senator conspicuously missed a Senate confirmation vote in Washington on President Obama's nominee to head the Consumer Financial Protection Bureau, Richard Cordray. Kerry's absence sparked questions from the Capitol Hill press corps about his whereabouts, which Kerry's office refused to answer. As it turned out, he was already on an overnight commercial flight to the Persian Gulf.

The next day, Kerry had an audience of more than two hours with Sultan Qaboos at his ornate palace on the outskirts of Muscat. The vast whitewashed facility overlooked the Persian Gulf's azure waters from a perch on Oman's dry coastline. "I began long conversations to try and lay the groundwork for" direct U.S.-Iranian talks, Kerry told me in describing the development of the Oman channel. "The sultan and I really became quite friendly. . . . We got to know each other very well, and he got to trusting me."

There was really only one topic on the meeting agenda: could the sultan actually facilitate a high-level discussion between the Americans and the Iranians in Muscat, solely focused on the nuclear issue? President Obama wanted to resolve the issue peacefully, Kerry told the monarch, but believed the time for such diplomacy was running out because Tehran was advancing to the point where it could produce a bomb. The White House wanted the discussion to be held in secret, shielded from the prying lenses of the global media. Not even the United States' closest Mideast allies, Israel and Saudi Arabia, could know about it, Kerry said. There were real fears these countries might try to sabotage the process, due to their deep distrust of Tehran.

Kerry returned to Washington and briefed President Obama's national security team about the sultan's offer. He directly described the channel to Hillary Clinton, who was open to it. "We didn't approach this with the sense this was definitely going to happen," Kerry said. "We approached it as a possibility."

The Americans were encouraged by the response from the Iranian side. Ismaily had been communicating with two of Supreme Leader Khamenei's closest advisors. This included his top foreign policy aide, Ali Akbar Velayati, and Foreign Minister Ali Akbar Salehi. Both men were U.S.-educated and had spent significant time living in Baltimore and Boston, respectively. But they were seen as hard-liners in the Iranian system and were understood to speak for Khamenei. The White House didn't seem to be at risk of communicating with officials who couldn't deliver in a negotiation.

Kerry, however, walked a fine line in his communications with the Iranians and tended to make assurances he wasn't authorized to make. The White House didn't want to offer any concessions before formal negotiations took place. But the senator did indicate that Washington would likely be willing to accept Tehran maintaining its capability to enrich uranium, provided there were strong safeguards put in place.

"Kerry was actually talking substance with the Omanis. . . . We were very careful to make clear that we were not taking negotiating positions," Ben Rhodes said of the senator's efforts. "Kerry actually was, in his non-official capacity, floating proposals, talking about things like enrichment."

So the Iranians came to negotiations believing they had already bagged a major concession.

———

SIX MONTHS LATER, Ismaily and the Omanis followed through on their promise to bring the Americans and Iranians together in Muscat. A motley diplomatic team led the U.S. side at this first meeting. Jake Sullivan was Hillary Clinton's deputy chief of staff in July 2012, and the youngest-ever director of the State Department's policy planning office. He was a golden boy inside the Democratic political and foreign policy establishment. A Minnesota native, the Yale-educated lawyer played a major role in shaping the 2008 presidential campaign, tutoring first Clinton and then Barack Obama on debating tactics and strategies. Sullivan had been a Rhodes scholar and edited the *Yale Law Journal*. Many Democrats assumed Sullivan, just thirty-six at the time, would one day become secretary of state or national security advisor on his own, particularly if Clinton was elected president.

Accompanying Sullivan was Puneet Talwar, a man who assiduously kept a much lower political and diplomatic profile in Washington. Talwar was the National Security Council's point man on Iran and issues dealing with the Persian Gulf. The Indian American was the White House's representative to all the international negotiations on Iran's nuclear program that had been held up to that point. Talwar purposely kept out of the public eye and almost never spoke to the media. He was the perfect "gray man," to use the espionage term, to take part in such a secret trip to Oman—loyal, dependable, and someone who easily blended in among the businessmen and traders who traveled to Muscat.

Talwar benefited from another asset no one else in President Obama's national security staff possessed: extensive dealings with Iranian government officials. During much of the 2000s, Talwar was a staffer on the Senate Foreign Relations Committee, then headed by Joe Biden. As part of his duties, Talwar intermittently attended international conferences focused on nuclear proliferation and ending the crisis over Tehran's program. The events were described as "track two" diplomacy, as no active American officials attended the meetings, which took place at universities and hotel conference rooms in European cities such as Stockholm and Vienna. Iranian diplomats who would gain top positions in the governments of Presidents Ahmadinejad and Rouhani, however, did take part. Among them were Javad Zarif and Ali Akbar Salehi.

The White House hoped Talwar could capitalize on his experience, and these contacts, to smooth the way for a direct dialogue with Tehran. He and Sullivan were a diplomatic one-two punch: Talwar the consummate low-key bureaucrat, and his younger partner a politically connected, emerging Democratic star. "In an administration where the White House dominates Iran policy, it makes sense that Puneet played this role" of interlocutor, said a former Western diplomat who discussed the secret diplomacy with Talwar at the time. His ties to Obama were crucial.

Sullivan and Talwar were uncertain whom they would meet upon their arrival in Oman on a warm July evening. Iranian media had run articles suggesting that a close advisor to Ayatollah Khamenei would likely be the emissary for any direct discussions with the Americans. Some of the stories focused on Ali Akbar Velayati, a physician and onetime foreign minister. Velayati would be a controversial choice: as previously noted, an Argentine prosecutor had issued an arrest warrant for him in 2007 after charging the Iranian with helping to plot the 1994 bombing of the Jewish community center in Buenos Aires. Tehran had repeatedly denied the charges. But the American delegation was reluctant to meet an Iranian official with such an allegedly bloody past.

Sullivan and Talwar met neither. A midlevel Iranian diplomat of whom very few Americans had ever heard arrived in Muscat as part of a small Iranian delegation. Ali Asghar Khaji was deputy foreign minister and headed the Iranian Foreign Ministry's North American division. He had extensive experience dealing with the West, having served as Tehran's ambassador to the European Union. He met regularly with then EU foreign policy chief Catherine Ashton while in

Brussels and even conferred with officials at the North Atlantic Treaty Organization, rare for an Iranian diplomat. He didn't seem to have real political power in Tehran or the direct line to Ayatollah Khamenei that Salehi or Velayati had. But the Americans were still encouraged. "The main purpose for us was: who were they going to send from their side? . . . The Iranians sent some real people," Rhodes said. "At that point, we knew the Omanis could set up a real meeting."

Sitting down with Khaji in Muscat, the Americans quickly realized the Iranian brought no new Iranian diplomatic overtures, nor was he empowered to do so. Instead, he repeated the same line Ahmadinejad's negotiators had presented during numerous earlier rounds of negotiations with the United States and other global powers. If the West lifted sanctions on Iran and accepted Tehran's right to produce nuclear fuel, then there could be discussions on how to address international concerns that Tehran was seeking to develop nuclear weapons. Until that happened, Khaji said, there wasn't much more to discuss. Sullivan, Talwar, and their team left Oman dejected and worried about the future of the diplomacy. "We essentially hit the same brick wall," said one of the Americans who took part in the meetings.

HASSAN ROUHANI WAS ELECTED Iran's new president almost a year later—in June 2013—and immediately shook up the global diplomatic establishment. His victory shocked Washington, which had expected a more hard-line politician to win. An Islamic cleric who studied judicial law in Glasgow, Scotland, in the 1990s, Rouhani campaigned on a platform of ending Iran's diplomatic isolation and reviving its moribund economy, ravaged by the West's international sanctions. He advocated for the immediate resolution of Iran's dispute with the West over its nuclear program through new negotiations. And he viciously attacked Ahmadinejad's eight-year rule for needlessly alienating Iran from a global community Rouhani believed Iran should help lead. The 2013 election showed that Iran, despite being a theocratic state with a supreme leader, still had one of the Middle East's more open political systems.

Rouhani's victory posed a quandary for the Obama administration and its allies in Israel and Saudi Arabia. While he preached moderation, the sixty-four-year-old was still a regime insider and a close confidant of Khamenei's. For a decade Rouhani had led the government's most powerful national security body, the Supreme National Security Council, which advised the supreme leader on foreign policy. And Rouhani was no stranger to the West, having served as Tehran's chief nuclear negotiator from 2003 to 2005, when talks took place between Iran and the so-called EU-3 (Britain, France, and Germany). In 2004, Rouhani's team had agreed to freeze Iran's nuclear work in exchange for economic incentives, a major breakthrough at the time. However, the deal later fell through as both sides charged the other with failing to follow through on their commitments. Rouhani perplexed the West: he appeared more moderate and accommodating but was still a regime stalwart.

Rouhani's political position offered both opportunities and challenges for U.S. foreign policy. The new president's close relationship to Khamenei meant Rouhani might facilitate a compromise with the West on the nuclear issue that Iran's previous reformist president, Mohammad Khatami, couldn't, because of his lack of political support in Tehran. Some U.S. officials compared Rouhani to Richard Nixon, seeing both men as conservative politicians who had the political and diplomatic strength at home to make peace with a long-standing enemy, be it communist China or the Great Satan. Engaging with Rouhani, American officials argued, could also strengthen moderate political forces in Tehran that had been marginalized during Ahmadinejad's rule.

Israeli and Saudi officials, however, feared Rouhani was part of an elaborate Persian ruse. They argued that in Iran's theocratic system, political leaders often fluctuated between hard-liners and moderates, but that ultimately it didn't matter, because only one man—Khamenei—made the policy decisions, and he was committed to conflict with the West. They also doubted Rouhani was seriously committed to dismantling Iran's nuclear program; rather, they thought, he was solely focused on removing the financial and diplomatic pressures being imposed on Iran by the West. They cited comments Rouhani had made in Tehran following his term as the nuclear negotiator, when he claimed his diplomacy provided Iran with cover to move forward with its nuclear work. "While we were talking with the Europeans in Tehran, we were installing equipment in parts of the facility in Isfahan [the uranium conversion plant], but we still had a long way to go to complete the project," Rouhani said in a 2006 speech. "In fact, by creating a calm environment, we were able to complete the work on Isfahan."

ROUHANI WASTED LITTLE TIME in projecting himself as a moderate and pragmatist who wanted to build bridges to the West. He spoke of loosening the social restrictions put in place during Ahmadinejad's tenure, attracting foreign investment, and ridding Iran of the corruption he said was a cancer eating away at the Iranian economy. He also called for a quick resolution of the nuclear stand-off. "The only way to interact with Iran is to have dialogue from an equal position, creating mutual trust and respect and reducing enmities," Rouhani said in his inaugural August 2013 speech. "Let me state it clearly that if you want a positive response, talk to Iran not with a language of sanctions but a language of respect."

To reach out to the West and Washington, Rouhani installed Javad Zarif as his foreign minister. The former ambassador to the United Nations had cooperated closely with the Bush administration in establishing a post-Taliban government in Afghanistan. To Obama administration officials, Zarif's appointment was an olive branch, and it was a signal Tehran was serious about returning to the negotiating table. They also saw the makeup of Rouhani's first cabinet as an effort by Iran's new president to reduce the power of the

Revolutionary Guard: only three ministers out of an eighteen-member cabinet were associated with the IRGC, compared to nine during Ahmadinejad's last year in office.

Zarif quickly reconnected with contacts he'd made in Washington, New York, and Brussels during his tenure at the United Nations. These included a mix of active and former American diplomats, U.S. lawmakers, journalists, and heads of prominent think tanks. He conveyed to them his belief that a deal on the nuclear issue based on some of the terms negotiated between Rouhani's diplomatic team and the Europeans in the early 2000s could be quickly negotiated. These included limits on Iran's production of nuclear fuel, curbs on the numbers of centrifuges it had enriching uranium, and greater monitoring of Tehran's nuclear facilities by the IAEA. In return, Zarif told his interlocutors, Tehran expected a rapid unraveling of the Western sanctions.

U.S. officials privately worried that Zarif was moving too fast to try to cinch a deal. They hoped he'd slow down the process. But the Obama administration saw Rouhani's arrival as a potential watershed. "The election of Rouhani likely opened things up a bit on their side," said Wendy Sherman, the State Department official who ran the day-to-day Iran nuclear policy. "If they didn't get a better economic future for their country, they could create a risk for themselves."

Zarif also sought to make clear to the world that the Ahmadinejad era—marked by the leader's Holocaust denial and threats to Israel—was over. On September 4, 2013, the diplomat took to the Internet and tweeted "Happy Rosh Hashanah" to the world's Jewry. His message astonished many in the Obama administration, considering that Ahmadinejad had regularly threatened to "wipe Israel off the face of time" and openly questioned the historical validity of the Holocaust. Many Iran watchers wondered if the tweet was genuine, given the ridicule Zarif was likely to face from conservative clerics and IRGC officers inside Iran.

Among those watching Zarif was Christine Pelosi, daughter of

Nancy Pelosi, a California congresswoman and former Speaker of the House. The documentary filmmaker was raised a Catholic, but her husband was Jewish and her daughter attended a Jewish pre-school. The younger Pelosi challenged the Iranian diplomat on Twitter: "Thanks. The New Year would be even sweeter if you would end Iran's Holocaust denial, sir."

Zarif wasted little time in responding: "Iran never denied it. The man who was perceived to be denying it is now gone. Happy New Year."

TOTALLY UNKNOWN TO THE outside world, the secret diplomatic channel established between Iran and the United States through Oman intensified once Rouhani took office, and at a significantly higher level. William Burns, the unflappable deputy secretary of state who had met with the Iranians earlier in Switzerland, joined Sullivan and Talwar in traveling to Muscat in the weeks after Rouhani's August inauguration.

Burns, Sullivan, and Talwar began a flurry of meetings with Iranian diplomats, not just in Muscat but also in Geneva and New York. The purpose of these meetings was to create an interim agreement that would freeze parts of Tehran's nuclear program and provide more time and diplomatic space for Washington and Tehran to forge a final deal.

The strategy drew heavily from the "fuel swap" agreement Burns thought he had secured with Iran in 2009. This plan held that the United States should get Iran to freeze its production of nuclear fuel in exchange for economic benefits. The American line continued to be that the United States wanted Iran to eventually dismantle its centrifuges to guard against Tehran diverting any nuclear fuel for military purposes. But Kerry and other U.S. officials had already begun signaling to the Iranians that the United States was flexible on this issue. On other areas, they still weren't: Iran should dismantle its heavy water reactor, which was seen as largely a bomb-making facility. Iran should also close its underground enrichment facility in the city of Qom, which was seen as having been built solely for the purpose of producing weapons-grade uranium. The United States at this stage showed no inclination that it would accede to Iran's other demands: the lifting of the UN resolution that barred Iran from developing ballistic missiles and a separate resolution that prevented countries from trading arms with the Iranians.

Concerns continued to mount at this time that Israel could launch unilateral military strikes against Iran later in 2013 if diplomacy wasn't effective in extending the time Tehran needed to build an atomic weapon. The White House was intensely focused on heading off such an Israeli attack and trying to forge some common ground with the new Rouhani government in Tehran.

PARTICIPANTS IN THESE MEETINGS said there was a lot of early jockeying between the Americans and Iranians in an effort to understand the other side's positions. Sullivan at one point quizzed Iran's deputy foreign minister, Abbas Araghchi, about the rationale behind Tehran's nuclear program. The Minnesota native said it was inconceivable to most Westerners that Iran's program could have any purpose other than to build atomic bombs. The economics behind it made no sense, Sullivan argued. Iran had massive amounts of oil and gas, and it could have developed much cheaper nuclear power simply by purchasing enriched uranium from foreign suppliers.

Araghchi pushed back. He cited the U.S. space program in the 1960s and 1970s and the quest to put a man on the moon. Washington derived little economic gain from the lunar walk, the former Iranian ambassador to Japan said. But the feat generated an enormous amount of national pride in the United States and bred scientific innovation. Iran's nuclear program "is our moon shot," Araghchi told the Americans.

———

KERRY'S FIRST DIRECT CONTACT with Zarif, which captivated the world, came at the September 2013 session of the United Nations General Assembly in New York. The annual event brings together the world's leaders for two weeks of speeches, dinners, and diplomacy in the spotlight of Manhattan. In the past, the meetings had been a showcase for President Ahmadinejad's radical views: he had used his appearances to question the Holocaust, Washington's narrative about the 9/11 attacks, and the wisdom of American foreign policy, and he had sought to rally the developing world against the United States and the cabal of imperialists, Zionists, and neocolonialists he claimed were exploiting Muslim, African, and Latin American populations globally. Ahmadinejad's presence sparked sizable protests every year from Jewish, Iranian, and human rights groups who assembled across the street from the UN's building in Turtle Bay.

But Rouhani and Zarif were committed to erasing Ahmadinejad's legacy and portraying Iran as a responsible actor on the global stage during their first General Assembly session. Trying to right the Iranian government's record, Rouhani gave a string of interviews to American media outlets as the September conference began. Tehran did acknowledge the Holocaust happened, Rouhani said, and he expressed his desire for better relations with Washington. The Iranian president and his top diplomat also began the process of trying to woo Western businesses back to Iran. At a gathering of the influential Asia Society, elite New York businesspeople, financiers, and intellectuals heard Rouhani make his pitch for rapprochement and Iran's reintegration into the global economy. "During my tenure in office as president, moderation and wisdom will guide my government in making and implementing policies in every field," Rouhani told hundreds of guests in the Hilton Hotel's ballroom on Sixth Avenue, including—for reasons most didn't comprehend—the boxing promoter Don King. "'Win-lose' approaches to international relations have already lost ground."

Beyond the media glare, the secret diplomatic track established in Oman between Washington and Tehran was working to organize an even greater event: a direct meeting (or at least a handshake) between Obama and Rouhani. No Iranian president had met his American counterpart, or even spoken with him, in more than thirty years. And both sides were eager to break the diplomatic ice and show visible support for the negotiations aimed at resolving the dispute over Tehran's nuclear program. Political opponents of rapprochement in both Washington and Tehran would attack such a meeting, Obama's and Rouhani's advisors understood. But they were eager to make history while the world's leaders were in New York.

Burns and Sullivan secretly discussed such a high-level meeting with their Iranian counterparts in Geneva and New York. President Obama's other close advisors also got involved. Susan Rice, the U.S. ambassador at the United Nations at the time, had developed a cordial working relationship with her Iranian counterpart, Mohammad Khazaee, during her four years in New York. Rice and Khazaee — despite the public acrimony expressed between their two countries — had privately tried to establish a formal hotline through which to reduce tensions between the American and Iranian navies in the Persian Gulf. There were growing concerns that any accident at sea involving the countries' ships could escalate into an all-out war.

Obama's and Rouhani's aides studied the UN General Assembly's agenda to identify a time and place where the two leaders might casually run into each other. They scoured hotel rooms in Manhattan where Obama and Rouhani could have a short meeting. The U.S. president's window of opportunity was narrow, as he was only staying in New York for a little more than a day.

American and Iranian officials identified the first Tuesday of the General Assembly session as the best venue for an encounter between Obama and Rouhani. Both men would be attending a lunch in honor of the heads of state at the UN offices. And they hoped the two men could shake hands and exchange a few words as the world's television cameras filmed.

But when the lunch guests arrived, Rouhani was noticeably not among them. Iranian officials said the president couldn't attend because wine was being served—an affront to a Muslim cleric. U.S. officials believed there was another reason: Iranian hard-liners were waiting to pounce on Rouhani for engaging the Great Satan. The Iranian president simply had had second thoughts because of political considerations, Iranian officials said. "We didn't have enough time to prepare," an Iranian official, Alireza Miryousefi, told me at the time outside the UN's offices.

American diplomats involved in the Iran diplomacy were concerned. If Rouhani couldn't even meet with Obama, how was he going to make concessions on the nuclear file? But the Obama administration wouldn't give up. Just hours before Rouhani was scheduled to fly back to Tehran, the White House patched President Obama through to the Iranian leader's cellphone as he drove to Kennedy Airport. For fifteen minutes they discussed global affairs and the need to resolve the nuclear dispute, with Foreign Minister Zarif serving as interpreter. Both men cautioned against the possibility of a dramatic restoration of relations between the United States and Iran, but both also said they believed there was a path forward. "While there will surely be important obstacles to moving forward and success is by no means guaranteed, I believe we can reach a comprehensive solution," Obama told a televised audience from the White House after the phone call. "The test will be meaningful, transparent, and verifiable actions, which can also bring relief from the comprehensive international sanctions that are currently in place" against Iran.

AFTER THE HISTORIC PHONE call between Obama and Rouhani, in October 2013 the quest for rapprochement shifted from New York to the Swiss lakeside city of Geneva. Geneva has long been a center for international diplomacy and intrigue, hosting major arms control conferences and secret meetings between American officials and Washington's nemeses—whether Iranian, North Korean, or Syrian. The "Peace Capital" hosts the UN's European headquarters and many of its international agencies, including the World Food Programme and the Office of the UN High Commissioner for Refugees, as well as the Red Cross. Luxury five-star hotels line Geneva's leafy streets and quiet shores, where Russian, Arab, and Persian businessmen watch over fortunes stashed away in the city's private banks—institutions hidden behind security cameras and darkened windows. Designer watches, chocolates, jewelry, and cheeses are sold from exclusive shops on the cobblestone streets of Geneva's Old Town.

Iranian diplomats and their counterparts from the United States, Europe, China, and Russia assembled intermittently in Geneva for five weeks in late 2013 in a high-profile attempt to resurrect the international negotiations on Tehran's nuclear program that had flagged during Ahmadinejad's tenure but gained momentum in Oman. Optimism was rekindled as the foreign minister stressed that a deal could be quickly concluded if the international community simply showed Iran respect and negotiated with it on equal footing. The Rouhani administration was engineering a massive makeover of Tehran's reputation, a public relations campaign the Israelis and the Arabs vociferously didn't buy. But the Russians, Chinese, and Europeans—and many in the White House—fully embraced it, wary of the prospects of another Mideast war if negotiations failed.

The Americans pursued a two-track strategy in Geneva, one that would only further alienate Washington from its Mideast allies and some in Europe. Officially, the American delegation was led by Wendy Sherman, the chief nuclear negotiator for the United States, backed by John Kerry, now secretary of state. Sherman was a veteran of the Clinton administration who had negotiated missile reductions with the North Koreans in the 1990s. But behind the scenes, and away from the prying eyes of the global media, the secret Oman

channel was also hard at work. The Iranians and the Americans believed the best way to reach a deal was without the complication of
the P5+1.

In early November, Sherman and her staff encamped in wood-
paneled rooms at Geneva's Intercontinental Hotel, just across from
the UN's offices at the Palais des Nations. Iranian, Russian, Chinese, and European diplomats joined them and busily moved between rooms and floors carrying position papers and legal briefs in a
frantic effort to seal an initial deal. Hundreds of journalists waited in
the hotel lobby, pestering tourists and businessmen alike while they
awaited news of an agreement. The reception area began to look
like a college dormitory, with Iranian, American, and European
journalists sleeping on the floor and littering the area with discarded
coffee cups and cigarette butts.

But across town, William Burns and Jake Sullivan were holding
separate negotiations in the serene lakeside rooms at another five-
star hotel. Thanks to the months of negotiations they'd already held
in Muscat and New York, the outlines of a deal were fast coming
into focus. The Iranians would scale back the most dangerous por-
tions of their nuclear program, particularly the production of near-
weapons-grade fuel and the installation of thousands of new
centrifuges used to enrich uranium. In return, the United States
and the Europeans would suspend some of their financial sanctions
and return billions of dollars in frozen oil revenues the Iranians had
been attempting to repatriate from overseas banks. Such an interim
agreement would address Western concerns that Tehran might rapidly move to produce nuclear weapons. It would also provide time
for a more permanent agreement to be reached.

The diplomacy in Geneva took on a schizophrenic nature as the
United States tried to rationalize the two tracks it was pursuing.
Puneet Talwar, the White House staffer, was one of the diplomats
tasked with shuttling messages between the two U.S. delegations
and forging a united front. Puzzled journalists saw Talwar taking
Geneva's public buses, not knowing he was going to attend the se-

cret meetings at the second hotel. He darted down the city's snowy streets in his business suit trying to make appointments with the Iranians as the clock ticked. The Obama administration still hadn't made public that there was a separate channel.

The diplomatic process reached a crescendo in mid-November when Kerry and the foreign ministers from the other negotiating countries arrived in Geneva, seemingly to clinch a deal. France had been taking a particularly hard line in the talks, hewing to the position that Iran must not be allowed to maintain any of the infrastructure it had developed to produce nuclear fuel. Paris's attitude, a marked role reversal on the international stage, where the Americans were normally cast as the diplomatic heavy, was led by French foreign minister Laurent Fabius. Fabius's role as France's top diplomat was seen as his last major position in the French government before retirement. A former prime minister, he'd spent more than four decades in France's political limelight, and wasn't going to go quietly.

Arriving in Geneva on November 8, 2013, the American and Iranian delegations presented a draft agreement to the rest of the P5+1, which had largely been inactive for a year. Expecting to begin deliberations, instead they realized an accord had nearly been completed behind their backs and that the goalposts had shifted. Many of the P5+1's most stringent demands weren't addressed. And there were clear indications that Iran would be allowed to maintain much of its nuclear infrastructure, including centrifuge machines and the Arak reactor, while beginning to get sanctions relief. The U.S. position had clearly softened, and this was only the interim deal.

Fabius wasted little time making France's presence felt. Iran and the P5+1 countries had all agreed not to discuss the substance of the deal with the press. But Fabius, feeling sufficiently burned by the United States, walked in front of the cameras at the Intercontinental Hotel and proclaimed that the Western countries were being duped by the Iranians. He specifically focused on the Arak reactor. "One wants a deal . . . but not a sucker's deal," Fabius told French radio.

Kerry and the U.S. delegations were livid. They privately accused Fabius of seeking to court the Israelis and Arab business by taking such a dramatic and public position. They accused the French diplomat of struggling to even understand the science behind the interim accord. "He didn't have any leverage and didn't know what he wanted," said one of the Americans in Geneva.

The fallout was swift. Israeli and Arab officials jumped on Fabius's comments as proof that the United States was preparing to accept a nuclear-weapons-capable Iran. Zarif and Iranian diplomats, meanwhile, felt the Americans had betrayed them, particularly after Kerry deferred to Fabius and consented to negotiating more stringent terms for the agreement. "We expect the West to have a united stance over the draft," Iran's foreign minister said.

The diplomatic contretemps proved short-lived. Two weeks later, Iran and the P5+1 returned to Geneva and agreed to an interim agreement not significantly different from what Burns and Sullivan had negotiated with Tehran in their secret channel. Three days of virtually round-the-clock negotiations concluded with Kerry, Zarif, and the other foreign ministers announcing an agreement that for the first time rolled back parts of Iran's nuclear program. Burns and Sullivan remained in the shadows.

Still, the interim agreement unnerved Israel and Washington's Arab allies. It strongly suggested that the Obama White House would ultimately accept a final agreement well short of what previous U.S. governments had once demanded. Tehran would likely retain much of its nuclear capacity, as well as the missiles to deliver warheads. Iran would remain a latent nuclear weapons state, which would significantly alter the power balance in the Middle East.

"What was concluded in Geneva last night is not a historic agreement, it's a historic mistake," Israeli prime minister Benjamin Netanyahu told reporters. "It's not made the world a safer place. Like the agreement with North Korea in 2005, this agreement has made the world a much more dangerous place."

CHAPTER 11

Khamenei's Shadow

I N 2014, AMERICAN DIPLOMATS JAKE SULLIVAN AND UNDERSECRETARY of State William Burns emerged from the diplomatic shadows as a July heat wave gripped Austria, including Vienna's Coburg Palace Hotel, where the United States and Iran were now trying to convert the interim nuclear deal into a final historic agreement. Critics of the negotiations, particularly in Israel, bristled at the location of the talks. The nineteenth-century royal home turned five-star hotel was less than a mile from where Adolf Hitler had addressed 250,000 Viennese after the Nazis annexed Austria in 1938. Israelis noted the irony that the United States was going to give ground to the Iranians on the nuclear issue in a city with such a dark history for their people. U.S. officials countered that the Coburg was situated on Theodor Herzl Platz, a downtown square named after the Austro-Hungarian founder of modern Zionism.

Even with the interim nuclear agreement in place, U.S. and European officials remained puzzled over the role of Supreme Leader Khamenei in the diplomacy. They assumed the cleric accepted Rouhani's winning the 2013 presidential election in a bid to relieve international financial pressure on Tehran. European governments viewed Rouhani and his foreign minister, Javad Zarif, as moderates who generally wanted an accommodation with the West and could be trusted. But did the supreme leader really want to make major concessions? Some cynics inside the diplomatic bloc were convinced the cleric was just using his media-savvy diplomats to divide the Western powers while continuing to grow Iran's nuclear capabilities. Khamenei said in speeches that his revolution would die if he made peace with the Great Satan in Washington. The White House, however, was betting the supreme leader would accept major long-term concessions as the process, and the sanctions, ground on.

U.S. negotiators continued to try to find some common ground with Zarif and his team at the Coburg that summer. Almost all the Iranians spoke fluent English. Some had attended universities in the U.S. heartland, such as the University of Kansas and the University of Denver, or elite eastern institutions, such as the Massachusetts Institute of Technology. Zarif had spent nearly twenty years in the United States working or studying in California, Colorado, and New York. American diplomats acknowledged he might have had an advantage inside the negotiating room because he knew their culture so much better than they knew his. Zarif was particularly adept at using the international media, sympathetic academics, and retired diplomats to make his case. His years at the United Nations had earned him a vast Rolodex of top contacts in the U.S. media, business, and academic elite.

U.S. and European diplomats struggled to understand the political power of the Iranian men across the negotiating table. For most of Ahmadinejad's eight-year rule, the affable Zarif had been exiled to a Tehran think tank, out of sight of the cameras, where he could only grumble privately to a selected few that Ahmadinejad was incompetent and was destroying Iran's international standing. Zarif was resurrected only after the election of President Rouhani in 2013, when the regime was desperate for some form of rapprochement with the West. Tehran knew of his connections in Washington and New York.

Zarif's number two, Deputy Foreign Minister Abbas Araghchi, was viewed as more of a hard-liner by the American team. Kerry thought the diplomat had stronger revolutionary credentials than Zarif and was closer to the supreme leader's office and the Revolutionary Guard. Araghchi led the day-to-day negotiations in Switzerland and Vienna and regularly guided the Iranian media on the status of the talks. He was sober and reserved compared to the gregarious and smiling Zarif. His nationalist sentiments were made clear in his conversation with Jake Sullivan in which he compared Iran's nuclear program to the U.S. space launch.

Salehi, the atomic energy chief, oversaw the entire process, the Americans believed, whether he was at the talks or not. He spoke for Iran's nuclear bureaucracy, and as a former vice president, he had access to Khamenei. The Revolutionary Guard also was seen as trusting Salehi because of his central role in promoting the nuclear program, in which the IRGC was the major player. "The IRGC made out like bandits under the sanctions, because they controlled the black markets," said Wendy Sherman, the undersecretary of state. "They didn't want this deal . . . because it gave Rouhani more credibility. Yeah, the IRGC was very present in the negotiation."

U.S. negotiators in Vienna still hoped to make steady progress as they eyed a July 2014 deadline to reach a final nuclear accord. The target was essentially six months from when the interim deal was implemented. Washington was working to get Zarif to accept a sizable reduction in the number of centrifuges Tehran maintained to produce nuclear fuel—to a few thousand from nearly twenty thousand. The United States saw its significant concession in Geneva (that Iran would be allowed to maintain some capability to enrich uranium) as deserving a reciprocal step. A smaller enrichment capability would be that step, they said.

But as the Vienna round drew to a close that July, Khamenei gave a major speech from Tehran without notifying Zarif or any of his negotiators. Iran's ultimate aim was to have nearly two hundred thousand centrifuges, the supreme leader told his country, and Iran would never stop advancing its nuclear capabilities through research and development, citing their use in medicine, power, and science. This was nearly twenty times the capacity Kerry and Zarif were negotiating.

"On the issue of enrichment capacity, their [the West's] aim is to make Iran accept 10,000 SWU," Khamenei said, referring to an atomic work unit that required at least one centrifuge to achieve. "Our officials say we need 190,000 SWU. We might not need this [capacity] this year or in the next two or five years, but this is our absolute need and we need to meet this need."

Khamenei foresaw an industrial-scale enrichment program that could quickly produce enough weapons-grade uranium for hundreds of atomic bombs, if Tehran made the decision to weaponize. But the supreme leader hadn't conveyed his thoughts to his negotiators in Vienna. Zarif was "blindsided" by Khamenei's comments, said American diplomats who met with him at the Coburg. "He seemed to have no idea where it came from." Indeed, the technical nature of Khamenei's speech raised fears in Washington that the cleric was being advised by an entirely different scientific team. The Americans again started to worry that Khamenei wasn't really interested in forging an agreement.

"The personal interplay in all of this was fascinating," Kerry told me. "The moments of passions, the flare-ups, the moments of demanding decision. It was pretty dramatic at times."

DIPLOMATIC DEADLINES CAME AND went that July and November. And the failure to meet them presented the United States and its partners with two stark realities in pursuing their negotiating track with Iran. The first was that the aim of some inside the U.S. government to dismantle Iran's nuclear infrastructure was now a non-starter if a final accord was going to be reached. Tehran had amassed a large program since negotiations with the Europeans had started in 2003, consisting of uranium conversion plants, underground enrichment facilities, and uranium mines. Iran was also moving ahead with building the plutonium-producing reactor in the city of Arak.

Getting Tehran to give all that up, after the United States had already started to ease some of the sanctions, was a long shot, the White House concluded. Some American and European officials felt it had been a mistake to begin channeling billions of dollars in financial relief to Tehran after the interim agreement was reached in Geneva in the fall of 2013. Western countries were giving Iran around $700 million in cash every month as part of this interim deal. The White House was essentially subsidizing the Iranians to talk and reducing the United States' financial leverage. Critics in Congress argued the Americans should be increasing sanctions on Iran, rather than easing them, if they wanted a better deal. Massive concessions from Iran, they argued, would come only if Iran was on an economic cliff. American leverage gained through financial warfare had successfully brought the Iranians to the table, and that leverage appeared to be growing.

Kerry and the White House, however, didn't believe additional sanctions were an option. They said the international community had gone as far as it had only because of the U.S. commitment to talk with Iran. Seeking more sanctions at that time, the Americans believed, would irreparably split the P5+1.

"To squeeze them further was to guarantee this wouldn't have happened," Kerry said about the idea that more sanctions would have forced Iran to capitulate. "We were going to lose our allies. They felt strongly that we were over-squeezing." While this was definitely not the case with the French delegation, the Chinese and the Russians had publicly spoken out against more sanctions.

The other wild card, of course, was Khamenei. The White House believed it needed to continue to try to bring the supreme leader on board the diplomatic process, despite his public hostility. President Obama, in the weeks before the November negotiating deadline, penned his fourth letter to the cleric through the direct channel he had opened up with his first missive in 2009. This letter, rather than focusing on the nuclear program alone, for the first time specifically raised the possibility of cooperation between Washington and Tehran in fighting Islamic State militias that had taken over large swaths of Iraq and Syria in the preceding months. They posed a direct threat to both Iran and the United States, the president argued. Solving the nuclear issue could open the path for greater security cooperation.

The supreme leader was noncommittal in his reply, as he'd been in response to the three previous letters. He acknowledged that his country was open to better relations with Washington, but only if it stopped its "hostile policies" toward Tehran. The White House was divided over whether this presented an opportunity or more obfuscation. U.S. allies in Europe and the Middle East were astounded to hear of the White House offer on ISIS, as so far the Americans had refused to link the nuclear deal to other security issues.

Indeed, President Obama was about to significantly change his negotiating strategy to keep the diplomatic process going, paring back most of the harshest demands that were initially the West's negotiating positions. The United States accepted that Iran would possess many of the technologies used to make atomic bombs. But the focus now was on maximizing the time Tehran needed to amass the fuel for a bomb. Kerry and his negotiators, meanwhile, were seeking to gain as much access for international inspectors as possible. "To the Iranians, they wanted to hear the magic phrase, 'the right to enrich,'" Rhodes said. "We also knew, when we talked about it internally, obviously we envisaged enrichment. The president, in his mind . . . had made this decision a long time ago."

Yet for decades, the United States had made dismantlement a precondition for any final agreement. The White House had made a major concession.

———

THE UNITED STATES AND its allies initially orchestrated their campaign against Iran's nuclear program based on the argument that the country had repeatedly violated the UN statute governing the use of atomic energy, the Nuclear Nonproliferation Treaty. Beginning in 2006, the UN Security Council had passed six resolutions requiring Iran to suspend its enrichment of uranium until the country addressed evidence it had covertly developed nuclear weapons technologies. The United Nations imposed sanctions on Iran starting that same year on the grounds that Tehran had failed to abide by the Security Council's demands. Then between 2010 and 2012 the United States and the European Union constructed a much broader sanctions regime targeting Iran, using the UN resolutions as political cover.

As the negotiations in Switzerland and Austria gained pace in 2014, the American negotiators started significantly departing from this original policy strategy and weakening its terms. U.S. officials knew this was a dangerous approach. If Iran was allowed to maintain these technologies, its regional rivals, particularly Saudi Arabia, Turkey, and Egypt, might demand the same capabilities, and a regional nuclear arms race could ensue. U.S. officials, however, believed they might have to take that risk.

John Kerry, while still chairman of the Senate Foreign Relations Committee, had been the first senior American official to suggest to the Iranians that the United States would accept enrichment on Iranian soil, passing messages to Tehran via Oman in late 2011. His comments unnerved some State Department officials, who felt he offered the concession too soon, and without a formal green light from the administration.

In the winter of 2013, Jake Sullivan and Williams Burns also discussed, in theory, what type of enrichment program the Iranians might need in the future, but without making any commitments. The interim nuclear agreement reached in Geneva in November

2013 implied that Iran would maintain the ability to enrich uranium, though it didn't spell out the scope.

By late 2014, Secretary Kerry and his team came up with a new strategy to resolve the Iranian nuclear crisis. Iran would be allowed to possess thousands of the centrifuges used to produce nuclear fuel, they concluded. But the country's infrastructure would have to be scaled back to the point that any rush to acquire the fissile material for a bomb would take at least a year. The U.S. strategy was remarkably complex: negotiators needed to develop a formula based on the number of centrifuges Iran already employed, the size of its existing fuel stockpile, and the ultimate curbs on the sophistication of the centrifuges. It also required the White House to upgrade the scientific knowledge of its negotiators and to prepare the American public and U.S. allies for an agreement that wouldn't be nearly as far-reaching or constricting on Tehran as originally envisioned.

IT WAS AT THIS point that U.S. energy secretary Ernest Moniz quietly entered the Iran diplomatic process. It was early 2015 and the negotiations were shifting to Zurich, Switzerland's financial capital. Moniz, the seventy-year-old son of Portuguese immigrants, had the experience and knowledge of nuclear technology and weapons systems needed to assume a key role in the talks. He had been a professor at the Massachusetts Institute of Technology for four decades and was known as one of the world's leading nuclear physicists. He had also served in the Clinton administration's Energy Department during the late 1990s. After becoming secretary of energy in mid-2013, he navigated complex issues such as nuclear waste storage and the safeguarding of the United States' nuclear weapons arsenal.

Moniz didn't look the part of a globetrotting diplomat. He wore his silver hair down to his shoulders and greeted the press with a puckish grin. He looked like an aging folk singer or an English professor at a northern California university in the 1960s. But this laid-back appearance belied a ruthless political acumen. Moniz had gained the trust of both President Obama and Secretary Kerry. He regularly attended all the White House's National Security Council meetings on Iran once he took over the Energy Department in the summer of 2013. He liked to finish his nights in quiet bars or his office drinking bourbon or scotch.

The White House dispatched Moniz to Switzerland to counter Iran's decision to send Ali Akbar Salehi, the head of the Atomic Energy Organization of Iran and one of Iran's top nuclear scientists. He had also served as Tehran's ambassador to the IAEA, the UN's nuclear watchdog, during the mid-2000s, as scrutiny of Iran's nuclear program intensified. IAEA personnel believed Salehi had more knowledge of Iran's nuclear program, and possibly its atomic weapons activities, than any other senior Iranian official. He was mild-mannered, spoke fluent English and Arabic, and was capable of charming foreign governments.

Kerry and his team were initially worried about Salehi's direct involvement in the talks. They saw it as Khamenei potentially hardening the Iranian government's line and marginalizing Zarif. Salehi regularly told Iranian newspapers that the government wouldn't dismantle any of its nuclear facilities. Back in Tehran, he rallied the country behind the need for nuclear power, though he supported the direct talks with the Americans.

Ironically, Salehi had earned his doctorate in nuclear physics from MIT in the 1970s, at the same time Moniz had taken up a position as an associate professor there. The two men had never met during their time in Cambridge, according to American and Iranian officials. But their relationship emerged as one of the most important in the final stages of the nuclear talks. The contrast between Salehi in his dark suits and tieless shirts and the boyish Moniz captivated the world's cameras.

The two men were the best positioned to negotiate the technical terms of the agreement that was now aimed at achieving the one-year breakout time. Starting in Switzerland in March 2015, they held marathon one-on-one discussions focused on the numbers of centrifuges and Iran's stockpile of fissile material. The United States also wanted Tehran to dismantle or repurpose its plutonium-producing reactor in the city of Arak, which offered a second path for the country to develop the nuclear fuel for a bomb.

In their talks, Moniz and Salehi sought to build on their common history. The American brought a onesie emblazoned with MIT's logo, the beaver, for the Iranian scientist's granddaughter. Salehi praised Moniz to the Persian press as a serious and honest diplomat and negotiator. "The Iranians could not move without Salehi at the table. He's a very influential person. And he built Iran's nuclear program, to a degree," Moniz told me in his Department of Energy office in early 2016. "He had to be there to decide what they could and would accept."

Vast scientific establishments in the United States and Iran backed the two men in their negotiations. To support his efforts, Moniz mobilized hundreds of nuclear experts at the U.S. National Laboratories in Oakwood, Tennessee; Sandia, New Mexico; and Livermore, California. The Americans assembled a mock-up of the Natanz uranium enrichment facility in Oakwood to gauge how the centrifuges at the site could be dismantled and kept offline to keep Tehran's stockpile at low levels. They also modeled how the Arak reactor could be repurposed to ensure that it produced significantly less plutonium usable in nuclear weapons. Part of the process involved taking out the core of the reactor and filling it with cement.

But as the talks proceeded, Salehi and other Iranian officials continued to test even the new American approach to the one-year breakout time. While the Iranians were open to limiting their country's enrichment capacity for a time, they stressed this wouldn't be permanent. Tehran was also demanding a rapid rollback of American sanctions, rather than the phased approach demanded by the Obama administration. The two scientists were having trouble bridging their countries' remaining negotiating gaps. Iran was demanding to keep all of its nuclear facilities and infrastructure.

Every U.S. red line was under attack.

IN LATE MARCH 2015, the negotiations moved to the Beau Rivage Palace, a massive nineteenth-century hotel and spa, in the Swiss city of Lausanne. The complex covered two city blocks and stared out across Lake Geneva and up into the Swiss Alps. The hotel had maintained an impressive guest list over the decades. European powers and the United States had met there in 1918 to negotiate the breakup of the Ottoman Empire following the end of World War I. Coco Chanel had lived there intermittently, in a lake-view suite, before her death in Paris in 1971. Her stylish grave is down the street from the Palace, daisies arranged in the logo of the luxury Chanel brand. The ruler of Zaire, Mobutu Sese Seko, convalesced at the hotel in the 1990s while receiving cancer treatments from a nearby clinic in a failed attempt to extend his life.

The Beau Rivage's long, eggshell-white corridors stretched out before Lake Geneva, often empty, or with just one foreign-born hotel staffer shuffling down its lime-green rugs. Diplomats congregated in a glass-encircled breakfast room dwarfed by the Alps to chart out their strategies during early morning meetings. Foreign ministers took breaks in the steam baths and swimming pools laid out on the hotel's lower floors. The Iranians went on long walks outside along the lakeside esplanade, trailed by photographers and camera crews.

Despite this picture-postcard setting, the politics of Washington were dogging Kerry, Moniz, and their team as they tried to reach a framework agreement with Tehran that would form the basis for the final nuclear accord. U.S. lawmakers and supporters of Israel, Republican and Democratic alike, were growing increasingly alarmed by the emerging terms of the agreement that were leaking out to the press. Iran was going to be allowed to maintain a sizable capacity to enrich uranium, they were told. The subsequent lifting of Western sanctions would release Tehran from its isolation and feed it with billions of dollars in funds to support its terrorist proxies in Syria,

Iraq, Lebanon, and the Palestinian territories. Washington's power circles were on high alert.

A little-known southern senator, Tom Cotton of Arkansas, took it upon himself to derail the process. On March 9, the Harvard graduate and Iraq War veteran directed forty-six other Republican lawmakers to sign a letter directly addressed to Ayatollah Khamenei warning him that Kerry and the White House didn't have the power to deliver a nuclear deal that wasn't supported by the majority of Congress. "It has come to our attention while observing your nuclear negotiations with our government that you may not fully understand our constitutional system," Cotton and his colleagues wrote. "We will consider any agreement regarding your nuclear-weapons program that is not approved by the Congress as nothing more than an executive agreement. . . . The next president could revoke such an executive agreement with the stroke of a pen and future Congresses could modify the terms of the agreement at any time."

Kerry and his team shuddered over the potential impact of the Cotton letter. Khamenei might use it to overturn a diplomatic process about which he was already suspicious. The cleric could also cite Congress's meddling as a pretext to toughen the terms demanded by his negotiators. He and other hard-line actors in Tehran could reassert themselves directly, as Khamenei had done from time to time. He continued to make speeches outlining terms that were at odds with those discussed in Europe.

The political pressure from both Washington and Tehran, strangely enough, drew the American and Iranian negotiating teams closer together in Lausanne. Immediately upon arriving at the Beau Rivage on a cold morning, Kerry convened a meeting with Zarif where he sought to assure the Iranian diplomat that Cotton was "dangerous" and didn't have the power to derail the White House's negotiating strategy. "Although we see the letter as a political move, we need to know the U.S. government's stance on this issue," Zarif said, seeking the Obama administration's support in pushing back

Congress. Kerry said they must keep their talks focused solely on the negotiating room and not be distracted by outside agitators.

U.S. officials reached out emotionally to President Rouhani's brother, Hossein Fereydoun. Fereydoun was a regular in the negotiations and known to pass messages to his older sibling. Days into the Lausanne session, the Rouhani brothers' mother died in Iran. Kerry and his aides warmly embraced the diplomat and politician before he flew back to Tehran for the funeral. "We hope this is a year that can bring us prosperity and peace," Mr. Kerry told the Iranian delegation ahead of another hours-long negotiating session. Beau Rivage staff tried to brighten the mood by assembling a traditional Persian *hafsin* table, stocked with goldfish, eggs, grass, and candies, to welcome the spring and commemorate the Iranian New Year, Nowruz, outside the negotiating room.

THE PRESSURE OF TRYING to forge the framework for a final agreement was building on Kerry and his negotiators. The secretary of state had repeatedly warned that the Americans were prepared to walk away from the talks if Iran didn't make the necessary concessions to secure the framework. His aides said that on two occasions in the winter of 2015, Kerry bluntly told Zarif the U.S. team wouldn't turn up at the negotiating venue if Iran did not display some flexibility. Kerry at one point asked Zarif if he needed to return to Tehran for instructions. But the secretary never made good on his threats, feeding the perception among some diplomats that he wanted the agreement more than the Iranians did—this despite the continued deterioration of the Iranian economy, made worse by the steep drop in global oil prices.

The United States, meanwhile, continued to offer concessions to keep Tehran engaged. In addition to giving ground on enrichment, the Americans suggested that the White House was prepared to allow Iran to maintain other core parts of its nuclear program that just a year earlier the United States had said absolutely needed to be shut down, including the underground enrichment facility in Qom that had been exposed by French and American intelligence in 2009 and the heavy water reactor in Arak, the so-called bomb-making factory.

Washington's slackening position placed it at odds with some of its closest allies, and not just Israel. France was a key player in the negotiations at the Beau Rivage and had a history of being hawkish on nuclear proliferation. U.S. officials believed that Fabius had nearly sunk the interim agreement in 2013, when France pushed for denying Iran any enrichment capacity, while Paris was deeply skeptical of Zarif and the other Iranian diplomats because of the earlier failed negotiations in the 2000s in which he had taken part. The French believed at that time the Iranians had used diplomacy as cover to advance their program, and were doing so again. French officials were nervous when Kerry and Zarif met alone, assuming the secretary of state would make even more concessions.

French diplomats in Lausanne pressed the United States to take its time and not rigidly stick to any specific deadline. They believed that there had been so many arbitrary deadlines that it didn't make sense to force the process into one now. The sanctions were crippling the Iranian economy, they argued, and time was on the West's side. France's ambassador to the United States, Gérard Araud, a former nuclear negotiator, took to Twitter to press his government's case. "Making the end of March an absolute deadline is counterproductive and dangerous," Araud wrote. "No agreement without concrete decisions on issues beyond the enrichment capability question," he said, specifically mentioning the need for extensive monitoring of Iran's nuclear sites and clarity on Iran's alleged past weaponization work. French foreign minister Laurent Fabius called his team in Lausanne and told them to hold the tough line. French diplomats were virtually the only ones briefing the international press at the Beau Rivage, making clear their uneasiness about the process.

France's outspokenness drew a stiff reprimand from the White House. President Obama called French prime minister François Hollande as the Lausanne talks ground on and told him to quiet his negotiators or risk blowing up the deal. Kerry's team seethed at what they saw as French insubordination, and belittled them as minor players in the talks. These tensions would continue until the end of the process.

But the French concerns were real. Iran pocketed the carrots the White House dangled in Switzerland. And the framework agreement that was announced showed that Tehran would be able to maintain, if not grow, its nuclear program over time. It accepted that the centrifuges and the heavy-water reactor at Arak would remain in some form.

The White House's dogged pursuit of its agreement became clear in the final days of negotiations in Lausanne. The night before the April deadline, President Obama ordered a satellite teleconference with his negotiators on the ground, including Kerry and Moniz. They congregated in a white tent on the lawn outside the Beau Rivage on a secure link. The Iranians could see the Americans gathering in the cold winter air away from their hotel rooms, as could the television cameras.

Obama wanted to make clear to his team that the United States would maintain a tough line, according to participants in the call. But at the same time, the president ordered Kerry to allow the talks to continue beyond the stated April 1 deadline, if required. The nuclear agreement was too important to the United States and the world not to push on, he said. The White House wanted to send a message of assertiveness. But negotiators in Switzerland said the meeting conveyed the absolute opposite—that the United States would keep talking indefinitely. "There was little doubt at that point that the Iranians had boxed us in," said a European diplomat in Lausanne. "The Americans had ensnared themselves in the process."

———

VIENNA'S COBURG PALACE WAS the site of what was expected to be the final round of negotiations in June 2015, which were aimed at formalizing the framework nuclear agreement set forth in Lausanne. Kerry and the Americans targeted July 1 as the deadline to complete the diplomatic process. But many inside the negotiating bloc, particularly the French, were skeptical the deal would get wrapped up by then. Kerry arrived in Austria only seventy-two hours before the self-imposed deadline. He hobbled around the Austrian capital on crutches after having broken his femur in three places during a bicycle ride weeks earlier in Switzerland, and he needed painkillers and regular physiotherapy in order to keep up his hectic pace. Members of his entourage said they expected to be at the Coburg at least a week, as a summer heat wave drove temperatures above a hundred degrees. U.S. embassy staff were already planning for a Fourth of July party for Secretary Kerry and his entourage in the gardens of the scenic hotel.

As he had done in the past, Ayatollah Khamenei tacitly intruded into the negotiations. Just days before they started, the cleric gave another nationally televised speech in which he laid out new red lines for his negotiators, again apparently without their knowledge. The address, which marked the beginning of the Muslim holy month of Ramadan, said no outside inspectors would be allowed entry into Iran's military sites and that any restraints on Tehran's program would be limited. Khamenei also said the country's research and development would continue. "Contrary to the Americans' insistence, we do not accept long-term, ten-year and twelve-year restrictions, and we have told them the acceptable number of years for restrictions," Mr. Khamenei said in his address.

Khamenei's speech fed into the sense of uncertainty in Vienna. U.S. lawmakers were champing at the bit to impose fresh sanctions on Tehran if the process appeared to stall. And while President Obama still had eighteen months left in office, U.S. diplomats felt they needed to get a deal in the coming weeks or the administration wouldn't have enough time to implement it. The clock again was ticking, but the Iranians seemed calm. Zarif and other diplomats said they didn't feel the pressure of committing to any American timeline. Party politics in Iran were much less of a factor.

Moniz and other negotiators, meanwhile, were worried about the health of Salehi. The physicist and diplomat underwent emergency stomach surgery just weeks before the Vienna round began. Diplomatic sources in Tehran suggested he had cancer and might die. Moniz voiced fears that the Iranian team might not be able to conclude an agreement without Salehi's presence. Salehi eventually turned up in Vienna, but he was gaunt and had lost more than twenty pounds.

The negotiations, meanwhile, were taking on a carnival-like atmosphere. Journalists camped out in a giant white tent in front of the Coburg or in the coffee shop of the neighboring Marriott Hotel. Pro-Israel groups appeared on the sidelines to protest the Iranian delegation and raise the specter of another Western betrayal of the Jews, akin to Neville Chamberlain's peace agreement with Hitler in 1938. An even larger pro-deal, if not pro-Iranian, camp also sat outside the Coburg to pressure the U.S. delegation to make an accommodation with Tehran. It included an odd assortment of Iranian Americans, Vietnam-era leftists, and former U.S. diplomats who seemed to be angling for business opportunities in Tehran once the sanctions got lifted. They blamed the United States, not Iran, for the impasse, which they viewed as a manufactured crisis. They argued that the United States had more to gain from any agreement than did the ayatollahs in Tehran, because of the wars the United States was trying to end in Syria, Iraq, and Yemen. "The Obama administration is saying this is only a transactional deal focused on Iran's nuclear program," Flynt Leverett, a onetime national security staffer in the George W. Bush White House, told me at a coffee shop across from the Coburg. "I think this should be part of a much more comprehensive agreement."

———

THE RELATIONSHIP BETWEEN KERRY and Zarif emerged as the center-piece of the negotiations. This wasn't how many in the Obama administration had initially thought it would play out. When the talks had started in Oman three years earlier, the diplomacy was dominated by midlevel diplomats and White House staffers. But Kerry and other high-level American and Iranian diplomats took over after the process became public in the fall of 2013. Some U.S. diplomats felt a secretary of state shouldn't engage in the day-to-day work of a negotiation, instead only coming in at crucial points to push the process forward. They also didn't believe Washington's top diplomat would be able to devote himself to one issue when so many other crises were demanding his attention, including civil wars in Ukraine and Syria and territorial disputes between China and other Asian nations in the South China Sea.

But once Kerry took the reins at Foggy Bottom, he made it clear that he was going to dominate a diplomatic track that he believed he had started and conceptualized. The Vietnam War veteran had boundless energy and stamina and deeply believed that the only alternative to diplomacy would be a war. A breakdown in talks would likely lead to more U.S. sanctions on Tehran and an acceleration of Iran's nuclear program. "So many wars have been fought over misunderstandings, misinterpretations, lack of effective diplomacy," he told me in 2016. "War is the failure of diplomacy."

Kerry privately told his staff that he wasn't seduced by Zarif, who was notorious for his infectious smile and charismatic demeanor. Kerry said he knew the U.S.-schooled diplomat was an Islamic revolutionary and a loyal follower of Khamenei, and Kerry repeatedly sought to play down the idea that an agreement was preordained or even likely. Still, as the process moved forward from 2013, the two men spent hundreds of hours directly negotiating in Vienna, Zurich, New York, Geneva, and Munich. They would take long walks together to burn off the stress of the talks. In Geneva, camera crews followed the diplomats as they walked along Lake Geneva in a light snowfall. Video of the two caused controversy in Tehran, as hard-liners believed Zarif was becoming a tool of the Americans. The two men became wary that their collaboration was making them suscep-tible to political attacks in their own capitals.

Still, the Iranians were successfully wearing down the Americans and their partners as the negotiations extended beyond the Fourth of July and into a hot European summer. Most of the United States' initial positions from the start of the Obama administration were no longer hard and fast. Iran was going to be allowed to maintain five thousand centrifuges to produce nuclear fuel at the Natanz facility. This was below the nearly twenty thousand Iran had amassed by 2015. But Kerry and his team agreed that Iran would then be allowed to build an industrial-scale nuclear program, with hundreds of thou-sands of machines, after a ten-year period of restraint.

By early July, Iran had pocketed another concession: the Arak reactor, initially seen as a bomb-making factory, would be allowed to remain open. It would be altered to produce less plutonium. But after a decade Iran would be able to construct additional heavy-water reactors. The Qom enrichment site, fortified under a moun-tain, also would be allowed to remain open and to continue developing faster centrifuges, though without actually producing fissile material.

The United States and its partners, in return, were preparing to lift most of the international sanctions that Stuart Levey and his col-leagues at Treasury had spent a decade putting in place. Tens of billions of dollars of Iran's oil revenues, frozen under the sanctions, were to be released from banks in Asia and the Middle East. The aim was to reintegrate Tehran back into the international economy. U.S. officials said sanctions could be "snapped back" if Iran cheated on the deal. But the logistics would be daunting, given how long it had taken to put them into effect in the first place.

———

THE FINAL DAYS OF VIENNA were marked by frayed nerves and Iranian efforts to squeeze even more out of the agreement. U.S. officials, meanwhile, continued to try to determine if Khamenei was truly behind his diplomats or if there could be a reversal at the last minute, as in previous negotiations.

Zarif and his team specifically focused on two issues most reporters didn't even realize had been on the negotiating table. Iran wanted the lifting of United Nations statutes that barred the country from testing ballistic missiles and engaging in the conventional arms trade. The Iranian foreign minister argued, with some merit, that these prohibitions had been put in place as part of broader UN laws specifically aimed at curbing Iran's nuclear program. An agreement on the nuclear issue, Zarif argued, meant all these restrictions had to be repealed at once. U.S. officials knew this risked legitimizing Tehran's shipments of arms to its military proxies, such as Hezbollah and the Assad regime. Americans also believed there was no reason for Iran to develop ballistic missiles unless they eventually planned to mount them with nuclear payloads.

This Iranian hard line fueled fireworks in Vienna as the P5+1 diplomats grew irritated and fatigued. On July 5, Kerry and Energy Secretary Moniz scrapped with Zarif and Ali Akbar Salehi in the basement at the Coburg about the duration of the curbs on Iran's nuclear program. The Iranians were seeking as short a timeline as possible and pressing for more concessions from the Western side. The exchange got so heated that an aide to Kerry had to enter the negotiating room and tell the secretary to tone it down, as the Coburg's well-heeled clientele were complaining. "The whole hotel could hear you," Germany's foreign minister, Frank-Walter Steinmeier, joked with Kerry the morning after the contretemps.

Another blowup occurred as Zarif sought to rewrite terms that many of the P5+1 parties thought had been agreed upon months earlier. Zarif's position caused the coordinator of the P5+1 team,

European Union foreign policy chief Federica Mogherini, to warn that she might instruct her diplomatic partners to go home. "Don't threaten an Iranian," Zarif barked back at the normally mild-mannered Italian, unnerving diplomats in the room. Russia's foreign minister, Sergei Lavrov, known for his scowl and tailored suits, sought to lighten the mood by interjecting: "Or a Russian."

The Iranians, though, played hardball on the missile issue and arms embargo to the end. Calling foreign journalists to a late night briefing at the Coburg on July 6, Iranian diplomats cast the United States as the recalcitrant party. One Iranian official said he believed the nuclear deal was largely done, but the West's unbending position on the arms embargo could reverse all the progress. He said no country should be prevented from arming itself. "So this is a question that should be posed to our European and American partners . . . What was the reason that you put this issue in the agenda of the Security Council?" the official said, suggesting there was a wider international conspiracy against Iran.

Within a week, the United States and its partners caved to Iran's positions, but with a twist. The arms embargo would be lifted in five years and the missile bans in eight years, rather than immediately. A new UN resolution was drafted to codify the agreement, but its language was weak. Rather than banning missile tests, it only "called" on Iran to refrain. There was no formal document to be signed by the P5+1 as part of the Vienna agreement, so the Security Council resolutions were the closest thing to an enforcement mechanism.

IN ANOTHER WORRYING SIGN, the United States vastly scaled back its demands that Iran come clean on the past nuclear weapons work it was accused of conducting through the Physics Research Center. The IAEA, the UN's atomic watchdog, had been seeking for more than a decade to understand just how close Iran had come to building a bomb, but received almost no cooperation from Iran on the probe. IAEA attempts to meet with Fakhrizadeh, Abbasi-Davani,

and other nuclear scientists were repeatedly rebuffed, as were requests to visit military sites. Iran called documents the IAEA had
amassed on Iran's covert work "fakes."

Through the Vienna process, Iran did agree to take some additional steps in late 2015 to answer the IAEA's questions about its
suspected bomb work. But U.S. officials, in private, acknowledged
that Tehran would probably never own up to developing a bomb,
nor would it fully cooperate in the agency's investigation. The
Obama administration said it could live with this. It was more important to block Iran from developing a weapon in the future than
to bring it to task for its previous violations of United Nations statutes. The White House believed it knew exactly what Iran had done
in Parchin.

Many nuclear experts, however, feared the United States and
global powers were letting Tehran off the hook. It would be very
hard to verify Iran's compliance with a new nuclear deal if the IAEA
and P5+1 didn't fully understand the scope of Iran's capabilities.
And Tehran's unwillingness to cooperate with IAEA inspectors was
a cautionary sign about the integrity of any agreement in the years
ahead. "This decision on weaponization will haunt the international
community for a long time," said Olli Heinonen, a former IAEA
weapons inspector who spent decades studying Iran's program and
emerged as a critic of the Vienna talks. "It sets an incredibly bad
precedent."

THE ANNOUNCEMENT OF AN agreement came on the afternoon of July
14 in Vienna, another oppressively hot day in Austria. P5+1 diplomats had stayed up until three in the morning finalizing it. Ministers took showers and tried to catch some sleep before descending
on a convention center to announce the deal. More than two years
of talks—from Oman through to Austria—had finally come to an
end.

Kerry and the other world leaders privately gathered in UN offices and spoke about the impact of the deal. They presented in the alphabetical order of the countries they represented and described the accord as a historic one. Fabius, who'd been coerced into playing ball, noted it had been reached on Bastille Day and hoped it would have the same long-term relevance. Zarif confidently said the Vienna deal would mark the end of Iran's international isolation. And Kerry, citing his experience as a soldier in Vietnam, repeated his mantra that diplomacy must be exhausted before any use of force. He choked back tears as he spoke.

Still, in the final days, U.S. officials continued to wonder whether Khamenei and the IRGC really supported Zarif. Hard-liners in Tehran chastised the Iranian negotiating team for its work in Vienna, despite terms many analysts viewed as favorable to Iran. Khamenei continued his rhetorical attacks on Washington throughout the process.

Kerry and his team confronted Zarif in the hours before the talks concluded and asked him whether he really spoke for the supreme leader. "He assured us that he did," said one of Kerry's aides. "Only history will show if he was right."

Kerry, reflecting on the process months later, said it remained unclear to him whether the deal marked just a short-term truce between the United States and Iran or an opening for a real rapprochement. Ever the optimist, he focused on the latter. "My hope is that Iran will change some of its behavior further so that they can take advantage of what they opened the opportunity for," Kerry told me outside his office on the seventh floor of the State Department. "That would be the lost opportunity. Hopefully, what we're doing in Syria, what we're doing in other places, allows us to make the most out of these things so that we avoid that other war."

TWO MONTHS AFTER THE Vienna agreement, the head of the International Atomic Energy Agency, a Japanese diplomat named Yukiya Amano, visited Iran. The sixty-nine-year-old's mission was straightforward: to complete the IAEA's probe into Iran's suspected efforts to develop an atomic weapon. Specifically, his team of inspectors was visiting the Parchin military base, where bomb testing was believed to have happened more than a decade earlier. Agency staff were taking soil samples to test them for the remnants of nuclear materials.

Iranian authorities didn't make Amano's work easy during his trip, despite the landmark agreement. Tehran denied the IAEA interviews with its top nuclear scientists, including Mohsen Fakhrizadeh and Fereydoun Abbasi-Davani. Tehran also demanded that its staff, not the IAEA's, physically conduct the sampling at Parchin, worried about outsiders roaming the secretive base. Scores of Revolutionary Guards were massed at the site when Amano and his delegation arrived on a late September morning.

Still, the IAEA obtained the samples and tested them at the agency's laboratory in the woods outside Vienna. The results only deepened the mystery of Parchin and the questions about just how close Tehran had come to building a bomb. The IAEA found particles of man-made uranium there, possible evidence of nuclear weapons work. The agency said in a report that Iran's claims that only conventional weapons testing had occurred at Parchin simply weren't credible.

I asked Amano about his trip to Parchin and the tests during a spring 2016 interview in Washington. "The samples . . . the samples," he replied cryptically, before pausing for thirty seconds of silence. "The samples did not support [the] Iranian story. The Iranians weren't telling us everything in this regard."

Conclusion

———

War and Peace

T
EN DAYS AFTER THE VIENNA ACCORD WAS REACHED, MAJOR
General Qasem Soleimani secretly boarded an Aeroflot jet in
Tehran and made the four-hour flight to Moscow's Sheremetyevo
International Airport. Despite the nuclear deal, Soleimani remained
under a UN travel ban in the summer of 2015 for his role in developing Iran's nuclear program. UN member states were obligated to
prevent the Revolutionary Guard commander from traveling on
their soil. U.S. officials believed countries largely respected the UN's
ban, except for Iran's closest allies, including Iraq, Syria, and Lebanon, where Soleimani regularly visited. He was supposed to be a
marked man in the rest of the world. But the nuclear agreement
seemed to have given him carte blanche to enter the international
community.

The Russians and Iranians both moved quickly to pocket the
Western concessions made in Vienna, including the end of the international sanctions and the arms embargo, to fortify their military
and economic alliance. Indeed, even before the nuclear talks ended,

Supreme Leader Khamenei sent his top foreign policy advisor to Moscow to meet Russian president Vladimir Putin. The Iranian envoy, Ali Akbar Velayati, passed on a letter to the Kremlin's czar that called for greater strategic cooperation between the two countries. Putin responded by announcing Moscow's intent to move forward with the sale of an anti-aircraft missile system, the S-300, which could guard Iran's nuclear facilities from Israeli or American air attacks. The Kremlin and Tehran also outlined plans to develop a fleet of new nuclear power reactors in Iran. And the Kremlin eyed selling more conventional weapons to the Revolutionary Guard.

Soleimani's summer trip, however, had a much more specific and immediate goal—saving Russia's and Iran's closest Middle East ally, President Assad of Syria. Through the winter and spring of 2015, the dictator's military opponents had gained control of large swaths of northern Syria and threatened to cut off the capital, Damascus, from the coastal territory of Latakia, the stronghold of the Assad family and its Alawite sect. Many of these rebel groups were tied to al Qaeda, and some were the forward troops of the Islamic State. The Syrian regime controlled most of Syria's major towns and cities but only a fifth of the country's total territory. Assad appeared to be on the brink of falling from power.

In Moscow, Soleimani met with Defense Minister Sergei Shoygu and the heads of Russian military intelligence and the Kremlin's defense industries. Unfurling a map in front of his Russian hosts, the Iranian general charted out the areas where the rebels were making gains, but also the choke points where their militaries could bolster Assad and drive back the insurgents. He stressed that the Syrian opposition remained divided, with little to no real support from the United States and the West. "The Russians were very alarmed, and felt matters were in steep decline and that there were real dangers to the regime," said a senior Middle East official briefed on the meetings. "The Iranians assured them there is still the possibility to reclaim the initiative. At that time, Soleimani played a role in assuring them that [they] haven't lost all the cards."

Soleimani's trip set the stage for Russia's direct military intervention inside Syria in the fall of 2015. Moscow's airstrikes in the ensuing months were matched by ground operations coordinated by General Soleimani and the militias he controlled on the ground, including Hezbollah and Shiite forces recruited or conscripted from Afghanistan, Iraq, and Yemen. The Revolutionary Guard sent in hundreds of its own military advisors and troops to oversee the operation. This combination allowed President Assad to intensify strikes and begin reclaiming territory from the opposition.

The joint Russian-Iranian operation challenged the Obama administration's hopes for how Tehran would behave in a post-deal environment. President Obama and Secretary Kerry optimistically told journalists and lawmakers after the July agreement that a deal might pave the way for greater cooperation with Iran in ending many of the Middle East's crises, including those in Syria and Yemen. Kerry and his European counterparts talked about using the P5+1 diplomatic format to engage with Tehran in a process to bring about a political transition in Damascus.

But the White House and State Department at times appeared tone-deaf to the messages that were coming out of Tehran. Supreme Leader Khamenei repeatedly told his followers that the nuclear deal would bring no change in Tehran's regional policies and that there would be no discussions with Washington aimed at ending his government's support for Hezbollah, the Assad regime, or the Palestinian factions at war with Israel. "Negotiations with the United States open gates to their economic, cultural, political, and security influence. Even during the nuclear negotiations they tried to harm our national interests," Khamenei said in the weeks after the talks concluded. President Obama's critics, meanwhile, concluded that the Russians and Iranians had colluded to manipulate the American negotiators at the end of the talks. "One reason Iran was able to negotiate so successfully was because of Russian support for a deal that would be antithetical to America's interests," Senate Republican leader Mitch McConnell told lawmakers shortly after the nuclear agreement was reached in July 2015. "No surprise then that just days after the deal was accounted, the commander of Iran's Qods Force reportedly flew to Moscow to secure Russian support for their mutual ally in Syria."

WHILE THE IRANIANS AND RUSSIANS were plotting their moves into Syria, the Obama administration was executing its own war: this one a political campaign to ensure that the nuclear deal passed through Congress. The administration characterized the deal and its approval as the most important initiative of its second term and the defining foreign policy legacy of Barack Obama's presidency. But there was staunch opposition in Congress. Republicans were keen to deny Obama a major political victory in his last months in office. Even many leading Democrats were deeply skeptical of the agreement. They believed it afforded Iran too many concessions without any assurances Tehran wouldn't eventually get a nuclear bomb when the terms of the agreement ended. At that point, with sanctions lifted, the United States' ability to contain Iran would be severely limited.

Under the deal, many of the United States' opponents in Iran would be taken off international sanctions lists, either immediately or in a phased process. This meant they could again travel, open bank accounts overseas, and engage in international business. These included General Soleimani and the alleged masterminds of Iran's secret atomic weapons work in Parchin, Mohsen Fakhrizadeh and Fereydoun Abbasi-Davani. A range of the Revolutionary Guard's top brass, including some implicated in international terrorist attacks, were also given sanctions relief. A decade of U.S. efforts to constrict Iran financially and militarily was being unwound by the nuclear deal.

Israeli prime minister Benjamin Netanyahu's hard-line stance against the agreement harnessed congressional opposition, with many pro-Israel groups in the United States lining up behind him.

Netanyahu took the almost unprecedented step of speaking to a joint session of Congress in March 2015, even before the deal was concluded, to say that its emerging terms posed an existential threat to his country. Netanyahu rallied Israel's supporters in Washington, urging them to spare no expense in their efforts to sink the agreement. "This is a bad deal. It's a very bad deal. We're better off without it!" Netanyahu said in a forty-minute address that drew repeated standing ovations in a House chamber packed mostly with Republican lawmakers. "It would be a farewell to arms control. And the Middle East would soon be crisscrossed by nuclear tripwires. A region where small skirmishes can trigger big wars would turn into a nuclear tinderbox."

Arab governments were also stunned by the terms of the agreement. None of them were willing to take to the political stage like Netanyahu. Nor did they have the same lobbying apparatus in Washington to amplify their voices. But diplomats from Saudi Arabia, the United Arab Emirates, Qatar, and other countries made it clear to Washington policy makers that they too believed the agreement could stoke an arms race in their region, with some saying they'd be forced to follow Iran's lead and develop nuclear technologies. "There's no way the Saudis won't match whatever Iran has," an Arab foreign minister said at a dinner party for foreign policy experts held in Washington weeks before the agreement was finalized in Vienna. He noted Riyadh's financial support for Pakistan, which had an expanding nuclear weapons arsenal. He said the Saudis could basically call in a bomb from Islamabad.

The White House responded by setting up an "anti-war room" in the basement of the West Wing to mobilize its campaign for the agreement. Computer screens remained logged on to Twitter to monitor commentary from opponents, and a small television helped staffers keep tabs on the cable news debate. For weeks the operation buzzed with senior White House officials, digital gurus, and rank-and-file aides running a rapid-response operation. The "anti-war" name of the room underscored the White House's realization earlier that year that the nuclear deal was unlikely to win any Republican votes in Congress and would require a battle plan focused on mustering support among Democrats skeptical of the deal.

The heart of the message crafted by the Obama administration during months of political plotting was a sharp yet divisive one: those who opposed the agreement were lobbying for another Middle East war. Despite the fact that only a few on the right were advocating military strikes, the White House weeded out nuance in its messaging when selling the deal. "Are you for solving this diplomatically or being forced . . . to war?" Ben Rhodes, one of Obama's closest foreign policy advisors, privately told Democratic activists in describing the message they should sell to Congress and their constituents back home. In an interview, Rhodes said about the congressional brawl: "I loved it. I thought it was healthy. . . . Maybe we didn't change minds on the other side, but we answered their questions."

CONGRESS DEMANDED ITS SAY on the nuclear agreement, and some form of oversight. President Obama had made it clear he would veto any moves to block the deal. But with Democrats joining the Republicans, lawmakers succeeded in winning a ninety-day period over which to review the terms of the deal. A vote would be scheduled at the end of the fall to show either support for the deal or the announcement of legislative efforts to kill it. Republicans needed to win over two-thirds of the Senate to garner enough votes to block the agreement and override an expected presidential veto.

Obama and his supporters pressed forward with the White House's plan to typecast the deal's opponents as warmongers. They specifically sought to tie critics of the agreement to those in Washington who supported the invasion of Iraq. The White House grumbled about the neoconservatives who were seeking to sabotage Obama's most important international initiative. Jewish leaders were worried the White House's campaign was taking on a not-so-subtle anti-Semitic tone, with its references to moneyed lobbyists and their ties to Prime Minister Netanyahu.

Mobilizing opposition to the deal in Congress was the American Israel Public Affairs Committee, or AIPAC. AIPAC has historically sought to be bipartisan and maintain good ties to both Democratic and Republican administrations. The organization took no position on the Iraq War (nor did the government of Israel). But AIPAC came out forcefully against the Iran agreement and oversaw a $20 million ad campaign to try to overturn it.

The White House was livid. In early August, President Obama met with two AIPAC leaders to fire a shot across their bow. The president accused the organization of spreading false messages about the terms of the agreement and of failing to allow his administration to correct those messages before AIPAC's members. Some Jewish groups had run ads describing the president as an appeaser and comparing him to the British prime minister Neville Chamberlain, who had signed the Munich Agreement with Adolf Hitler in 1938. Obama told them he wanted to maintain good relations with AIPAC, but also that he would challenge what he thought was a distorted position on the Iran deal.

A day later, Obama gave a nationally televised speech at American University. His aides chose the school specifically in order to dust off memories of John F. Kennedy—the Democratic icon had given a speech there at the height of the Cold War to warn against the dangers of a nuclear war with the Soviet Union. Obama raised similar concerns about the threat of conflict with Iran during his comments. But he also sent a clear warning to AIPAC and many in the pro-Israel crowd that his administration would not take the attacks on the agreement lying down. "If the rhetoric in these ads and the accompanying commentary sounds familiar, it should," Obama said. "Many of the people who argued for the war in Iraq are now making the case against the Iran nuclear deal."

A number of Jewish leaders worried that the White House was essentially blaming them for the string of Middle East wars that had consumed the United States and dredging up old tropes about Jews and their power to control politicians and governments. "Words have consequences, especially when it's authority figures saying them, and it's not their intent, perhaps, but we know from history that they can become manipulated," said Malcolm Hoenlien, executive vice chairman of the Conference of Presidents of Major American Jewish Organizations, who was among those who met with Obama in August. "Of all political leaders, he certainly should be the most sensitive to this."

Almost a dozen Republican presidential candidates, meanwhile, ganged up on the nuclear deal and uniformly rejected it. Many used their opposition to the deal to enhance their pro-Israel credentials, often through hyperbolic language and personal attacks on Obama. "By doing so, he will take the Israelis and march them to the door of the oven," former Arkansas governor Mike Huckabee said. "This is the most idiotic thing, this Iran deal. It should be rejected by both Democrats and Republicans in Congress and by the American people."

THE BATTLE FOR THE NUCLEAR DEAL at home grew personal, with critical coverage in the press targeted by the White House and its army of supporters as the fight in Congress intensified. The ghosts of the Iraq War still hadn't been exorcised in Washington in the spring and summer of 2015. The middle ground in the Iran debate essentially evaporated. Those in the media who voiced criticism of the emerging deal were often typecast as hawks or pro-Israel activists. Other reporters seemed to turn into cheerleaders for the merits of the agreement and how Obama was ushering in a new era of foreign policy.

Traveling to Switzerland in March 2015, I found it difficult to navigate the divide between the administration and its opponents, both at home and abroad. Even before the talks concluded, I was briefed by European diplomats that there was growing concern

about the terms on which Kerry and his team were making concessions. France wanted the United States to press Iran to provide access to a number of nuclear scientists and military sites in order for
the IAEA to gain clarity on just how far Iran had gone in developing
nuclear weapons technologies. They were worried Kerry had re-
lented on this point.

I followed up on the topic of France's ire and asked senior U.S.
administration officials in Lausanne if discord with France could
undercut the push for an agreement. I was assured this wasn't the
case. These American diplomats privately belittled the French as
being minor players in the talks and two-faced. They said that for all
of Paris's tough talk and bravado, the French would be the first to
travel to Iran to seek business deals once the agreement was forged.
They also said that at the end of the day, the Americans were making all the tough calls.

I continued to follow up on the issue of the French concerns
with a colleague who covered the White House. President Obama
had called French president François Hollande in the middle of the
talks in Switzerland to discuss tactics. We wanted to know from the
White House if the president had browbeaten the French leader for
insubordination. The administration wasn't amused by our inquiry:
I was informed I had been kicked off Kerry's next flight to the nuclear negotiations, which was coming up in just a few days. They
said I had violated the terms for traveling with the United States' top
diplomat, because I'd followed up on issues I'd heard discussed on
his plane—a zone of silence—and in particular the tensions with
the French. I'd never realized there was such a rule. The last reporter kicked off a State Department flight had broken a news embargo on when Secretary of State Hillary Clinton's plane would
land in Iraq, raising widespread concern inside the State Department's diplomatic security bureau about the future presidential candidate's safety. I didn't feel my questions equated to a national
security threat.

Others in the press corps got it even worse. David Sanger of *The*

New York Times was subjected to a coordinated White House–State Department Twitter assault after writing that Iran might not have the technical capabilities to dispose of its nuclear stockpile, as required by the nuclear accord. George Jahn of the Associated Press, meanwhile, was accused by White House supporters of being an Israeli asset after receiving a leaked document from the IAEA. His story documented how the Iranians wouldn't allow agency personnel to conduct their own soil sampling at a suspect military site. Instead, they would provide their own samples and would videotape the process, which Jahn equated with "self-inspections." Supporters of the White House, including in the nonproliferation community, charged that the document was forged and that Jahn had no journalistic ethics. Weeks later the agency announced that the major points raised in the AP's story were accurate.

THE ULTIMATE FAILURE OF REPUBLICANS to derail the deal was greeted with euphoria in the White House and State Department and among President Barack Obama's closest political supporters. Democrats hailed the Iran deal as a victory for a new era of U.S. foreign policy dominated by diplomacy rather than war and coercion. They raised hopes that an opening to Tehran would put an end to five decades of enmity between the United States and Iran and breed regional cooperation and business ties. They cited the deal as a major advancement in the quest to stop the spread of nuclear weapons.

"The new agreement doesn't overthrow the clerical regime ruling Iran. It doesn't change Iran's policies toward Israel or its Arab neighbors. And it doesn't force Iran to end the repression of its own people," wrote Joseph Cirincione, president of the Ploughshares Fund, an organization that emerged as one of Washington's biggest champions of the Iran deal. "The agreement forged between Iran and the world's powers does only one thing, but it is a big one: It reverses and contains what most experts consider the greatest nuclear proliferation challenge in the world."

On the day the Republican gambit failed in the Senate, President Obama made an unannounced trip to the State Department to meet with the U.S. negotiating team. John Kerry wasn't in his office when the president arrived, causing him to make a beeline up to the exclusive seventh floor to greet his boss. They cracked champagne and made toasts near a balcony that overlooked the National Mall, the presidential memorials, and, in the distance, the Potomac River. They discussed the many obstacles that had stood in the way of achieving the agreement, and how they had been overcome step by step.

At the heart of Obama's philosophy was a sense that they had righted history. The United States had rushed into a war in Iraq a decade earlier, and the president and his team believed they had narrowly avoided the same mistake in Iran, thus rewarding the voters who elected him. The era of a militarized foreign policy was over, they believed. "The president was proud that we found a diplomatic solution," said a senior U.S. official who joined in the State Department celebration. "Without an agreement, the likely fallout would have been a conflict. Sooner or later."

FAR FROM OPENING IRAN UP to Western ideas and communications, the nuclear deal, at least initially, hardened the regime both against Washington and against its own internal opponents in Tehran during the months around the deal's completion in July 2015.

The Revolutionary Guard continued its pattern of arresting American citizens in a bid to gain leverage over the United States and the White House in any dispute, whether concerning the nuclear deal or regional issues. Exactly a year before the deal, the IRGC's intelligence unit arrested *The Washington Post*'s Tehran bureau chief, Jason Rezaian, and charged him with espionage. This was in addition to two Americans already held in Iranian prisons. The Revolutionary Guard then arrested four more U.S. nationals after the deal, including a prominent Iranian American businessman named Siamak Namazi and his eighty-year-old father, who had worked at the UN.

The Obama administration responded to the arrests by again returning to a secret negotiating track with Tehran, this time through Geneva, Switzerland. Many of the United States' interlocutors were Iranian intelligence officials, rather than the smooth Westernized diplomats who ran the nuclear channel, such as Foreign Minister Zarif and Vice President Salehi. In January 2016, the White House approved a prisoner swap that resulted in the release of four Americans—including Rezaian, though not the Namazis—in exchange for seven Iranian nationals convicted of arms smuggling in the United States, as well as the dropping of extradition requests for fourteen Iranian government officials and business executives. The administration hailed the deal as another sign of the strength of direct negotiations with Tehran. But critics accused the White House of bowing to Iranian extortion. The day before the Americans were allowed to leave Tehran, the U.S. Treasury sent $1.7 billion to Iran. The administration said it was repayment for debts that went back to the shah's rule, but many in Congress viewed it as ransom. The money was later deposited in Iran's Ministry of Defense.

By early 2016, Iran had made good on its pledges under the nuclear deal to scale back its program. It took thousands of its centrifuges off line, shipped out most of its fissile material, and poured cement into the core of the Arak reactor. This was no small achievement, given that both the United States and Israel feared Iran had been just months away from building a nuclear bomb. The administration's claim it would take Iran a year to build a bomb if the Iranians mobilized now appeared to be accurate. "There are serious constraints on their nuclear program for fifteen years," Energy Secretary Moniz told me. "Fifteen years, with serious verification measures, should give considerably more comfort to our allies in the region."

But progress on the Iran deal was undercut by Iranian aggression elsewhere. Khamenei and the Revolutionary Guard stepped up ballistic missile tests, defying UN bans and raising fears they were moving ahead on a nuclear weapons program, even if the production of fissile material had largely been mothballed. U.S. officials have long acknowledged that there's little need for an Iranian missile program unless the country eventually plans to mount its rockets with nuclear payloads.

The joint Iranian-Russian moves into Syria, meanwhile, only stoked fears in Israel and the Arab states that Iran was going to use the end of its economic isolation to extend its regional role. Tehran was expected to get around $100 billion of its frozen oil revenues returned, in addition to the lifting of most international sanctions. Israeli officials said the Revolutionary Guard was using its presence inside Syria to plan joint military operations with Hezbollah on the Golan Heights. U.S. naval ships on numerous occasions interdicted Iranian ships ferrying arms to insurgents in Yemen, the Houthis, who had toppled the Saudi-backed government in San'a, fueling a furious air war launched by Riyadh in an attempt to drive them back.

In the Arabs' eyes, the defense of Assad and the Houthis were just the latest Iranian power grabs, greatly abetted by the U.S. invasion of Iraq and the Iran deal. "Iran is an occupying force in Syria," Saudi Arabia's foreign minister, Adel al-Jubeir, said on the sidelines of the UN assembly shortly after the deal. "We will devise a military solution if President Assad doesn't cede power." The Saudis believed Iran was essentially in control of four Arab capitals — Baghdad, Damascus, Beirut, and San'a.

Counter to the White House's hopes that the Iran agreement could help stabilize the Middle East, signs were emerging in the months after its completion that a broader war was a possibility. The Sunni states vowed to increase their support for co-religionist rebels who were fighting against the Russian-Iranian-Syrian alliance. And jihadist groups, including the Islamic State, were using Moscow's and Tehran's entrance into the Syrian war to mobilize their ranks. European officials worried that a new wave of refugees would flood into their countries from Syria and Iraq. They believed that the Islamic State could use the influx to send in terrorists, or recruit refugees, to launch more attacks on European cities like the ones in Paris and Brussels in 2015 and 2016. "This is the most dangerous time in the Middle East in decades," said Emile Hokayem, a regional analyst at the Institute for Strategic Studies in London. "A fuse has been lit, and the White House has diminished its ability to confront it."

U.S. AND EUROPEAN OFFICIALS involved in the Iran diplomacy say it is too early to gauge how the nuclear agreement will impact Tehran in the long term. President Obama has told aides that he believes the deal will strengthen moderate leaders such as President Rouhani as the country's economy improves and reconnects to the West. The Ayatollah Khamenei, who's battled cancer over the past decade, will eventually exit Tehran's political scene, possibly bringing an end to the theocratic system he helped bring into being in 1979.

In a positive sign, Rouhani's political allies gained seats in the Iranian parliament in January 2016, after many campaigned on the merits of the nuclear deal. Even though the regime marginalized many of Iran's democratic leaders after the 2009 uprising, the international community saw the vote as possibly the beginning of an era of reform. Iran is expected to reap considerably more economic gains in the coming years if the nuclear deal holds. "Historically, whether in Russia or eastern Europe, these types of political openings tend to bring political reforms. And you could make a good argument that the same will happen in Iran," said Michael McFaul, who served as the Obama administration's ambassador to Russia and worked on democracy promotion in the White House. "But is it a slam dunk? No!"

Secretary Moniz told me: "I think the real issue is what's going to happen on a decadal timeline on a range of behavior. The deal is a deal. It's not based on trust. It's really a verification-based deal on top of the rollback. But, obviously, we'd all love to see this maybe becoming the beginning of a reestablished relationship with us and the world community."

QUESTIONS ALSO REMAIN OVER whether the United States' own political system will allow a rapprochement with Iran to take root. Democratic leaders, including Hillary Clinton, have supported the nuclear deal, but Clinton has vowed to aggressively challenge Tehran's regional activities if elected. She's also bluntly said she'd bomb Iran's nuclear facilities if Tehran is found to be cheating on the deal. Republican leaders have been even more aggressive, vowing to tear up the agreement in the years ahead.

Barack Obama, meanwhile, has resigned himself to the fact that his Iran diplomacy will likely define the success or failure of his presidency, at least on the international stage. "Look, 20 years from now, I'm still going to be around, God willing. If Iran has a nuclear weapon, it's my name on this," Obama told *The Atlantic* in the weeks after the deal's signing. "I think it's fair to say that in addition to our profound national-security interests, I have a personal interest in locking this down."

THE IRAN WARS THAT have played out over the past fifteen years have consumed the United States' foreign policy agenda unlike any other single issue on the international stage. The Obama administration argues that the restraints placed on Iran's nuclear capabilities will offer a window for more responsible political actors to gain power in Tehran and forge a better relationship with the West. The diminished threat of an Iranian nuclear weapon, at least in the near term, reduces the threat of the United States' being ensnared in yet another Middle East war, President Obama has calculated. Washington can then shift its focus to Asia and Latin America, where booming economies offer Americans the opportunity to profit rather than fight.

But the history of Iran since the 1979 Islamic revolution suggests that the next U.S. administration must be prepared to confront an Iranian regime just as hostile to the West as past ones. Indeed, the conflict that has raged between the two countries over the past two decades has deepened, in many ways, the animosity that exists between the countries' militaries and spy agencies. New forms of warfare have emerged that have led Washington and Tehran to take their fight into new theaters, particularly cyberspace and the financial markets, and away from the traditional battlefield. Oil and sanctions are now part of each country's arsenal, adding an even more complex dynamic to the conflict.

The Iranian regime has shown little sign of toning down its animosity toward Washington and its allies in the aftermath of the Vienna agreement. The Revolutionary Guard continues to develop increasingly sophisticated weapons systems, including ballistic missiles inscribed with threats against Israel on their nose cones. Khamenei and other revolutionary leaders, meanwhile, fine-tune their rhetorical attacks against the United States, seeming to need the American threat to justify their existence.

The constraints placed on Iran's nuclear program over the next fifteen years offer an opportunity to calm the Middle East, as even critics in Israel and many Arab states acknowledge. But there are also real risks that a much bigger and broader war is brewing in the region, and that the United States will inevitably be drawn in.

The conflict between Iran and the United States' closest Arab allies, particularly Saudi Arabia, has intensified over the past two years. It's been fueled, in some ways, by Washington's attempts to build ties with Iran. Arab leaders obsess about a new U.S.-Iranian compact eclipsing the power of the Sunni states in favor of a "Shiite axis." They've made clear to the White House and Pentagon that they'll go it alone and confront Tehran across the region if the United States won't support their cause.

The principal battle line in this Sunni-Shiite and Saudi-Iranian conflict has been Syria. Tehran's unbending support for the Assad regime has fueled the flow of arms to anti-government militias from Saudi Arabia, Turkey, Qatar, and the United Arab Emirates. But it's also hastened the emergence of powerful, and radical, Sunni militias such as the Islamic State. This battle has spread into Yemen, Jordan, Lebanon, Iraq, and Turkey.

This rivalry raises the prospects of a nuclear arms race spreading across the Middle East as Saudi Arabia and its Sunni allies seek to match the technologies Iran has been allowed to amass. The costs of the Vienna agreement could only grow, and this Iran deal, rather than calming the world's most combustible region, risks further enflaming it. The Iran wars could just be entering a new chapter.

Acknowledgments

I N THE SUMMER OF 2006, I WAS IN LAGUNA BEACH, CALIFORNIA, ON A lazy summer vacation, when I received a phone call from an editor at *The Wall Street Journal* and was told to get ready to travel to the Middle East. The Lebanese militia and political party, Hezbollah, had just kidnapped two Israeli soldiers, and killed three others, after ambushing an Israeli tank near the Lebanese border. The Israel Defense Forces were beginning to retaliate by launching airstrikes on Lebanon, and the *Journal* wanted me in the position to cover a potentially widening regional war.

At the time, I'd barely stepped foot in the Middle East, despite working for more than a decade as a foreign correspondent. I'd covered conflict and Islamic terrorism in countries ranging from Indonesia to Pakistan. But I was a novice in understanding the history of the Arab-Israeli conflict and its entrenched politics and raw emotions. I'd also never faced firsthand the violence fueled by the Middle East's ethnic, religious, and clan feuds.

Arriving in Amman, Jordan, that July, I had little time to acclimate myself to the rapidly changing story before I was ordered to drive overland to Lebanon. The Israelis had blown out Beirut's international airport. I hired a local taxi for thousands of dollars and drove surreptitiously from Jordan through Syria and then over the border into Lebanon. My driver snaked through the steep mountain passes of the Bekaa Valley en route to Beirut, calling ahead to spotters to make sure we wouldn't be targeted by Israeli aircraft or come across bombed-out bridges. Convoys of cars and trucks were on the road. But they were all headed in the opposite direction—an ominous sign.

I was stunned by what I saw after eventually arriving in Beirut. The Mediterranean city, known as the Paris of the Middle East, wasn't exactly the hellhole I'd imagined after reading about Lebanon's decades of civil war. Spectacular ocean views and sunsets greeted me from my hotel veranda. Many nightclubs were still open. And scantily clad Lebanese women strolled the streets of Beirut's eastern enclave.

But the city was under siege, and the Israelis seemed determined to punish the Lebanese collectively by blowing up their country's power grids, freeways, and even its coastal lighthouse. The Beirutis seethed and cursed the Israelis as the bombings continued deep into the summer and the death toll rose. But many also blamed an invisible actor in the tragedy—one they said was driving Hezbollah to confront the Israelis from behind the scenes. The Lebanese militia would never have attacked the Jewish state without the green light of Iran, Hezbollah's chief financier, arms supplier, and religious guide, Lebanese leaders fumed. The Iranians were happy to sacrifice thousands of Lebanese in support of their regional rivalry with Israel and the United States, but without placing Tehran's own men at risk.

Iran was out of sight that summer in the Levant. But it was definitely not out of mind. The Islamic Republic, far from its borders, was inserting itself in the region's most intractable conflict through its support of Hezbollah, and seeking to lead the Islamic world against the West. This was a direct challenge to the United States.

The Lebanon war sparked my fixation on Iran and its role in the Middle East. And this would drive my coverage at *The Wall Street Journal* for the next decade. The battle that summer wasn't just about the Arab-Israeli dispute. It was about Iran's quest for regional dominance.

In the wake of the September 11, 2001, terrorist attacks on the

United States, the American public became consumed by the hunt for al Qaeda's leadership and the wars in Afghanistan and Iraq. But behind the headlines, the conflict between the United States and Iran, as well as their proxies, emerged as perhaps the single most important factor driving the region's carnage, from Iraq to Lebanon to Syria. Revelations of Iran's covert nuclear program and apparent designs to develop an atomic weapon only added more fuel to the fire.

I, therefore, set out to cover the U.S.-Iran conflict in the years following 9/11 from every angle that emerged and from every region. This proved to be a daunting task as Washington's efforts to check Tehran—and vice versa—grew to consume the entire U.S. national security apparatus. Military might and traditional espionage were key parts of this endeavor. But cyber warfare, financial sanctions, and, ultimately, secret diplomacy dominated as President Barack Obama radically shifted U.S. foreign policy away from that of the George W. Bush administration.

The Iran Wars is the fruit of this past decade of work. And, in all honesty, I had my doubts at times it would be completed. Initially envisaged in 2012 as a look at the U.S.-Iranian rivalry, and whether it might lead to a direct military conflict, the story radically shifted as news broke out the following year about the secret diplomacy in Oman. A book that at first sought to assess the potential for another Middle East war quickly morphed into a study of diplomacy and the prospects for two historical enemies coming to an accommodation with each other.

At this writing, the chances for success remain highly uncertain. But the nuclear accord in Vienna has fueled tremendous hope for a new relationship emerging between the United States and Iran and for Tehran to be reintegrated into the global community. I've tried in these pages to inject a healthy amount of honesty and skepticism into what's become a highly polarized debate on Iran. Walking a straight line, and threading a loop, is not an easy task when writing about U.S.-Iranian relations, as I found out. This was particularly the case in a political environment where the middle ground in Washington evaporated. I hope the readers of this book will recognize the sincere effort I made to chart a balanced path.

I owe an enormous amount of gratitude to *The Wall Street Journal*, and its editors and reporters, for helping me complete *The Iran Wars*. The paper gave me tremendous freedom and resources to track the Iran story in recent years as it raced across the Middle East and into the hotels and conference rooms of Europe. The story became so dominant that I worried at times I was neglecting my broader job as the paper's foreign affairs correspondent. But the *Journal*'s leadership understood the global importance of the Iran story and how it will almost certainly define President Obama's legacy. I'd particularly like to thank the *Journal*'s Washington bureau chief, Jerry Seib, and national security editor, Robert Ourlian, for putting up with my disappearing for a few weeks now and then to finish the manuscript. I also greatly appreciate the support of Editor in Chief Gerard Baker and his deputies, Rebecca Blumenstein and Matt Murray, as well as page one honcho Matthew Rose.

The Wall Street Journal's reporting staff both in Washington and the Middle East is exceptional. Carol E. Lee at the White House and national security reporter Adam Entous broke numerous scoops on Iran as the story played out during President Obama's second term. Julian Barnes and Gordon Lubold at the Pentagon assessed the potential for U.S. conflict with Iran, and Felicia Schwartz at the State Department followed Secretary of State John Kerry's endless globe-trotting in search of the nuclear deal.

Our reporters based overseas did a crack job of tracking Iran's efforts to profit from the Arab Spring and to spread its influence regionally. I'd particularly like to acknowledge Farnaz Fassihi, the top Iran expert at the paper; Sam Dagher, who raced in and out of Syria after the onset of the civil war there; Nour Malas, who also took exceptional risks reporting on her native Syria; and Asa Fitch and Benoit Faucon, who were great collaborators in covering the financial war on Iran.

A close-knit, but not always agreeable, group of journalists and analysts closely followed the Iran diplomacy as it took root in Switzerland, Austria, and New York in late 2013. My Brussels-based colleague Laurence Norman was an incredible ally in enduring the grueling negotiations that stretched on for weeks on end in Geneva and Vienna. It was no secret that he was always on the beat well before I stumbled down from my hotel room. Lou Charbonneau of Reuters, Julian Borger of *The Guardian*, Michael Gordon and David Sanger of *The New York Times*, and Bradley Klapper and Matthew Lee of the Associated Press were all wonderful colleagues over the past three years. I'm only sad that Michael Adler, the great correspondent of Agence France-Presse, didn't get to report on the final negotiations. He passed away in the summer of 2014. No journalist tracked the Iranian nuclear program more closely over the past decade than Michael, from both Washington and Europe.

In the United States, Middle East, and Europe, a skilled group of Iran analysts, nuclear experts, and sanctions aficionados helped me understand the incredibly complex dimensions of the Iran standoff. In the nuclear field, I'd like to thank David Albright, Olli Heinonen, and Robert Einhorn for spending hours explaining to me the history of Iran's nuclear program. Mark Dubowitz, David Asher, Juan Zarate, Avi Jorisch, and Stuart Levey were invaluable in describing the often-arcane laws and strategies tied to running a financial war. And on the broader issue of Iran in the world, I'd like to thank Karim Sadjadpour of the Carnegie Endowment for International Peace, Hossein Mousavian of Princeton University, Andrew Tabler of the Washington Institute for Near East Policy, and Emile Hokayem of the International Institute of Strategic Studies.

Former colleagues and mentors were instrumental in helping my journalism career over the years. John McBeth of the *Far Eastern Economic Review* took me under his wing in Indonesia during the late 1990s and taught me how to be a foreign correspondent. I'll always remember talking and writing in his lime-green Jakarta office as we covered the final months of President Suharto. My first editors at the *Journal*, Marcus Brauchli, Peter Waldman, and Michael Williams, were critical in helping me learn how to make the complexities of international stories accessible to U.S. readers. They were also all good friends.

The Iran Wars was initially conceptualized in 2012 with my agents Gail Ross and Howard Yoon, when talk of war with Iran was still rife. I want to thank both of them for sticking with me through a process that took far longer than I think any of us initially imagined. But they were patient with me as the news took control of the project and led it in new directions. I appreciate their confidence in me.

At Random House, Will Murphy and Molly Turpin were great co-pilots in navigating a book that definitely took on a life of its own. Will, a fellow Berkeley alum, knew exactly when to step in, and when not to, over the past two years as Iran dominated the global news headlines. Molly was tireless in going through literally every page of the book with me after the Vienna agreement was completed in mid-2015. Her fresh eye and enthusiasm repeatedly picked me up when I was spent mentally and too close to the writing.

Finally, I want to thank my family for bearing with me through the final stages of the book. My father, Richard, and his wife, Anne Solomon, always gave me encouragement and pep talks during Sunday dinners at their Washington home. My mother, Carol, encouraged me to write, even in my younger years when I spent way more time playing volleyball than studying in high school and college. My sister, Lisa Solomon, and brother-in-law, Randall Davidson, cheered me on throughout the project. And my son, Hudson, arrived as a blessing in early 2013, not long after I committed to writing *The Iran Wars*. I was comforted and inspired by him looking over my shoulder as I typed away. I look forward to spending much more time with Hudson now that the project is completed.

Notes

PROLOGUE: A DIPLOMATIC RUSE

3 **On September 26, 2013, Secretary of State John Kerry:** Author's notes from covering P5+1 meeting on Iran in New York at the UN General Assembly.

5 **"We hope to be able to make progress":** Ibid.

6 **"I think all of us were pleased":** Ibid.

7 **A scheduled fifteen-minute meet-and-greet:** Author interviews with three U.S. officials briefed on the Kerry-Zarif meeting.

7 **"The president and I both had a sense":** Author interview with John Kerry.

11 **"there was definitely a fear that strikes":** Author interview with Fred Hof.

11 **"Whether the deal is approved or disapproved":** Ayatollah Ali Khamenei, Iranian state television, July 18, 2015.

11 **"The White House bet the farm on reaching an accommodation":** Author interview with senior Israeli official, who spoke on the condition of anonymity.

CHAPTER 1: THE PERSIAN DOMINO

12 **In the northern hills of Tehran lies a tribute:** Author's notes from 2014 visit to the Holy Defense Museum in Tehran.

13 **"How could you have worked with Saddam?":** Ibid.

18 **"You both respect them, but also realize":** Author interview with Bill Murray.

19 **"An effective policy on Iraq offers the United States":** David Wurmser, *Tyranny's Ally: America's Failure to Defeat Saddam Hussein* (Washington: AEI Press, 1999), 72.

20 **"Lebanon-based terror is a major tool used by Iran":** Ibid, 110.

21 **"You think we wouldn't have checked":** Author interview with senior Iranian official, who spoke on the condition of anonymity.

22 **"We thought we were being set up":** Author interview with Ambassador Zalmay Khalilzad.

22 **"I never understood the rationale for the war"**: Author interview with Michael Oren.

24 **"You couldn't read the key judgments"**: Author interview with John Bolton.

24 **"We just thought this would be a catastrophe"**: Author interview with Benjamin Rhodes.

28 **"There are two futures"**: Robin Wright, "Javad Zarif on Iran's Nuclear Negotiations," *New Yorker*, May 21, 2014.

CHAPTER 2: THE MISSED CHANCE

29 **"In the final analysis, we doubt"**: Ayatollah Ali Khamenei, Iranian state media, September 26, 2001.

30 **"Everybody should know that Iran"**: Ibid.

31 **"A huge opportunity appeared after 9/11"**: Author interview with Hossein Mousavian.

35 **"My first day at the CIA"**: Author interview with Gary Berntsen.

35 **"I told the Afghans"**: Author interview with Henry Crumpton.

35 **"[This] horrified the Afghans"**: Author interview with Gary Berntsen.

35 **"This was a good thing for us"**: Author interview with Henry Crumpton.

36 **"It turned out that the Iranian Revolutionary Guard Corps"**: Gary Schroen, *First In: An Insider's Account of How the CIA Spearheaded the War on Terror in Afghanistan* (New York: Presidio Press, 2005). Kindle edition, chap. 17.

37 **"Massoud was a gentleman"**: Author interview with Gary Berntsen.

37 **"The only reason they even pretended"**: Author interview with Henry Crumpton.

38 **"The Iranians had given much more lethal"**: Author interview with former CIA officer based in Afghanistan and Pakistan.

38 **"Qasem is a very pragmatic commander"**: Author interview with Hossein Mousavian.

40 **"Zarif was the face the regime liked to put forward"**: Author interview with Karim Sadjadpour.

41 **"They were pretty specific that they were willing"**: Author interview with James Dobbins.

42 **"Powell thought that our interests"**: Ibid.

42 **"The Iranians would sometimes beat down my door"**: Author interview with Zalmay Khalilzad.

43 **"Should we not insist that the new Afghan regime"**: James Dobbins, *After the Taliban: Nation-Building in Afghanistan* (Washington: Potomac Books, 2008). Kindle edition, p. 83.

44 **"Iranians do not consider their own weaknesses"**: Author interview with Harold Rhode.

46 **"Ghorbanifar, in the end, was only"**: Author interview with George Cave.

47 **"This was good information"**: Author interview with Michael Ledeen.

48 **"None of the information bore any ties"**: Author interview with Bill Murray.

50 "This was a remarkable moment": Author interview with James Dobbins.

50 "The Iranians were very supportive in London": Author interview with Zalmay Khalilzad.

52 "We felt like we couldn't keep this going": Ibid.

CHAPTER 3: THE SHIITE CRESCENT

56 "[Military maneuvers in Tehran] are aimed": Harmony Documents, Combating Terrorism Center at West Point.

57 "During his visit to Kuwait, Mohammad Baqir al-Hakim": Ibid.

57 "We certainly sought to shake things up": Author interview with Douglas Feith.

59 "If you can release Najaf, you can": Author interview with Ladan Archin.

61 Chalabi and his aides viewed establishing ties: Author interview with Francis Brooke.

63 "We should be very, very careful": Author viewed personal diary of Michael Rubin written during his Iraq tour.

64 "It seems like the Iranians knew": Ibid.

66 "People simply are afraid to come out": Ibid.

67 "The Iranians are thinking three or four steps ahead": Ibid.

69 "In 2006, Iran seemed to make a tactical decision": Author interview with Stephen Hadley.

70 "Soleimani can be brutal or cunning": Author interview with Mouwaffak al-Rubaie.

72 The Kurdish politician Noshirwan Mustafa reported angrily: State Department cable sent from Baghdad, June 4, 2009.

73 "He came to get rid of Jaafari": Author interview with Zalmay Khalilzad.

75 "The instructors were members of Lebanese Hezbollah": Harmony Documents, Combating Terrorism Center at West Point.

75 "Everyone in JAM tells everyone": Ibid.

76 "Iraqi [Special Group] trainees do not like": Ibid.

77 "They were totally shocked": Author interview with retired general Stanley McChrystal.

78 "The Americans came to detain this delegation": Associated Press, "Kurd Leader Says U.S. Troops Tried to Capture Revolutionary Guards in Raid," April 7, 2007.

79 "Daqduq contends that the Iraqi special groups": Brigadier General Kevin Bergner, Department of Defense briefing, July 2, 2007.

79 "They did a very good job": Author interview with Stanley McChrystal.

80 "General Petraeus, you should know that I": Author interviews with two U.S. defense officials who saw the correspondence.

80 "General Petraeus mentioned that we continue": State Department cable sent from Baghdad, November 15, 2009.

81 "If we sustain casualties from one of these IRAMs": Author interview with senior U.S. defense official briefed on the exchange.

CHAPTER 4: THE AXIS OF RESISTANCE

82 "It was a very cynical alliance in every respect": Author interview with Mouwaffak al-Rubaie.

83 "The United States and Britain will not be able": President Bashar al-Assad interview with *as-Safir* newspaper, March 27, 2003.

83 "Muslims must use all possible means": Statement released by Sheikh Ahmad Kuftaro, Grand Mufti of Syria, March 26, 2003.

85 "The Damascus fairgrounds are owned and operated": Author interview with David Schenker.

89 he told Hariri he would "break Lebanon over Hariri's" head: Author interviews with Rafik Hariri's political allies, including the Druze politician Walid Jumblatt.

90 In December 2004, Badreddine and three other Hezbollah men: Special Tribunal for Lebanon report on Hariri assassination, June 2011.

92 A seventeen-year-old Libyan national named Muhammad Anwar Rafiia'a Yahiya: "Al-Qa'ida's Foreign Fighters in Iraq: A First Look at the Sinjar Records," Harmony Documents, Combating Terrorism Center at West Point.

93 "Syria has an interest in keeping the U.S.-backed regime": Ibid.

94 "the cooperation the Syrians provided in their own interest": Congressional testimony of William Burns, assistant secretary of state for Near East affairs, June 2003.

95 Elliott Abrams, one of President Bush's closest Middle East advisors: Author's interviews with three Bush administration officials who described White House debate on whether or not to bomb Damascus International Airport.

97 "Be careful when you're there": Author's interviews with two former U.S. officials present at the meeting with Hillary Clinton.

97 "Now we can begin to pursue new projects": Author interview with Adib Mayaleh.

99 "He doesn't want to lead a religious-based country": Author's interviews with two Arab Americans who attended Kerry dinner in 2009.

100 "I thought what I brought back": Author interview with John Kerry.

100 "My judgment is that Syria will move": John Kerry speech at Carnegie Endowment for International Peace, Washington, D.C., March 16, 2011.

101 "I never argued Assad was a reformer": Author interview with John Kerry.

102 "You have to be there in forty-eight hours": Author interview with Imad Moustapha.

103 "And now they're turning to us": Author interview with Bouthaina Shaaban.

105 "It is not my democracy as a person": Author interview with Bashar al-Assad.

105 "Syria is stable. Why?": Ibid.

105 "What you have been seeing in this region": Ibid.

106 "How can you accuse anyone": Ibid.

106 "If they believed it was nuclear": Ibid.

106 "We need to have normal relations": Ibid.

110 One of them, Alois Brunner, settled in Damascus in the late 1950s: Jodi Rudoren, "A Long-Sought Fugitive Died Four Years Ago in Syria, Nazi Hunter Says," *New York Times*, December 1, 2014.

111 "We along with other Palestinian factions": Author interview with Khaled Meshaal.

112 "If Israel doesn't accept a halt": Ibid.

CHAPTER 5: THE PHYSICS RESEARCH CENTER

115 "Many secretive nuclear activities are at work": National Council of Resistance of Iran press conference, August 14, 2002.

116 Jafarzadeh, however, didn't expose the MeK's secret collaborator: Author's interviews with three current and former U.S. officials who outlined intelligence relationship between the MeK and Israel.

117 "They seemed to have trouble digesting this thing": Author interview with Alireza Jafarzadeh.

118 One of the sites disclosed by Jafarzadeh: National Council of Resistance of Iran press conference, August 14, 2002.

120 Shortly after it was established, the Physics Research Center began sending: David Albright and Paul Brannan, "The Physics Research Center Telexes: New ISIS Studies and Findings," Institute for Science and International Security, May 16, 2012.

122 The telexes also show that a "Department 70": Ibid.

122 One of these was Ali Akbar Salehi: Ibid.

122 "We have strongly marked our opposition": Ali Akbar Salehi, "We Do Not Want Nuclear Weapons," *Washington Post*, April 12, 2002.

123 First it merged into an office inside the Defense Ministry: *Implementation of the NPT Safeguards Agreement and the Relevant Provisions of Security Council Resolutions in the Islamic Republic of Iran*, International Atomic Energy Agency, November 8, 2011.

123 "Our [nuclear] capabilities are adequate at the moment": Eric Follath and Holger Stark, "The Birth of a Bomb: A History of Iran's Nuclear Ambitions," *Der Spiegel*, June 17, 2010.

123 A breakthrough for Fakhrizadeh's program came: *Implementation of the NPT Safeguards Agreement and the Relevant Provisions of Security Council Resolutions in the Islamic Republic of Iran*, International Atomic Energy Agency, November 8, 2011.

124 So began a six-year relationship that became central: "Revisiting Danilenko and the Explosive Chamber at Parchin," Institute for Science and International Security, September 7, 2012.

126 Not long after Jafarzadeh's disclosure in Washington in 2002: Author's interviews with two U.S. intelligence officials briefed on the intercept of Fakhrizadeh's phone conversation.

127   Regardless, Fakhrizadeh's communications ended up forming: *Iran: Nuclear Intentions and Capabilities*, U.S. National Intelligence Council, November 2007.

128   Intelligence on Iran's nuclear work continued: Eric Follath and Holger Stark, "The Birth of a Bomb: A History of Iran's Nuclear Ambitions," *Der Spiegel*, June 17, 2010.

129   The CIA began secretly communicating with a researcher: Author interview of former CIA officer directly involved in Shahram Amiri operation.

130   A year after Amiri's arrival in the United States: Shahram Amiri videos posted on YouTube between June and July 2010: https://www.youtube .com/watch?v=GSr8ck7Pqj4; https://www.youtube.com/watch?v= V1FgM4jQdRE; https://www.youtube.com/watch?v=HMLJQ5vuYao.

131   "I don't think that any Iranian": Shahram Amiri statement to Iranian media upon arrival in Tehran on July 15, 2010.

131   "This was an intelligence war between the CIA and us": Unidentified Iranian intelligence official to Fars News Agency, July 21, 2010.

132   Fashi, in a lengthy account of the assassination: Fashi's confession was broadcast on Iranian state media and detailed in government news accounts. Author corroborated claims with Iranian government officials.

136   One of Soleimani's deputy generals: "Treasury Sanctions Five Individuals Tied to Iranian Plot," Treasury Department press release, October 11, 2011.

136   Shahlai's reach stretched far beyond Iraq: *United States of America vs. Mansor Arbabsiar, Gholam Shakuri*, Department of Justice, October 11, 2011.

138   "How are your efforts going to buy the Chevrolet?": Ibid.

138   "This was directed and approved by elements": Eric Holder press conference at Department of Justice, October 11, 2011.

141   "The Islamic Republic of Iran and North Korea": Ayatollah Ali Khamenei's comments to Fars News Agency, September 1, 2012.

141   "Six years ago the intelligence service of the U.K.": Fereydoun Abbasi-Davani press conference at IAEA headquarters in Vienna, September 20, 2011.

CHAPTER 6: THE RIAL WAR

144   "We learned that denying access to the dollar": Author interview with Juan Zarate.

146   "We wanted to find a way to put the Iranian regime": Author interview with Stuart Levey.

147   "We saw an escalating financial war that had": Ibid.

148   "As you make your business decisions": Stuart Levey speech to the 5th Annual Conference on Trade, Treasury and Financial Management in Dubai, March 7, 2007.

149   "We were concerned that . . . [if we were] so abrupt": Author interview with Benjamin Rhodes.

154   "'Don't test us' was our message": Author interview with senior Treasury official who spoke on the condition of anonymity.

154 "As their financial options get narrower": Author interview with Adam Szubin.

156 "If there is a buck to be made with the Iranians": Author interview with Robert Morgenthau.

158 "I have to be kept informed, and I have to be able": *United States District Court Southern District of New York, in Relation 650 Fifth Avenue and Related Properties*, September 16, 2013.

159 The processing steps were laid out in an internal document: *United States of America v. Lloyds TBS Bank PLC*, January 9, 2009.

160 Jahedi was among a coterie of Iranian government officials: *United States District Court Southern District of New York in Relation 650 Fifth Avenue and Related Properties*, September 16, 2013.

161 "I don't think anyone realized that the Iranians": Author interview with Eitan Arusy.

161 Lawyer Steven Perles: Author interviews with Steven Perles and his legal associates.

165 In early 2009, Levey surprised Perles: Author interviews with current and former Treasury officials involved in the Clearstream case.

165 "We couldn't believe, in many ways": Author interview with Steven Perles.

166 "The case [made] it clear to Iran": Ibid.

CHAPTER 7: THE CLENCHED FIST

170 "In particular, I would like to speak directly": President Barack Obama, Nowruz address, March 20, 2009.

171 "They chant the slogan of change, but no change": Supreme Leader Ayatollah Ali Khamenei nationally televised speech, March 21, 2009.

171 "He left the door open": Author interview with former U.S. official who saw Khamenei's written response to Obama.

172 "I think I would closely coordinate with my advisors": Hillary Clinton during Democratic presidential debate, April 16, 2008.

172 "He decided that instead of backing off it": Author interview with Benjamin Rhodes.

174 "Senator Obama wants to sit down, without any precondition": John McCain during Louisiana campaign stop, June 4, 2008.

174 "Our willingness to pursue diplomacy": Barack Obama speech to American Israel Public Affairs Committee, June 4, 2008.

175 "What was interesting about Iran is that lots of things": Author interview with Benjamin Rhodes.

177 "Our eyes are wide open" when it comes to Iran: Author interview with U.S. official who attended Clinton meeting.

178 "Because Iranians seem willing to take risks": Author interview with Jennifer Windsor.

178 "The White House clearly didn't want to rock the boat": Author interview with Karim Sadjadpour.

181 **Administration officials who took part in the debates:** Author interviews with four current and former U.S. officials who took part in the debate on the Green Movement uprising.

181 **President Obama ultimately decided to remain silent:** Author interviews with two CIA officers working on Iran during 2009 Green Movement uprising.

182 **" 'Let's give it a few days' was the answer":** Author interview with senior official involved in White House deliberations, who requested anonymity.

182 **"If you were working on the nuclear deal":** Author interview with Michael McFaul.

182 **"Although there is amazing ferment taking place":** President Barack Obama, interview on CNBC, June 16, 2009.

182 **"It is up to Iranians to make decisions":** President Barack Obama, White House statement, June 16, 2009.

184 **"In 2009, no iron fist is strong enough":** President Barack Obama, White House press conference, June 23, 2009.

185 **"There were a few days where the opposition":** Author interview with Karim Sadjadpour.

188 **"This limits Iran's ability to have the breakout":** State Department briefing on Iran negotiations, October 1, 2009.

189 **"The failure of the Geneva agreement really marked":** Author interview with Dennis Ross.

190 **"America is angry over the proximity":** Parisa Hafezi, "Turkey, Brazil Seal Deal on Iran Nuclear Fuel Swap," Reuters, May 16, 2010.

191 **"The confidence that the original . . . deal would have":** Author interview with State Department official who requested anonymity.

191 **"For reasons known only to them, the leaders":** President Barack Obama, Nowruz address, March 20, 2010.

CHAPTER 8: BLACK GOLD

194 **"If you sanctioned the Iranian central bank":** Author interview with Stuart Levey.

196 **In talks with the Chinese, Ross and other U.S. officials:** Author interviews with U.S. and Arab officials involved in Ross's oil deliberations.

197 **"Iran is very vulnerable in the oil sector":** Saudi prince Turki al-Faisal in a private speech to British and American servicemen at RAF Molesworth air base outside London, June 8, 2011.

197 **"In 2011, every bilateral meeting that the president":** Author interview with Benjamin Rhodes.

198 **"We spent many hours in these consultations with them":** Author interview with senior U.S. official involved in the Israel consultations.

200 **"There's not an issue we worked on as intensively":** Author interview with Benjamin Rhodes.

200 **"You have rebuffed [sanctions on Bank Markazi]":** Senator Robert Menen-

dez during Foreign Relations Committee hearing on "U.S. Strategic Objectives Towards Iran," December 1, 2011.

200 **"I am writing to express the administration's strong opposition"**: Treasury Secretary Timothy Geithner's letter to Senate leaders, December 1, 2011.

201 **"That was the statistic I found most surprising"**: Author interview with Adam Szubin.

201 **the Foundation for Defense of Democracies**: Author interviews with Mark Dubowitz and Richard Goldberg.

203 **Senior executives of the global financial institutions**: Society for Worldwide Interbank Financial Telecommunication's corporate bylaws.

204 **"no specialized financial messaging shall be provided"**: European Central Bank guidelines.

205 **"The sanctions were a catalyzer that exposed"**: Author interview with Akbar Komijani.

206 **Industry in the country seized up**: Farnaz Fassihi and Jay Solomon, "In Iran's Factories and Shops, Tighter Sanctions Exact Toll," *Wall Street Journal*, January 3, 2013.

206 **"From the owner to the line worker"**: Ibid.

CHAPTER 9: THE ARAB SPRING

209 **As the year progressed, the Obama administration**: Author interview with senior U.S. intelligence official, who spoke on the condition of anonymity.

210 **General Soleimani and his staff concluded**: Ibid.

211 **"Some countries might have concluded"**: Author interview with U.S. defense official, who spoke on the condition of anonymity.

212 **The popular movements in the region "indicate a fundamental change"**: Supreme Leader Ayatollah Ali Khamenei in Persian New Year speech, March 27, 2011.

212 **"From the outside, what is the role of the West?"**: Author interview with Bashar al-Assad.

213 **"In too many places, in too many ways"**: Hillary Clinton speech to the Forum of the Future in Doha, Qatar, January 13, 2011.

214 **In March 2011, the State Department's top Mideast official**: Author interviews with two State Department officials involved in the Bahrain mission.

215 **"We were straightforward with the Americans"**: Author interview with Saudi advisor to the royal family.

216 **"We needed to send a clear signal"**: Author interview with senior White House official involved in Libya deliberations.

217 **"I was amazed at what I saw that Iran had done"**: Author interview with senior Pentagon official involved in Middle East policy.

218 **"There's a different leader in Syria now"**: Hillary Clinton on CBS's *Face the Nation*, March 27, 2011.

218 **In late April, Syrian security forces entered Deraa**: Nour Malas, "Syria Revolt Fueled by Roof Fires and Tweets," *Wall Street Journal*, July 15, 2011.

219 **Protestors were using calls for reform "to fragment Syria"**: President Bashar al-Assad speech before Syrian parliament, March 31, 2011.

220 **"We have consistently said that President Assad"**: President Barack Obama, written statement, August 18, 2011.

221 **He personally dispatched one of the IRGC's top commanders**: Author interviews with U.S. and Arab intelligence officials.

222 **Iran's widening military presence inside Syria**: Farnaz Fassihi, "Tensions Rise over Iranian Hostages," *Wall Street Journal*, August 2, 2012.

222 **"Assad asked for them to be on the ground"**: Author interview with General Yahya Bittar, Free Syrian Army intelligence chief, Reyhanli, Turkey.

223 **"We feel safe, we don't want them to leave"**: Farnaz Fassihi, Jay Solomon, and Sam Dagher, "Iranians Dial Up Presence in Syria," *Wall Street Journal*, September 16, 2013.

223 **"We could have butchered them all"**: Ibid.

224 **"We did the heavy lifting"**: Ibid.

224 **"They are told that the war in Syria is akin to Imam Hussein's epic battle"**: Ibid.

225 **"Syria is the front line of resistance"**: Ibid.

225 **"They're trying to reconstitute the Persian Empire"**: Author interview with senior Jordanian intelligence official in Amman, Jordan.

226 **"We've seen almost nothing in terms of help"**: Author interview with General Yahya Bittar, Free Syrian Army intelligence chief.

228 **"We are getting ready and mobilized for the strikes"**: Author interview with Abu Mohammad al-Attar, Free Syrian Army commander.

229 **"The Iranian diplomats said it wouldn't be their decision"**: Author interview with Iranian official who spoke on the condition of anonymity.

230 **"The U.S. gave us the impression that they"**: Author interview with Saudi prince Turki al-Faisal in Monaco.

231 **"Is there a symbiotic relationship between Iran and ISIS?"**: Author interview with senior Pentagon official involved in Middle East policy.

232 **"When the Syrian army is not fighting the Islamic State"**: Maria Abi-Habib, "Assad Policies Aided Rise of Islamic State Militant Group," *Wall Street Journal*, August 22, 2014.

232 **"We have seen what appear to be credible reports"**: Senior State Department official on Syria peace talks in Geneva.

233 **"The network . . . uses Iran as a transit point"**: "Treasury Targets Networks Linked to Iran," Treasury Department press statement, February 6, 2014.

233 **"U.S. policies in Iraq and Syria were subjected"**: Joseph Bahout, Brookings Institution Middle East forum, November 24, 2015.

CHAPTER 10: THE ROAD TO VIENNA

234 **Salem ben Nasser al-Ismaily was hardly a high-profile player**: Author interviews with Arab, U.S., and European officials directly involved in Ismaily's work.

235 "The policy of peace is good for everyone": Salem ben Nasser al-Ismaily comments at World Economic Forum, Dead Sea, Jordan, October 24, 2011.

237 "We always must walk a cautious line": Author interview with Salem ben Nasser al-Ismaily.

237 "Iran is a logical export destination": State Department cable from Muscat, Oman, January 7, 2010.

239 Beginning in 2010, Ismaily began shuttling between: Author interviews with U.S. and Arab officials involved in the negotiations; Shane Bauer, Joshua Fattal, and Sarah Shourd, *A Sliver of Light* (New York: First Mariner Books, 2014).

241 "The Omanis came to us indicating": Author interview with Benjamin Rhodes.

242 "I began long conversations to try and lay the groundwork": Author interview with John Kerry.

243 "We didn't approach this with the sense": Ibid.

243 "Kerry was actually talking substance with the Omanis": Author interview with Benjamin Rhodes.

245 "In an administration where the White House dominates": Author interview with retired Western diplomat who took part in Track II talks with Iran.

246 "The main purpose for us was": Author interview with Benjamin Rhodes.

246 "We essentially hit the same brick wall": Author interview with U.S. diplomat involved in the Oman talks.

248 "While we were talking with the Europeans": Hassan Rouhani, "Beyond the Challenges Facing Iran and the IAEA Concerning the Nuclear Dossier," speech, April 19, 2006.

248 "The only way to interact with Iran": Hassan Rouhani, inaugural speech, August 4, 2013.

249 "The election of Rouhani likely opened things up": Author interview with Wendy Sherman.

249 "Happy Rosh Hashanah": Mohammad Javad Zarif Twitter feed, September 4, 2013.

250 "Thanks. The New Year would be even sweeter": Christine Pelosi Twitter feed, September 4, 2013.

251 Iran's nuclear program "is our moon shot": Author interview with U.S. diplomat involved in the talks.

252 "During my tenure in office as president": Hassan Rouhani, speech before Asia Society in New York, September 26, 2013.

254 "We didn't have enough time to prepare": Author interview with Alireza Miryousefi.

254 "While there will surely be important obstacles": President Barack Obama, televised address, September 27, 2013.

257 "One wants a deal . . . but not a sucker's deal": French foreign minister Laurent Fabius, France Inter radio, November 9, 2013.

257 "He didn't have any leverage": Author interview with U.S. official involved in talks with the French.

258 "We expect the West to have a united stance": Javad Zarif, Iranian state television, November 21, 2013.

258 "What was concluded in Geneva last night": Israeli prime minister Benjamin Netanyahu, statement, November 25, 2013.

CHAPTER 11: KHAMENEI'S SHADOW

260 U.S. and European diplomats struggled to understand: Author interviews with U.S. and European officials who took part in the talks.

261 "The IRGC made out like bandits under the sanctions": Author interview with Wendy Sherman.

262 "On the issue of enrichment capacity": Supreme Leader Ayatollah Ali Khamenei, nationally televised speech, July 8, 2014.

262 "He seemed to have no idea where it came from": Author interview with senior U.S. negotiator.

262 "The personal interplay in all of this was fascinating": Author interview with John Kerry.

263 "To squeeze them further was to guarantee": Ibid.

264 "To the Iranians, they wanted to hear the magic phrase": Author interview with Benjamin Rhodes.

268 "The Iranians could not move without Salehi": Author interview with Ernest Moniz.

270 "It has come to our attention while observing": Tom Cotton, letter to Iran's leadership, signed by 47 Senate Republicans, March 2, 2015.

270 Kerry convened a meeting with Zarif where he sought: State Department briefing in Lausanne, March 16, 2015.

270 "Although we see the letter as a political move": Javad Zarif, comments to reporters in Lausanne, March 16, 2015.

271 "We hope this is a year that can bring us prosperity and peace": Author's notes from covering Kerry-Zarif meeting, March 20, 2015.

272 "Making the end of March an absolute deadline": Gerard Araud Twitter feed, March 20, 2015.

273 "There was little doubt at that point": Author interview with European diplomat at Lausanne talks.

274 "Contrary to the Americans' insistence, we do not": Supreme Leader Ayatollah Ali Khamenei, speech commemorating Muslim holy month of Ramadan, June 24, 2015.

275 "The Obama administration is saying this is only": Author interview with Flynt Leverett.

276 "So many wars have been fought over misunderstandings": Author interview with John Kerry.

278 "The whole hotel could hear you": Indira A. R. Lakshmanan, "Iran Deal: The Inside Account," *Politico*, September 25, 2015.

279 **"Don't threaten an Iranian":** Laurence Norman, "New Tensions Emerge in Iran Nuclear Talks," *Wall Street Journal*, July 9, 2015.

279 **"So this is a question that should be posed":** Iranian briefing for foreign reporters in Vienna, July 6, 2015.

280 **"This decision on weaponization will haunt the international community":** Author interview with Olli Heinonen.

280 **Kerry and the other world leaders privately gathered:** Indira A. R. Lakshmanan, "Iran Deal: The Inside Account," *Politico*, September 25, 2015.

281 **"He assured us that he did":** Author interview with U.S. official involved in Vienna talks.

281 **"My hope is that Iran will change some of its behavior":** Author interview with John Kerry.

282 **"The samples . . . the samples":** Author interview with Yukiya Amano.

CONCLUSION: WAR AND PEACE

283 **Ten days after the Vienna accord:** Soleimani's trip to Moscow described by U.S. and Arab intelligence officials who tracked it.

284 **The Iranian envoy, Ali Akbar Velayati:** Velayati's trip to Moscow reported by Russian and Iranian state media on January 29, 2015.

284 **"The Russians were very alarmed, and felt matters":** Laila Bassam and Tom Perry, "How Iranian General Plotted Out Syrian Assault in Moscow," *Reuters*, October 6, 2015.

285 **"Negotiations with the United States open gates":** Supreme Leader Ayatollah Ali Khamenei, nationally televised speech, October 7, 2015.

285 **"One reason Iran was able to negotiate so successfully":** Senate Republican leader Mitch McConnell during congressional debate, September 17, 2015.

287 **"This is a bad deal. It's a very bad deal":** Israeli prime minister Benjamin Netanyahu, speech before U.S. Congress, March 3, 2015.

287 **"There's no way the Saudis won't match":** Author's notes from an off-record dinner with senior Arab diplomats in Washington.

287 **The White House responded by setting up an "anti-war room":** Carol E. Lee and Siobhan Hughes, "Obama Methodically Wooed Democrats to Back Iran Nuclear Deal," *Wall Street Journal*, September 11, 2015.

288 **"Are you for solving this diplomatically":** Tape of conference call involving White House deputy national security advisor Benjamin Rhodes and liberal activist groups, January 2014.

288 **"I loved it. I thought it was healthy":** Author interview with Benjamin Rhodes.

289 **Obama told them he wanted to maintain good relations:** Julie Hirschfeld Davis, "Fears of Lasting Rift as Obama Battles Pro-Israel Group on Iran," *New York Times*, August 7, 2015.

289 **"If the rhetoric in these ads and the accompanying commentary":** President Barack Obama, speech at American University, August 5, 2015.

290 **"Words have consequences, especially when"**: Julie Hirschfeld Davis, "Fears of Lasting Rift as Obama Battles Pro-Israel Group on Iran," *New York Times*, August 7, 2015.

290 **"By doing so, he will take the Israelis"**: Former Arkansas governor Mike Huckabee, Breitbart News, July 25, 2015.

292 **"The new agreement doesn't overthrow the clerical regime"**: Joseph Cirincione, "A Huge Deal," *Slate*, July 14, 2015.

293 **"The president was proud that we found"**: Author interview with State Department negotiator.

294 **"There are serious constraints on their nuclear program"**: Author interview with Ernest Moniz.

295 **"Iran is an occupying force in Syria"**: Saudi foreign minister Adel al-Jubeir, press briefing in New York, September 30, 2015.

296 **"This is the most dangerous time in the Middle East"**: Author interview with Emile Hokayem.

296 **"Historically, whether in Russia or eastern Europe"**: Author interview with Michael McFaul.

296 **"I think the real issue is what's going to happen"**: Author interview with Ernest Moniz.

297 **"Look, 20 years from now, I'm still going"**: Jeffrey Goldberg, "President Obama: The Middle East Interview," *Atlantic*, May 21, 2015.

Index

ABOUT THE AUTHOR

JAY SOLOMON is the chief foreign affairs correspondent for *The Wall Street Journal*. For nearly two decades, he's written from Asia, Europe, and the Middle East, including stints in Jakarta, Indonesia; Seoul, South Korea; New Delhi, India; and Washington, D.C. *The Wall Street Journal* has nominated him for three Pulitzer Prizes. Solomon was the first American journalist to uncover the secret meetings between the United States and Iran that took place in Oman. He led coverage of the nuclear negotiations for the *Journal* from 2011 through 2015.

ABOUT THE TYPE

This book was set in Electra, a typeface designed for Linotype by renowned type designer W. A. Dwiggins (1880–1956). Electra is a fluid typeface, avoiding the contrasts of thick and thin strokes that are prevalent in most modern typefaces.